Best wishes,
James Cabezas

Eyes of Justice: A Career Crime Fighter Battles Corruption . . . and Blindness

A Memoir

James Cabezas

James Cabezas
With Joan Jacobson

ISBN: 9781727093636

For Pop and the Cabezas Family

Thanks to Joan Jacobson. This memoir would not have been written without her knowledge and experience.

Reviews for Eyes of Justice

"For aficionados of Maryland's robust culture of organized crime, disorganized crime and political culture, the memoir of legendary investigator Jimmy Cabezas arrives to occupy some essential space. From his early undercover work on Baltimore's Block, the red-light district once home to gambling czars and burlesque queens, to his long campaign with the Maryland State Prosecutor's Office and investigations of corrupt politicians -- up to and including Baltimore's mayor -- Cabezas provides an honest insider's view on the quotidian, unending and always unfinished battle for clean government."

--David Simon, executive producer *The Wire, The Deuce*

Jim Cabezas is a true rarity, someone with a unique story to share. His experiences in law enforcement alone would have made for a terrific read, but his personal battle makes this memoir all the more resonant. Some people say God is in the details, others say it's the devil. Cabezas's life story has both.

--Laura Lippman, New York Times bestselling author of Sunburn

Jim Cabezas' memoir is a first-hand account of the good and bad of the Baltimore Police Department. Nothing is sugarcoated as he describes scandals inside the department, dating back a half century. This book is a must-read for senior law enforcement leaders and young officers alike. Widely respected as one of the area's top criminal investigators, Jim Cabezas is an inspiration to those who share his passion to investigate corruption regardless of the consequences.

--John J. McEntee, Jr.

Retired Deputy Commissioner, Baltimore Police Department

"In my half-century in journalism, I've never met a finer person, nor a braver one, than Jimmy Cabezas. He is unconquerable, and his life story is remarkable and inspiring. Joan Jacobson's done a wonderful job telling it."

--Michael Olesker, Author and Journalist

A riveting true-life story of a street cop who overcomes blindness to become Maryland's chief political corruption investigator during one of the darkest days in Baltimore's history – the downfall of Mayor Sheila Dixon. James Cabezas is the epitome of honesty and determination who represents the best in law enforcement.

--Robert Rohrbaugh, Former Maryland State Prosecutor

PROLOGUE

My alarm was set for 4:45 a.m., but I suspected I had awakened earlier. I felt on the night table for my talking wrist watch and listened. It was only 2:37 a.m. I tried to fall back to sleep, but it was hopeless. Not wanting to wake my wife, Laura, I quietly pulled off the covers and firmly planted my feet on the carpet. I felt for the bureau, then the wall that led to the bathroom. I didn't bother to turn on the lights. That would be silly.

Once showered and shaved, I opened the door. Laura was awake. "Should I call you an early bird or a night bird that doesn't sleep?" she asked. "Yeah," I sighed. "I guess you haven't had the chance to lay out my clothes, have you?" The night before, I told Laura I would need my black suit, a white button-down oxford shirt and my red power tie.

She knew nothing about the raid planned for this morning and knew not to ask. Very sensitive matters, I always believed, must operate on a need-to-know basis. In my many years in law enforcement I had become a master at keeping secrets; when I worked as a deep covert for the Baltimore Police Department, I did not even reveal my true identity to a previous wife. For two years, she thought I was a taxi driver.

When Laura walked into the kitchen, she said, "What, no coffee?"

"Not this morning. I would appreciate it if you would drive me to the office." Once we arrived in Towson, Laura parked. As I did every day, I waited for her to grab my arm to walk me to the elevator where she punched the button for the fourth floor. We arrived at the Office of the Maryland State Prosecutor, the agency that investigates political corruption, theft of government funds and election law violations. I was the agency's chief investigator.

As we said our goodbyes, I heard Laura's voice turn back to me. "I am thinking that if you told me what's up, you would have to cut my head off

2

and put it in the oven." My wife can always make me laugh. "Have a nice day," I told her with a chuckle. "I love you."

My colleagues have described me as a person of above-average intelligence with a gifted memory, streetwise and blessed with the ability to change my behavior like a chameleon. In police uniform, in the precarious days before bulletproof vests, I got drug addicts to inform on their dealers and captured a fleeing armed robber. In a coat and tie, as polite as could be, I gained confessions of theft from elected officials—a sheriff, a state legislator and more than one county councilman. Calm and collected, I pretended to take bribes from a Baltimore sheriff—and caught it on audio tape. I turned the filthy job of sifting through trash for evidence into an art form. As a deep covert working the sleaziest block of Baltimore, I grew long hair with a Fu Manchu mustache and spoke a dialect called "Balamerese" to earn the trust of strip-club owners, prostitutes, drug addicts and outlaw bikers.

Throughout my career I was honored to serve my city and my state as an honest Baltimore police officer and investigator, working alongside many other principled cops. I am equally as proud to have survived and outsmarted the many corrupt, racist and inept cops I met along the way who tried their damnedest to prevent me from doing my job. For years I kept a little figurine of the lion from "The Wizard of Oz." It reminded me that it takes courage to do the right thing.

During all my dangerous years in law enforcement, I had no fear. The only thing I ever feared was blindness. I knew, since I was a child, that I would one day go blind. There were so many cruel reminders in the decades that followed: the blurred and cloudy vision, the early cataracts, 15 surgeries and each dreaded detached retina, moving—like a black curtain—across each eye, shutting me off from the glorious world of sight.

Blindness stripped away my independence, one agonizing step at a time. My last trash rip, my last raid on a suspect's home. My ability to drive, to watch a movie. I would never again see my wife's beautiful face, never watch my grandchildren grow.

Some people ask, "Why me?" I say, "Why not me?"

No one is immune to tragedy; but I am a man who learned to turn misfortune into opportunity. When I was going blind and could no longer carry a firearm, I found a career investigating political corruption and became a lawman without a gun.

I am in fact a lucky man, forever grateful to the many talented doctors who kept me seeing for years. I even had a devoted boss who found me a talking computer and kept me in my job after a government doctor tried to violate my rights as a disabled worker and end my career.

Cutting my career short because of my disability would have been especially cruel for a workaholic like me. Still, there were parts of the job I had to give up. As a blind criminal investigator, a raid with a search and seizure warrant was the investigative tool I missed most. In the years when I could see, it was my favorite day of a criminal investigation, coming months after we painstakingly collected other evidence: subpoenaed bank records, informant interviews, wiretapped phone conversations, evidence of secret business dealings found in a suspect's trash, irregularities in campaign finance records and financial disclosure statements signed by elected officials under penalty of perjury.

Before I went blind, I led many successful raids that gathered thousands of dollars in stolen cash, guns and drugs, valuable photo equipment, hundreds of illegal gambling machines, even sticks of dynamite.

I investigated and helped prosecutors win convictions of business owners and bureaucrats who stole millions from the government, and elected officials who took bribes and raided their campaign accounts. Once, we caught Baltimore's third-highest elected official siphoning tax dollars through a fictitious employee.

On this day, June, 17, 2008, though, the stakes were even higher because of the prominent person we were investigating.

Instead of being on the scene, I would be in the office, monitoring events by phone. Investigator John Poliks would lead the raid in my absence. John and I had known each other for almost 30 years, going back to our days in the police department. He had been an investigator for the Maryland Prosecutor's Office for more than a decade.

There was no one I trusted more than John to be my eyes.

As we gathered in the state prosecutor's conference room early in the investigation, I made it clear to the staff the importance of this case.

"Ladies and gentlemen, there is no room for a single mistake," I told them.

"If we are right, no one can hurt us. If we are wrong, no one can save us."

Now, two years later, we were ready for the final search. Later he would describe the scene to me in copious detail.

A little after 6 a.m., John led the small team of investigators and state troopers to the scene of the raid on a quiet street in West Baltimore.

Before he knocked, John could not help noticing the red front door with a large decorative oval window. "This is a really nice door," he thought. He knocked hard. A few minutes went by before it opened.

The mayor of Baltimore, Sheila Dixon, stood in a plain nightgown.

"I have a search warrant for your house," he said.

"You're not coming in here this time of the morning," the mayor told him. She slammed the door.

A few minutes later she reappeared.

"I have a search warrant," John repeated. "We have to come in one way or the other."

"I need an hour," said the mayor.

John knew a person could destroy a lot of evidence in an hour.

"No" he told her.

Again, she slammed the door.

John called me with the bad news.

"Take the door down if you have to," I told him, raising my voice.

John hesitated. This door, he thought, is almost too nice. What if it was a gift from a developer doing business with the city who might be under investigation, he thought.

"I can't destroy evidence."

The door opened again. Mayor Dixon handed John a cell phone.

"Hello Dale," said John before he heard a voice on the line.

"What do you have?" asked Dale Kelberman, a well-known white-collar criminal defense lawyer.

John told him about the warrant and handed the phone back to the mayor so Kelberman could tell his client she had no choice. Finally, the mayor stood back.

In went the team, to search for evidence of theft, embezzlement and misconduct in office. The list of items they were looking for filled ten pages of our search and seizure warrant: a burnt umber mink jacket, a coat of Persian lamb and mink, an Italian leather coat, Giorgio Armani shoes and Jimmy Choo sandals, an Xbox, video games, and many gift cards purchased by developers doing business with the city.

Here I was, overseeing one of the most significant investigations of my career. If anything went wrong, we would face catastrophic political fallout. Not to be part of every single step was frustrating. I felt very, very cheated. Still, I knew we were prepared and that the raid would go well.

Once inside, John called to tell me the mayor had left the house with her gym bag and that the search had begun.

I loosened my red power tie in the darkness.

"Here we go," I said to myself.

1
MY POOR LITTLE EYES

On the night of March 18, 1958, I went to bed as an eight-year-old boy with no cares in the world. I expected to wake up, eat my mother's delicious homemade biscuits for breakfast and head off to my third-grade class at St. Elizabeth's Catholic school, eight blocks from the small rowhouse my family rented in East Baltimore.

It was a wonderful place to grow up—just a few blocks from the magnificent Patterson Park where I played football with a tight group of friends. I could stand outside any number of houses, yell "football, football, football" and get 12 boys together in ten minutes. One football could keep a group of boys with little pocket money entertained for hours. It was that kind of place. We called ourselves the Port Street Rebels.

The weather report for that morning called for cloudy skies with a high of 46 degrees. But it was wrong. It was so very wrong. I woke up to a very different day, and I was thrilled. I sat in our basement kitchen looking at eye level out the window to our tiny back yard. I carefully spread a small amount of our family's precious butter on my mother's biscuits and drank my well-sugared Lipton tea. I watched fat snowflakes fall where my mother hung laundry on a clothesline. Those snowflakes, I thought, were surely an omen for a good day ahead. I would have an unexpected day off from school. And as the snow fell steadily—and in what seemed like blankets of white—I knew I would have a chance to make some money shoveling the walks outside the dozens of small rowhomes that line the narrow East Baltimore streets.

I already knew the importance of earning money in a family that struggled to pay the rent, buy groceries and afford Catholic school tuition for my nine-year-old sister Esther and me. Even though the tuition was discounted by my mother ironing the priest's vestments, it was still a challenge. But this morning I was thinking of all the baseball cards I could buy with my earnings.

I was a diehard Baltimore Orioles fan and I treasured cards of a 20-year-old third baseman and up-and-coming hitter named Brooks Robinson, a pitcher named Milt Pappas, and a catcher named Gus Triandos. I collected the cards (which cost five cents for five cards and gum) and stored them in shoe boxes. I didn't just collect them for the photos of my favorite players or the bubble gum which irritated my parents when we blew humungous bubbles that popped on our faces and in our hair. My friends and I also used them to play games. In one game we set up the cards against a wall, like bottles in a shooting gallery. We then each took a turn, throwing other cards to knock down the ones on the wall. The one who knocked down the most cards was the winner and got to keep all the cards.

I asked my mother if I could go out shoveling snow that afternoon and she gave me her permission, with the admonishment, "Make sure you dress warmly and don't be out for more than two hours." My mother was a worrier who always made sure Esther and I never left our home without our St. Christopher medals around our necks. She believed the medals, with an engraving of St. Christopher, the patron saint of travelers—shown walking bent over his staff—would protect us when we were away from home.

I then called my good friend and neighbor Dean Patterson, whom I called "Deany."

"Hey, you have a shovel, don't you?" I asked. Deany was an exceptionally bright kid, in fact the smartest boy I knew. We didn't go to school together (he went to the local public school, P.S. 83) but we were close neighbors

When I dressed to go out, I was careful to wear warm clothes, but in those days nothing was waterproof. I put on my one-piece long johns, blue jeans (we called them dungarees back then), a long-sleeve flannel shirt and a hooded sweatshirt. On top of all that I put on my green army tank jacket that zipped up. Most of my friends had the same jacket which we bought at Sunny Surplus and wrote on with magic markers, "Port Street Rebels," "Go Orioles" and of course, "Go Colts." I then put on short rubber boots that snapped closed and a pair of brown cloth gloves that got very cold and wet, very fast.

By the time we met up Deany already had a plan. "Why don't we go the furthest distance from home then work our way back," he suggested. I would never have thought of that: to arrange our day so that by the time we finished shoveling walks, feeling exhausted, we'd already be back home. What young boy thinks that far ahead? He also came up with the clever idea that we should knock on two doors at once, so we could give our sales pitch to two houses at a time, getting ahead of any competition. Here he was, eight years old and thinking about a competitive business edge.

We headed east, away from our homes. On our way, we planned out what we would charge for our services—or at least what we thought we could get. The streets had identical rowhouses, but some streets had longer walks to the front steps than others. If we were on Montford Avenue, we would charge 50 cents. We thought it was a fair price for the entire walk. If we could only get 25 cents we would just shovel a narrow path in the middle of the walk. On the smaller streets like Rose, Glover and Port, we would only charge a quarter.

By the time we got out at two in the afternoon, there was a lot of snow. We walked up unshoveled streets north toward Fayette Street. When we started knocking on doors, some of the housewives greeted us with concern. They thought it was too cold for us to be outside and invited us inside for cookies and hot chocolate. Their concern and generosity weren't unusual. In that neighborhood, it was just what people did for each other.

The snowflakes were some of the largest we'd ever seen, the size of Holy Communion hosts the priest gave out during Mass. And they were coming down fast and wet. We crossed over to Luzerne Avenue, then up to Fayette Street, a main thoroughfare of East Baltimore. We stopped dead in our tracks and looked at the scene. Tractor trailers were already jackknifed, blocking the road. We noticed cars that had pulled over, but the drivers were gone. We thought, geez, we're going to be off school for the rest of the week.

What we didn't know was that this freak blizzard, not even mentioned in the weather forecast, was wreaking havoc all over the city and beyond, up and down the Eastern Seaboard in fact, in a way more devastating than two eight-year-old boys could ever understand. Power lines and transformers fell from the heavy weight of the ice, leaving live electric wires dangling in alleys. Trees snapped, roofs caved, porches collapsed. Several people died of heart attacks trying to shovel snow. When it was over, there would be more than 40 deaths from heart attacks, exposure, electrocution and traffic accidents. More than a million homes and businesses were left without electricity from Virginia to Maine.

By the time we were done, we were close to home, as Deany had planned. We made $4.70 each that day and we were thrilled. But I had a problem. I'd been out for three hours, not two as my mother told me. And I was absolutely freezing.

As soon as my mother saw me, she scolded me in Spanish, the language we used at home.

"I told you two hours. We've all been worried. We didn't know where to find you," she said. She quickly pulled off my icy, wet clothes, wrapped me in a large blanket and ran upstairs and drew me a bath.

The rest of the evening was uneventful. I ate dinner, watched some TV and slept soundly.

I woke up the next day with a sore throat and a fever. My mother called our family doctor, Dr. Black, who came to the house. He examined me, took my temperature and listened to my heart and my lungs. Then he reached into his black bag and took out what looked like a very large needle. I didn't like the size of it. It hurt when he put it into my upper arm. I didn't know what he had injected me with, but I later learned it was penicillin.

About a day and a half later, I got very sick. My lips were so swollen that my top lip actually touched my nose. My facial skin started to blister, as well as the skin on my arms and my chest. I was very thirsty and had a hard time swallowing. My eyes hurt from a burning sensation. My mother had never seen me that sick and began to panic. My father was more no-nonsense, insisting I would be fine. But when my fever rose to 105, my parents (who did not own a car) called an ambulance. I only remember thinking one thing as the ambulance crew took me on a stretcher down our front steps: "I hope they don't drop me."

We lived between Johns Hopkins Hospital, one of the world's most prominent hospitals, and City Hospitals, a municipal hospital that served disadvantaged people in East Baltimore. The medics took me to City Hospitals because it had a special unit for burn patients—and I looked like someone whose skin, blistered and peeling, had been burned by fire. I remember nothing about the emergency room there and I don't recall being afraid.

But I do remember my parents worrying over me. They rode a bus each day to the hospital, trudging up long sidewalks to get to the entrance. They saw me hooked up to an IV. My skin was itching and blistering and very painful. To stop me from scratching, the nurses put cotton gloves on my hands and tied them to the bed rails. My eyes were so swollen I looked like a cicada. The nurses bandaged them so I couldn't touch them and applied drops every four hours, even through the night. They were called Prednefrin Forte, a strong steroid. I, of course, did not know it then, but I would take these drops for decades.

It was the first time in my life I could not see. I was not a shy boy, so I was always asking the kind nurses what they were doing as they replenished my IV liquids or changed my bed pan. Since my eyes were covered, the nurses helped me eat. They called me Jimmy. My parents brought me a transistor radio so I could listen to music. They set it to WCAO, a popular Baltimore station. The disc jockeys I loved were Kirby Scott, Alan Field and Frank Luber. That year I listened over and over to two popular songs: "Witch Doctor" and "Purple People Eater," both songs that really appealed to an eight year old.

Here are the lyrics to "Witch Doctor":

> *I told the witch doctor I was in love with you!*
> *I told the witch doctor you didn't love me true!*
> *And then the witch doctor he told me what to do!*
> *He said that:*

Ooh eeh ooh ahah ting tang wallawalla bingbang
Ooh eeh ooh ahah ting tang wallawalla bingbang
Ooh eeh ooh ahah ting tang wallawalla bingbang
Ooh eeh ooh ahah ting tang wallawalla bingbang

The lyrics to "Purple People Eater" were just as catchy:
It was a one-eyed, one-horned, flyin' purple people eater
One-eyed, one-horned, flyin' purple people eater
A one-eyed, one-horned, flyin' purple people eater
Sure looks strange to me (one eye?)

I lay there for 40 days, my parents trudging up the long walk from the bus to the hospital entrance in the biting cold, sitting at my bedside, reciting the rosary over me each day. My mother worried and wept, as my father tried to console her. "My poor little eyes," she said in Spanish. Over and over. "My poor little eyes." (*Mis pobres ojitos.*)

I was diagnosed with Stevens-Johnson Syndrome, a rare, acute reaction to the penicillin Dr. Black gave me after the blizzard. Stevens-Johnson has been described as attacking patients as if they were burning from the inside out. That explained my blistering, peeling skin, the swollen lips and bulging eyes. Patients who survive can go blind, but those lucky enough to keep their sight can still be left with a painful dry-eye syndrome or have an extreme sensitivity to light. While I was left with scars on my chest that would last for years, the most debilitating effect for me would be the scarring on the inside of my eyelids. Every time I blinked, more than a dozen times a minute, my eyes were scratched, leaving them red and irritated.

When I finally came home it was springtime and I was very weak. I looked like a person who had been exposed to radiation. My fingernails and toenails had fallen out and my skin was left so thin that my mother refused to allow me to play baseball or swim. She worried I could get cut or that the chlorine in the water would irritate my eyes. Though my parents wouldn't let me play sports, they did let me go outside and bang pans after the Baltimore Colts won the 1958 championship game against the New York Giants. For extra spiritual protection they presented me with a new St. Christopher medal that I wore for many years.

My friends stuck with me. They must have sent 50 get well cards. That meant so much to me that I saved them for many decades in a grocery bag and would look at them from time to time. They were endearing to me. When I got home, my buddies came over to the house and played Monopoly and other board games since I couldn't go outside to play sports. My sister, just 11 months older, was mostly very quiet during this time. She worried that her little brother might die.

One day after I came home from the hospital, my father sat me down in our little living room. Even at my young age I considered him to be a very religious, loving and optimistic man. He had a serious and compassionate look on his face and I could tell he was going to say something very important because he did not sit next to me or stand over me. Instead, he got down on one knee and faced me at eye level. Then he took my hand. When I was in the hospital, he told me, the doctors explained the devastating effects of Stevens-Johnson Syndrome and told him that I was a very lucky boy.

"God has treated you in a very special way," my father said in Spanish. "You should never forget that if it wasn't for God's miracle, you would not be here. You should never forget this," he repeated, "so that one day you should serve God in a special way."

He said the doctors told him I was one of only 11 patients with the syndrome in the Baltimore area that year and they revealed to him a chilling statistic. I cannot confirm the accuracy of what he said because the state health department doesn't keep records of Stevens-Johnson Syndrome. Accurate or not, his powerful words have stayed with me—and played a role in my brief decision years later to become a priest. This is what the doctors told my father: of the 11 patients, nine died, one immediately went blind and one walked out of the hospital with his sight intact. That was me.

2
COMING TO AMERICA

I was born to Latin parents. My father, Isidro Cabezas, grew up in Nicaragua, in a small pueblo near Managua. My mother, Rebecca Mendoza, came from a small village near Santiago, Chile. Since I was a child, I knew that their proudest moments (in addition to the births of my sister and me) came when each took the oath to become a United States citizen.

Becoming a citizen meant something extra special to my father. Like his father before him, he had worked for the brutal Nicaraguan dictator Anastasio Somoza. The dictator financed private education for my father and while serving in the Nicaraguan army, he became Somoza's personal secretary, handling his most confidential communications. The job gave him an insider's view of the man who, with absolute control of the military, courts and legislature, turned Nicaragua into a corrupt country during his 20 years in power before being assassinated in 1956. (His namesake son later succeeded him.) My father never talked about the Somoza regime, though I'm sure he had an intimate understanding of its brutality. Being an honest and fair man at heart, he must have yearned to break free of it.

My father always impressed upon me the significance of living in a society with judicial and legislative systems that are separate from the country's presidency. He understood, in ways other Americans could not, the importance of living in a free democracy with three independent branches of government. I too would one day come to marvel at the vital autonomy of the judiciary when I investigated scores of corrupt elected officials with the independence that all American criminal investigators and prosecutors deserve. Being a United States citizen, my father told me many times, "is a gift from God." And he would always add, "But don't forget that you are of Spanish blood."

I have heard two stories from relatives of how my father came to work at the Nicaraguan embassy in Washington in the 1940s. In one version he was sent there as an attaché for his own safety as the Somoza regime was losing power. In the other version, Somoza personally sent my father to Washington to get him out of the way. Apparently, the story goes, my father had wandering eyes that set their sights on Somoza's wife. Transferring him to the embassy kept my father thousands of miles away from her.

I know less about my mother's history. She left Santiago in 1941 to work in Chile's U.S. Embassy in Washington when she was 25. A relative recently told me my mother was a Jew who gave birth to two daughters before she came to the United States, but I have been unable to confirm this and I never knew what happened to these other children. I do know that she came to the U.S. on the S.S. Aconcagua from Valparaiso, which stopped in the Canal Zone, Panama and Havana, Cuba before docking in the United States, just ten months before the Pearl Harbor attack. She came to work as a maidservant to the Chilean ambassador.

My mother never told us about her work there. She was a quiet and stoic woman who did not reveal much about herself. Years later my sister, Esther, realized our mother had suffered from depression, though that word was never used when I was a child. She met my father in Washington, presumably through their embassy work, and they were married in 1947, but not until my mother agreed to convert to Catholicism. Both were 31 at the time of their marriage. My mother became a devout Catholic, always honoring the holy days of obligation and never missing Mass. She said the rosary nightly, kneeling before a makeshift altar that was adorned with a statue of the Blessed Mother and St. Joseph. She was more devoted to the Blessed Mother Mary than to Jesus Christ. I think she felt the Blessed Mother could provide her with the grace she needed to keep her family safe. My parents' move to Baltimore is quite an unusual story. During the 1940s and 1950s, while other immigrants and working class Baltimoreans worked in dangerous and dirty industries making cars at the General Motors plant, or steel and ships at Bethlehem Steel's Sparrows Point, my father and mother went to work (he as a butler and she as a maid) in what may have been the most elegant, pristine, and genteel place in all of Baltimore.

Evergreen House, a 48-room historic mansion on a 36-acre estate on North Charles Street, belonged to generations of the very wealthy Garrett family, whose patriarch, John Work Garrett, was president of the B&O Railroad during the 19th century. The mansion was adorned with the finest tapestries, carpets and intricate Italian mosaic tile floors. Tiffany chandeliers hung from the ceilings. The last Garrett to live there was John Work Garrett, former U.S. ambassador to Italy, who shared his grandfather's name. He and his wife, the former Alice Warder, decorated the mansion with original paintings and drawings by Picasso, Degas and Modigliani. Famed Ballet Russes scenery and costume designer Léon Bakst designed a theater inside the mansion for Alice, a singer, to perform for friends.

My parents found a place to rent on Keswick Road, a good walk to the estate. I can only imagine their awe when they first saw the mansion, and especially the finest room of all, the Garrett Library of elaborately carved walnut wood, with a 20-foot high ceiling. It contained thousands of the world's oldest and most rare books, many more than 600 years old, ornately bound in leather, on subjects including architecture and natural history. And one day I would learn how to dust them—very carefully. I would also visit the mansion's most peculiar and opulent room: its gold bathroom, complete with a gold bathtub and gold-plated toilet seat. It was enveloped by thousands of tiny Italian tiles, one-inch square, from the floor, up the walls and across the ceiling.

Garrett left Evergreen to the Johns Hopkins University when he died. By the time my parents went to work there, his widow still lived there but the mansion and its pastoral grounds were being turned into a museum. (The public can still visit today and see it in much the same condition that my parents found it.) For me, the acres of natural beauty that surround the mansion would become a place where I would spend many moments in complete tranquility, especially sitting on a very old stone wall overlooking a brook, contemplating my future.

But it would also one day prove to me in an excruciating way that no place, no matter how genteel or protected from the outside world, is safe from horrific violence that could change your life in an instant. At Evergreen House I would learn a hard lesson; that there is no separation between a protected world and a cruel outside world. There is just one world.

My earliest memories of home go back to a small, rented two-story rowhouse in one of East Baltimore's many working-class communities, just a few miles from Evergreen House, but light years away in social class. This particular house was on North Washington Street, just above North Avenue, the city's major East-West thoroughfare. In those days, the early 1950s, Baltimore's population was at its peak of nearly 1 million. But then the population began to drop for the first time and by 1960 the city had lost 10,000 people. It was the beginning of "white flight" to the suburbs, aided by the "blockbusting" tactics of unscrupulous realtors, who preyed on racial fears to cause panicked white residents to quickly sell their homes. Meanwhile, job loss, redlining and other forms of disinvestment hastened the city's decline and caused a rise in poverty. Today, my first East Baltimore home is in one of the poorest, most dangerous and vandalized parts of the city, where some abandoned houses are marked with a large red "X" to let firefighters know the buildings might collapse when they come to extinguish a fire.

But back then it was a stable, though segregated, working-class community, where we could walk to the Clifton Park swimming pool. Homicides were in single digits each year and the only gang we knew was *Spanky and Our Gang*, a Saturday morning children's TV show. I remember the day when my father came home with a large box with the word "Philco." My sister and I were so excited to have our first TV. My parents were grinning from ear to ear.

The corner store was run by a kindly man I remember as Mr. Cohen, who gave credit to those who could not pay up front. Our rented house was heated by coal and wood, with a coal chute that went right into the basement. Once when I helped my father bring in wood, I fell down the steps and had to have stitches in my chin.

I will never forget the house's French doors because my parents used them as a stage curtain of sorts. My father was a gregarious man who invited friends from Washington for parties a few times a year. He put a Spanish record on the Victrola, usually tenor Mario Lanza singing the song "Granada," and open the French doors to reveal my sister and me, two tiny children dressed in colorful costumes my mother made. We performed dances our parents taught us—the tango, the rumba and the cha cha.

After a few years we were one of only two families left on the block who were not black. Eventually the landlord sold our house amid the blockbusting frenzy. We moved to another rented house about a mile away on the 1800 block of Greenmount Avenue, where I would one day walk a police beat in the years after the 1968 riots that followed the assassination of Martin Luther King Jr. Our new home was also near the famous Greenmount Cemetery, final resting place of Lincoln assassin John Wilkes Booth—not to mention Johns Hopkins, the founder of the hospital where ophthalmologists spent years attempting to save my eyesight.

For kindergarten and first grade I went to a public school called Samuel Gompers (P.S. 99) and remember leaving my stuffed bear there one day. I cried until my mother took me back to the school, only to find the doors locked. I remember desperately looking for the bear through the windows with tears running down my face. I eventually retrieved it when school reopened. Nearly 20 years later, as a rookie police officer, I would respond to the same school building to investigate why an alarm had gone off. While searching the building, my sergeant, who was white, laughingly told me what his police dog had once deposited in the cafeteria for the African American children. I would never get over the depth of racial bias by some of my fellow police officers.

From Greenmount Avenue we moved southeast to 121 North Montford Avenue, where I entered my first Catholic school, St. Elizabeth's, a large, handsome building bordering the north side of Patterson Park. Second grade did not go smoothly because English was a second language for me. I got in hot water when I spelled the word "sheet" as "shit" on a spelling test. My teacher was Sister Teresina (we called her Terrible Teresina, though not to her face). She summoned my parents to school for my blasphemous spelling and I was ordered to repeat the second grade. Though it upset my mother, it was not such a bad idea. I was a little behind in my English, though my Spanish (which didn't count for anything in school) was excellent.

3
IN A TOUGH SPOT

Soon after my 40-day hospital stay my father took me to see Dr. Roy O. Scholz, an ophthalmologist recommended by the doctors at City Hospitals. Since we did not have a car and could not afford a taxi, we took two busses to get to his office at the intersection of Fayette and Charles streets in downtown Baltimore. The doctor's office was in a 12-story office building. I marveled at the elevator ride—my first—which took us to the third floor.

There we met Mrs. Jones, a very attractive lady, who was the doctor's receptionist and assistant. She oversaw a waiting room filled with about 20 patients. I found the last empty seat and my father stood. Soon Mrs. Jones gave me an exam with an eye chart, which showed that my vision was good. We then waited another 45 minutes before meeting the doctor.

When we entered the doctor's examination room, I met a short man who wore glasses. Dr. Scholz's whitish hair did not seem to me to be combed. He wore a white shirt with a loosely knotted necktie and his pants were bunched around his shoes. I was used to my parents who were always impeccably well-groomed. That day my father wore a formal black suit, a white shirt and a plain tie. He always knotted his ties fastidiously. To me Dr. Scholz looked disheveled, a little bit like a wild man. I would eventually learn that Roy O. Scholz, M.D., was one of the most prominent ophthalmologists at the world-famous Wilmer Eye Clinic at Johns Hopkins Hospital, visited by patients from all over the world. He had graduated from Johns Hopkins Medical School in 1939, so by the time I became his patient, in 1958, he was already revered in the profession. To me, he certainly did not look or act like someone who was an internationally famous doctor. He was a soft-spoken gentleman who addressed me and my father as if we were his next door neighbors. He would be the first in a long line of brilliant and dedicated ophthalmologists who would keep me from going blind for many decades.

His office in Baltimore's Mt. Vernon neighborhood near downtown was always full of patients who waited for hours to see him, including many senior citizens whom he treated for free.

He was clearly passionate about the wonders of eyesight and helping anyone in danger of losing it. At the time I became his patient, he was about to publish a book, called *Sight, A Handbook for Laymen, The Structure, Functions, Malfunctions, and Diseases of the Eye; a concise appraisal of the help and hope modern science offers those with impaired vision."* Although it is a practical book describing how the eye functions, Dr. Scholz chose this poetic quote from the play *William Tell* as the preface:

> O the eye's light of all the gifts of Heaven,
> The dearest, best! From light all beings live –
> Each fair, created thing – the very plants
> Turn with a joyful transport to the light…

He directed me to a stool in front of a large machine I had never seen before. It was a slit lamp, though I didn't know its name that day. He told me to rest my chin on a plastic cup and lean forward so my forehead rested against a metal bar. He shined a bright light into my right eye. The light went from right to left several times. He then used his thumb to gently lift my eyelid. He repeated his exam with the light in the left eye. He told my father he needed to dilate my pupils by putting drops in each eye and said I would have to wait 45 minutes to an hour. Once he reexamined my eyes, the doctor pushed his chair away from the slit lamp and stood up. He removed his eye glasses and rubbed his own eyes with his index fingers. He used his tie to clean his glasses and began to explain his evaluation.

He told us that dry eye syndrome, a result of the Stevens-Johnson Syndrome, causes the eyelashes to grow inward. The only known remedy at the time was to use tweezers to pluck the eyelashes out. If the procedure was not done, the eyelashes would continuously scratch my eyes, creating irritation and possibly infection. He did not remove any lashes that day, but I was frightened at the mere thought. He did not mention the scars on the inside of my eyelids that were already starting to irritate my eyes.

He also explained that in order to reduce the vascularization, or swelling, when blood vessels get irritated and make my eyes bloodshot, I would need to take strong steroid eye drops every day. He handed my father a prescription for Prednefrin Forte. The drops, he said, were absolutely necessary, but came with pros and cons. The drops would save my eyes in the short run by reducing inflammation and preventing infection. But long-term use could give me premature cataracts. I had never heard the word cataract until then and had no idea what it meant.

He made it clear that I would be spending many future hours in his office, not something an active eight-year-old boy wants to hear from any doctor.

Later Dr. Scholz would tell me, "We're in a tough spot." But I did not have a clear understanding of what the doctor told me and my father that first visit. It was just too much information for a small boy to comprehend. Pop and I walked out of the office without speaking, but he hugged my shoulders. As we walked to the bus stop I felt very hungry. We had started our trip after breakfast at 7:30 a.m. and now it was almost four in the afternoon. On the bus home I worried that the doctor visits would interfere with my playtime. Pop tried to reassure me. He told me that my problem was not as serious as it sounded, but he didn't say it in a convincing way. I'm sure he was as shocked as I was by what the doctor said.

When we got home, my mother was anxious to hear the doctor's report, but Pop said, "Let's eat first." Mom fed us hamburgers, which I remember because she made delicious hamburgers with chili pepper. After our late lunch Mom and Pop went upstairs to talk. When they finished their discussion my father went to the pharmacy to fill my eye drop prescription. That day I began a lifelong regimen of two steroid eye drops a day. My mother called me upstairs. She embraced me tightly and said in Spanish that I should not worry because the Blessed Mother would watch out for me. I felt reassured, but as I walked down the steps I could hear her crying as she prayed. When I reached the bottom step I saw Esther looking my way, but my big sister didn't say a word.

4
A HAPPY BOY

In my childhood our idols were professional ballplayers, not the pop stars of today. We were fanatical football fans who loved the Baltimore Colts. The 1958 championship game between the Colts and the New York Giants changed the popularity of football forever. This was in the days before the Super Bowl, when most fans followed college football. But just months after my bout with Stevens-Johnson Syndrome, that game, now called "the greatest game ever played," was nationally televised, an unusual event in those days. Our Colts won in overtime, 23 to 17. The year 1961 was especially memorable because it was the year Yankees Roger Maris and Mickey Mantle competed to break Babe Ruth's record of the most home runs in one season. Even though we were Orioles fans, all season while playing ball in Patterson Park, each boy pretended to be either Maris or Mantle. We listened for the scores each night to hear which player was in the lead. Maris won with 61 home runs on October 1, my birthday.

East Baltimore was known at the time—and for many years—for its pristine white marble steps. Rowhouses for hundreds of blocks were graced with three or four of those steps leading to the front door, proudly scrubbed by housewives (my mother included) who also swept the sidewalks daily of debris. The steps were so emblematic that they became a cliché for any out-of-town writer describing working-class Baltimore. They were even in the first scene of John Waters's movie, *Hairspray*. Those steps were a mainstay of the community. People sat on them during heat waves to escape their stifling homes. Adults rested on them while their children played hopscotch and jumped rope on the sidewalks, since there were no front yards (and only tiny back yards.) And when the Orioles were playing, baseball fans would sit on them with transistor radios listening to the game. I could walk for blocks and follow the game just by passing by random neighbors with radios and asking them for the score, always hearing the deep voice of Orioles announcer Chuck Thompson. He also was a Colts announcer and did local beer commercials. His voice was so familiar that he felt like an uncle to us. He was later honored at the National Baseball Hall of Fame.

In those early days of my childhood many parents of my friends worked in manufacturing jobs, especially at steel plants, like Bethlehem Steel, that employed more than 30,000 people, and at GM, where 7,500 people worked making cars. Today all those plants and all those jobs are gone. But back then, those were good, secure union jobs. I remember that my friend

Bob Dillon's father worked for GM because they always had a new car to take us to Rocky Point State Park. My pal Ernie Sheppard's father was a police officer. Many parents were recent immigrants like mine, bringing up their children in the "American Dream." Bill Pompa's parents were from Italy and worked at an Italian restaurant. Then there was Fred Nagle, whose parents came from Germany. His father was an accountant. When we went out to play in the rain his dad would always tell us in his thick German accent, "Jimmy, Fred, don't get vet." I especially remember his mother's delicious German cooking: homemade poppy seed rolls and potato pancakes with sour cream. Many of my friends came from large, very poor homes. One German boy, whom we called "Dirt Ball," was so poor, I only ever saw him wearing a T-shirt with pants that were way too long. His belt was so long, it looped over five inches below his waist. He always had holes in his shoes that were lined with cardboard.

After a few years at the well-mannered world of Evergreen House, my father, too, had joined the manufacturing sector. He got a better paying job at Crown Cork & Seal, an East Baltimore company that made cans, bottles, tops and lids of all sorts for beer, soda and other food products. My father's work was described proudly in a 1953 company newsletter. The article was accompanied by a photo of him sitting with a serious look on his face next to an industrial machine.

Notice how, in those days when immigrants were welcomed to the U.S., the company was pleased to have a man working for them who had just become a citizen. The only headline to the article is the word, "Nicaragua":

Isidro Cabezas, who first worked in the Pickling Mill and more recently moved to the Aluminum Mill, represents the Western Hemisphere among Crown's new citizens, having come to the United States from Nicaragua—the country most Americans think of as the source of their bananas—a tropical land bordering the Caribbean and Central America.

Isidro's introduction to this country was by courtesy of his own government, which sent him to Washington after successful completion of his duties as aid to Anastasio Somoza, Nicaragua's President in the years 1936 to 1942 while Isidro was in the army.

It was in Washington that he met the girl who later became his wife, a Chilean likewise in America by virtue of her employer, the Chilean government.

While Isidro's tour of duty was finished, he returned to Nicaragua, but he could not forget either his girl or America. In 1947 he returned, married his girl and moved to Baltimore where they have established their home. Their family now includes a boy and a girl and all four are fast becoming full-fledged Americans. His own citizenship requirements were completed last June and he is noticeably proud of his newly acquired status of "citizen."

My father worked at Crown Cork & Seal for several years until he was laid off when the company moved to Philadelphia. The timing was catastrophic for our family: only months earlier, we were visited by a tragedy that no amount of praying to the Blessed Mother could help.

5
ENDEARING MEMORIES

In late March 1961 I sat alone on the front steps of our East Baltimore rowhouse, trying not to cry. My life after my near-death experience three years before had returned to normal and my eyesight was still intact. I was dutifully taking the prescribed eye drops twice a day and visiting Dr. Scholz every six weeks. He would pluck my irritating eyelashes as they grew inward, though sometimes my mother would do the plucking at home. The procedure was always painful, but something I could not avoid. I was particularly concerned that I would not be able to clearly see the baseball thrown by a pitcher when I played baseball with my friends in Patterson Park, but thank God that was not a problem.

Now I faced new misfortune. It was late in the afternoon, about 3 p.m. on a Saturday. An elderly African American woman slowly walked up the street. She looked very tired. I thought perhaps she had just come from work. I did not know her, since I only had white neighbors. She must have been heading beyond my stoop to the next block of North Montford Avenue where only African Americans lived. She wore sturdy shoes and a plain, dark blue raincoat, the clothing a woman might wear to clean other people's houses in the early 1960s. She certainly did not clean anyone's house in our block. We were all too poor to afford a maid.

I was hunched over with my hands covering my face. She came to the step and put her hand on my shoulder. "Child," she said, "Why you be cryin'?" She said it in the warmest, most sympathetic way possible for a child to understand she cared. She was truly concerned for me. In those days of segregated Baltimore my friends and I did not associate with black children. We only had four black students in my Catholic school. I did, however, have one secret African American friend. His name was Bumper and he lived a block away. I met him when I walked to Gordon's Seafood on Orleans Street to watch the workers unload dozens of bushels of feisty blue crabs which were transferred into giant steamers. Bumper and I played marbles inside his house, because we could not be seen in public together. I knew my parents would have welcomed him, but I did not introduce him to my friends, since it was taboo to have a friend of color. Perhaps this is the reason why I remember the African American woman so vividly today. She made a rare gesture of compassion across a racial barrier, perhaps going outside her comfort zone to alleviate my grief.

We had been a typical immigrant family, speaking Spanish at home, but enjoying an otherwise American lifestyle. Ours was a loving, religious home where grace was given over every meal as we made the sign of the cross. Over dinner, which often included a tough plank steak served with rice and frijoles, or refried beans, a Latin American staple, our parents asked Esther and me about our school studies and friends before excusing us from the table. They watched Walter Cronkite in the living room, while Esther and I waited for the evening game shows to come on. My mother often knitted and sat on her upholstered chair, encased with a cheap, uncomfortable plastic cover that was popular with fastidious homemakers. My father read *The News American*, the afternoon paper of the working class.

On Sundays we walked to Mass a few blocks to the beautiful St. Elizabeth of Hungary Church on the north side of Patterson Park. It was the largest congregation in the Archdiocese and could seat 400 people. There were four masses on Sundays back in those days. Behind the altar was an inscribed Beatitude that read, "What does it gain a man to conquer the world, but to lose his soul?" On the left side of the church was a dedicated area honoring the Blessed Mother. It was not unusual to see a few roses left by congregants for her. People also lit candles and left donations when praying for sick relatives, a lost job, or success for their children. The church was always packed with deeply Catholic believers. Sometimes it was standing room only, with Polish, German, Italian and Spanish immigrant families, all friendly to one another.

We would walk home to one of my mother's Sunday chicken dinners. My favorite was *arroz con pollo*, chicken cooked with rice, flavored with a tiny bit of aromatic, expensive saffron. She also made *empanadas*, dough stuffed with very spicy shredded beef that was first sautéed with onions, peppers and chopped olives. She baked it in the oven so the dough was perfectly crisp when she served it with a salad. Not surprisingly for a Spanish family, we had rice with almost every meal.

Esther and I rarely complained when we helped with family chores. I was the kind of boy who did not want to talk back to my father because I might hurt his feelings. I helped Pop tap small nails into clear plastic sheeting on the windows to help save heating costs in winter. I helped Mom hang up laundry on the clothesline in our little back yard. This was no fun when the temperature plummeted and we had to get the clothes off the line before they froze. Esther always helped Mom in the kitchen, learning how to cook her recipes. Mom also taught her how to sew well enough that Esther would one day make her living as a seamstress. Despite our poverty, we had a good home life. We not only loved each other, but we really liked one another.

In early November 1960, just before the presidential election, I came into the house and didn't see my mother. I called out, "Mom," but she didn't respond. This was really unusual. She then called my name as I reached the top step of the second floor. I found her in bed, lying on top of the bedspread looking emaciated and very tired. "What's wrong?" I asked. "I have these unbearable headaches that are making me nauseous," she told me in almost a whisper. I could tell she was in terrible pain. I stayed with her for about an hour and she hugged me tightly, almost desperately. "I'm going to say the rosary and I want you to say it with me," she said. In one hand she held the rosary beads and with the other she held me tightly. And so we began: "Our Father, who art in heaven, hallowed be thy name. Thy kingdom come, thy will be done on earth as it is in heaven. Give us this day our daily bread and forgive us our trespasses as we forgive those who trespassed against us. And lead us not into temptation but deliver us from evil. Amen."

Then we both cried.

A few days later Esther was in bed with Mom, playing with her hair, trying to make it look pretty. "Mom talked about Kennedy and how she hoped he would win the general election against Richard Nixon," Esther remembers. Kennedy would be the first Catholic president if he won. "I knew Mom was not feeling well, but I had no idea how serious her illness was," Esther recalls. "Jimmy and I were scared and worried."

Sometime on election night, November 8, an ambulance came to take our mother to City Hospitals, the same hospital where I was treated for Stevens-Johnson Syndrome more than two years before. We had tears in our eyes as we watched the medics lower Mom gently onto the gurney. Pop said everything would be fine and not to worry, but we were naturally frightened. Esther managed to calm me down. The TV was on, but we were not watching. We just sat in silence, feeling sad and wondering why Mom was so very sick. At 9 p.m. Esther told me it was time for bed. Tomorrow was a school day. I don't know when Pop got home, but he was there to make us breakfast. Pop was not himself. He looked worn out and his eyes were bloodshot. He had obviously been crying. We asked about Mom. Pop, a man who usually loved to talk, said little. He just told us, "Mom will be in the hospital for a while. The doctors are running tests." Then Esther and I left for school.

My mother had a brain tumor and would spend four months in the hospital.

A few days after she went in, we were coming home from school when Pop told us, "Keep your coats on, we're going to visit Mom." The weather was really cold. We waited for the #23 bus, which took us to City Hospitals.

We then walked for 20 minutes up the hill to the entrance. It was the same walk my parents took to visit me every day for 40 days. I thought to myself, "I hope Mom is not in the hospital as long as I was. My poor father. This is so unfair to him." We took the elevator to the sixth floor. When we entered the ward, I noticed an odd odor, not knowing at the time it was the smell of urine. There were about 20 beds in this very large room. My mother's bed was at the very end of the row next to a dirty window. Pop gently woke her up. She seemed to look at us but did not recognize us. Esther and I said "Hi" at the same time and then she smiled. Mom tried to speak but could not. She fell asleep so we left after about ten minutes. I felt very sad and had a horrible feeling of what might happen next. It was the first time I realized how very sick she was.

On Sunday the three of us went to Mass and the priest, Father William Newman, approached my father. Mass, he told Pop, would be said in our mother's honor. My father thanked him profusely as he fought back tears. That was a great honor for our family. The following week, when Esther and I arrived home from school, we found Pop sitting with his arms wide open and he waved us over. He dearly hugged us and said that Mom would be undergoing brain surgery. He told us not to worry, that God would take care of us.

A day or two after the surgery we visited her and found her head completely bandaged to the right side of her cheek. We didn't stay long. Mom just stared at the ceiling and did not respond to us. My father said some prayers and told us not to worry. On the way home Pop told us that Mom had fallen into a deep coma. "What's a coma?" we asked. He said, "She is in a deep, pleasant sleep." About two weeks after the surgery the bandages were removed to show a very large scar across her head and down her face. She had just one little tuft of black hair remaining near her forehead. Over the next three months Esther and I visited our mother, who never responded to us, but despite our sorrow, we never lost faith in God. She never regained consciousness.

Despite our sadness, Pop tried to make the holidays festive. We bought and decorated a Christmas tree and he gave me a Duke football he knew I desperately wanted. It was the brand used by the NFL. It had to cost him a bundle, so it was very special to me. What a wonderful gift, I thought. Not long after I received it, I was sitting on the front steps tossing the football when an older teenage boy passed by and yelled, "Hey, throw me a pass," so I did. The boy caught the ball and kept running. I never saw the ball again. I was shocked and really angry. I didn't have the heart to tell Pop the ball was gone. It has been my little secret until now.

One day in March at about 3 p.m. the Mother Superior knocked on the door of Esther's classroom at St. Elizabeth School. Without explanation, Esther was told to go behind the schoolyard on Belnord Avenue. She immediately saw Pop walking toward her. His eyes were bloodshot and tears ran profusely down his face. Esther started to sob. Pop hugged her. "Mom is dead," he told her. Although Esther is not sure, she believes that I was also pulled out of my classroom and sent behind the school to be with Pop and Esther. I don't remember.

My mother's death certificate gives her cause of death, "Rt. Parietal Astracytoma/Craniotomy (brain tumor); Craniotomy: surgery to remove tumor."

She died at 4:45 a.m. on St. Patrick's Day, March 17, 1961, four months after her operation. "Housewife" was listed as her occupation. Her citizenship was listed as "USA." She was 45 years old. Not long after her death, I saw a copy of the death certificate on my father's desk. I had no idea what those words next to "cause of death" meant. All I knew was that Mom died of cancer, a word I came to hate. Two days later Mom lay in a coffin at the Dabrowski funeral home. I know that the two-day viewing was crowded, but I remember very little. The next day Father Eckels, Mom's favorite priest, celebrated the Mass of Christian burial. Once the casket was placed into the hearse, Esther surprised everyone by refusing to go to the cemetery. Instead, she ran home alone. Pop and I knew she just could not bear the thought of Mom being lowered into a cold grave.

Our lives, of course, were very different in our once-happy home. The laughter was gone, replaced by sadness and a dark, scary feeling of the unknown. Pop, normally a funny man who loved to roughhouse with us, was no longer interested in playing games. He had lost his strength and confidence. Esther seemed to have lost her childhood as she, at the age of 12, carried on the many duties of cleaning house and making dinner. Often, my father did not even sit with us at dinner.

I did not cry during my mother's funeral, burial or wake, and I remember little about those events. But, I do remember her in bed when she first became ill. Because it was the last conversation I had with her, I suppose that is why it is such a powerful, endearing memory now, in fact the most endearing memory of my life.

I also remember so vividly that elderly woman who comforted me on my front steps days later, asking the simple question, "Child, why you be cryin'?"

When she put her hand on my shoulder, I thought, "Mom's never going to hug me again." It was a gesture so kind that it brought my tears flowing as I blurted out, "My mother died."

She only stayed a few minutes, but I am left with the tender memory of a stranger consoling me.

Later it would be my father who gave me the courage to move beyond our misfortune.

"It is not the tragedy which defines a person," he said, "But rather how she or he responds to it." Of course he said it in Spanish, but nothing was lost in the translation.

6
CULTURE SHOCK

In early 1961 ominous rumors buzzed at Crown Cork & Seal where Pop worked. Esther heard him nervously talking about it with a co-worker. They worried that new technology being developed by the bottling company's department of research and development would replace workers like them. The rumors turned out to be true. In the spring, three weeks after we buried Mom, Pop and most of his co-workers got the dreaded pink slips. The bosses kept their jobs, but had to relocate to a new plant in Philadelphia. The Baltimore plant, just across Eastern Avenue from City Hospitals, was shuttered forever. Two days later Pop had a breakdown. He sat in his living room chair, crying and shaking, unable to keep it from Esther and me. It was terrifying. In a matter of a few weeks the poor man lost his wife and his job. The sorrow so permeated his soul that Esther and I were scared beyond belief. Would Pop die too? I prayed every night, "Dear Lord, dear God almighty, Esther and I really need your help. Please make Pop better. Thank you Lord."

When Pop's jitters and crying jags didn't stop, Esther, at age 12, went next door for help. Her close friend Kitty lived there, and she asked Kitty's father, Mr. Phister, to come talk to Pop. A private talk between the two men helped Pop pull himself together. Thankfully, our father's life philosophy was "never say die." He was such a prideful man, he never let anyone see him sweat. So, he hit the reset button, much to our great relief.

We thanked the Lord that Pop was getting better. His first order of business was to find us a new home he could afford. It was clear we couldn't afford the rent in the Montford Avenue house. The thought of leaving home with all the tender memories of Mom really upset me. I wondered what would happen to Mom's shrine to the Blessed Mother that was still in my room. I also worried that we would move so far away that I would no longer be able to play with my buddies in the Port Street Rebels in Patterson Park. Esther had the same concerns about her friends and worried we might have to go to a new school.

Pop talked to an Italian neighbor named Bruno, whose daughter owned a house on Luzerne Avenue, just three blocks away. She had a second-floor apartment to rent, so we moved there, trudging with our heavy furniture up the narrow stairs. Just three weeks later we moved again, to an even cheaper place on the 2300 block of East Baltimore Street, sharing the rent with two Latin ladies. Boy, was our Italian landlady mad when she heard we were leaving so soon. "Had I known you would be moving in three weeks I would never have rented to you in the first place," she screamed at Pop. Then she began ranting at him in Italian, making a fist and shoving it upwards with a bent arm, while shouting "*fungool*," which I would later learn is the Italian version of the phrase, "go fuck yourself." Wow, that is one angry landlady, I thought.

After our second move, Pop read the daily employment ads in *The News American* and *The Evening Sun*, looking for work. He received weekly unemployment checks, but that was unacceptable to him. He didn't want to be on the government dole. To him, a man of honor was always expected to have a job. Finally, God answered our many prayers. Pop told us he was going back to work at Evergreen House. I did not know where that was, or exactly what it was, though Esther knew he and Mom once worked there. I was just so greatly relieved that he had found work. Esther believes that Pop returned there looking for work and begged the woman who managed the mansion for a job, that included a place for us to live.

On the day of our move (the third in just five weeks) Pop presented it in a positive light. Esther and I did not protest, even though we were not pleased to hear we would be transferring to a new school in the middle of the school year, somewhere in Baltimore where we had never been. What we didn't know is that the new school would be so different from our experience that we might as well be transferring to a school on the moon. He told us the school's name was The Cathedral School. I didn't like the name. All the Catholic schools I knew were named after saints like St. Dominic and St. Michael. That seemed appropriate to me—to give a school the name of an inspiring saint. Now I was going to attend a school with the name of a kind of building—a cathedral. And frankly, I had never seen a cathedral.

Once the word got out that we were leaving the neighborhood, the Rebels threw a party for me at the home of Mike Johnson. Six of my pals showed up. Mike's mom made us lunch and we sat down to a last game of Monopoly, that I hoped I would at last win. No such luck. I got the "Go to Jail" card. After saying warm goodbyes to the Rebels and thanking Mrs. Johnson, I walked home, thinking about what I was leaving behind. There would be no more Patterson Park, no more two-hand touch football on Port Street and no more Sister Nichols, my favorite teacher at St. Elizabeth's. Life isn't fair, I thought. Little did I know how very unfair life would become.

Finally it was moving day. A taxi picked us up as a family friend drove a small pickup truck with what little furniture we had left after we winnowed down our belongings with each move to a smaller place. Even Mom's cherished shrine to the Blessed Mother was left behind. The taxi took us through our East Baltimore neighborhood, past thousands of modest rowhouses just like ours, most with no lawns, just steps that led to the sidewalk.

Once downtown we headed north on Charles Street, cutting through the center of the city. Soon we began to pass houses that were the largest I'd ever seen, with huge porches, pillars and chimneys. There were vast lawns and flower gardens, and towering old trees. The taxi crossed Cold Spring Lane near Loyola College and turned right onto 4545 North Charles Street. As we rode up a long drive, we saw a house on a hill to our left standing alone that was much bigger and grander than all the houses we had just passed. Esther and I thought we were driving through a park on the way to our new home. We drove past an old building, not quite as large as the house on the hill, and continued past a creek with a small footbridge and a charming old stone wall. Dozens of acres of land, covered in perfectly manicured grass, sloped gracefully down to the creek near a garden that was full of flowers and benches, surrounded by a square brick wall. "This will take some getting used to," Pop said, though Esther and I weren't listening. The taxi continued past the creek and went up a hill, stopping in front of a small cottage. "We're home," said Pop. It took a few minutes for us to realize this enormous "park" was our new home.

It took only a few hours to unload. The cottage was already furnished with a large old desk and some old tables. Pop said they were expensive antiques. I had never heard of an antique. Our Latin friends arrived to help us settle in, and they began to cook a large chicken with rice, frijoles and a salad. A radio played Spanish music. They especially loved the music of Xavier Cugat, who popularized the rumba, and the Desi Arnaz Orchestra. I had to admit to myself that the cottage was already beginning to feel like home.

I told Esther I was going out to explore. "Don't get lost," she said in a tone that Mom might have used. I was back in an hour telling the others about the two large buildings. Pop said the larger building was a mansion and the other was a carriage house that used to be a horse stable. "What's a mansion?" I asked Pop. He explained that it was a house that had its own name—Evergreen House—that was once owned by a rich family that made their money in the railroad business. The mansion had 48 rooms, about the number of rooms in the houses on an entire city block of our old neighborhood.

In my later wanderings I found several peculiar graves marked in large stones of marble and granite. One inscription read, "The Old Gray, Nov. 29 1914, aged 29 years." Another was engraved simply: "Pet, A faithful friend, died January 1881." I was wide-eyed. These were graves of horses and pets marked with stones larger than any human gravestone I'd ever seen. "If they have this for animals," I wondered, "what do they have for themselves?" I had moved to a whole other world. "How can anybody be so rich?" I wondered. And that was even before I saw the mansion's gold bathroom.

If the culture shock from our new home wasn't enough, there was more alienation to come when school started. Pop told us we would be taking a bus to school for the first time and he would go with us the first day. I got up early and combed my hair "greaser style" with a duck tail in the back and a short curl coming down my forehead, just like rock-and-roll legend Jerry Lee Lewis. I put on white socks and pointy black shoes with Cuban-style heels. Breakfast was not my favorite meal, but I complied with Pop's orders to drink his "special vitamin" of one ounce of red wine mixed with a raw egg. Yuck. I certainly did miss Mom's fluffy biscuits. I put on my old tank jacket that all my friends in East Baltimore wore.

When we got off the bus Esther and I were surprised to see how palatial the Cathedral of Mary our Queen looked; it seated 2,000 people and its two spires soared 163 feet above North Baltimore. It took five minutes to walk to the school building. We watched in amazement as other students stepped out of Jaguars and Mercedes Benzes. Esther was sent to the seventh grade and I went to the fifth-grade classroom, where my teacher, Miss Alma, introduced me to the other students. They gave me an odd look. I quickly realized they were staring at my clothing and hair style. The other boys wore their hair very short and combed with a part on the side. They wore expensive-looking herringbone jackets and starched white button-down oxford shirts. It didn't take long for me to figure out that The Cathedral School of Mary Our Queen was also far more academically advanced than St. Elizabeth's. Now I felt like a freak who was stupid.

I also quickly learned that the students talked differently. I had to learn to be very careful not to speak in "Balamerese," the dialect of white working-class Baltimoreans, whose words get mangled beyond recognition. Esther and I pronounced Santa Claus "Sany Claus." We washed our hands in the "zink" and our mother carried a "pocky book." Our religion was "Cat Lick" and our country was "Merica." And we never pronounced the "T" in Baltimore. It was just "Balamer" to us.

The other students lived in houses with five or six bedrooms and three-car garages. They had private music lessons and went on overseas vacations. Wow, I thought. Can anyone spell ostentatious? Esther was fortunate to connect with another transfer student from a poor family named Beverly Mason. I was not so lucky. For weeks before the summer break, I took two buses on weekends to the old neighborhood to meet up with my old Port Street Rebels.

I was shocked one day to hear my best friend, Deany, tell me I had changed. "You're not the same guy," he said. "What do you mean I'm not?"

I asked. "You're not the same guy," he repeated. He then turned his back on me and walked away. I was crushed and angry. It was the last time I saw any of the Rebels. Finally the school year ended and I was relieved to be promoted to the sixth grade. Pop arranged for my teacher, Miss Alma, to tutor me during the summer in math and English because I was so far behind.

Sometimes I accompanied Pop to the Evergreen mansion. He did not allow me to explore the house alone, but always escorted me to every room, along with his cautionary comments, "be careful and don't touch anything." The experience made a big impression and gave me a clear understanding that there was another world out there. I was determined to become an active member.

Pop's duties included maintaining a spotless interior with its museum-quality valuables. He also scheduled meeting times and catering services for many groups, including the Daughters of the American Revolution, the Baltimore Bibliophiles, and the Society of the Ark and the Dove.

As the fall semester began I became more acclimated. One day I saw what seemed to be two cars in one. I asked my friend, Mark Jenkins, "Wow, what is that?" It was a white limousine. When it stopped in front of the school, a chauffeur dressed in full uniform got out to open the door for the Knott children, the sons and daughters of Henry Knott Sr., a developer who was one of the richest Catholics in Baltimore.

It wasn't long before the big announcement that football tryouts were scheduled. I became the starting fullback. You couldn't say much for the caliber of our team. We sucked big time. But that didn't matter. I was finally one of the boys. As for Esther, she didn't want anything except for the school year to end. In her class there was one quick witted, gregarious and exceptionally smart boy named Louis J. Otremba. Everyone called him Louie. One day Esther and I were waiting for the #11 bus when we heard a car honk. It was Louie with his older brother, Frank, in the driver's seat of a 1956 gray Dodge Coronet. "Get in," yelled Louie. As Esther and I jumped into the back seat, we had smiles on our faces. I yelled out, "I love America." Louie became my best friend that day. He opened my eyes to the lay of the land. He was the one who told me that the construction in the 1950s of Cathedral of Mary Our Queen was financed by Thomas J. O'Neill, who owned a popular department store downtown that miraculously survived the Great Baltimore Fire of 1904.

To cope with my alien surroundings, I began paying attention to a little voice in my head. It was telling me to be cautious, not to embarrass myself. When I got to The Cathedral School I was still thinking in Spanish and translating in my head, so I was always hitting the alert button to check myself. I began to protect myself, especially around other students who spoke of going to Killington, Vermont to ski or to vacation on St. Simons Island in Georgia or Bar Harbor in Maine, places I had never heard of. My little voice would tell me, "Just keep listening and you will learn what they are talking about." I jokingly considered giving this inner voice a nickname.

As the school calendar moved on, I played first-string guard for the basketball team, which wasn't much better than the football squad. But we had fun. On the roster was Lou Schmidt, who played center, and Jimmy Lacy, who played point guard. Lacy's father was a Loyola College legend. His remarkable basketball statistics continue to stand today. In 1964, while in the eighth grade, Lou was honored with the Unsung Hero Award for his dedication to school sports. He might not have been the best player, but no one played harder. Often Lou and I would shoot hoops behind his house. We enjoyed hanging around his sisters Robin and Kelly. Years later Jimmy was driving drunk when he crashed the car, killing Lou. Lou was a business student at Loyola College at the time of his death.

In the fall of 1963 I saw Pop reading a small pamphlet. "Pop what are you looking at?" I asked. "It's the Maryknoll missionary magazine," he answered. "Can I see?" He handed it to me and explained that the Maryknoll fathers and brothers devote their lives to the Holy Lord by carrying the word of God to economically depressed areas in China and Central and South America. "If you are interested, you should speak with the school sisters," Pop told me. I took his advice to heart. We both knew that my mother's greatest wish before she died was for me to become a priest. Later, Sister George Mary, my seventh-grade teacher, who I considered a surrogate mother, sat with me for hours talking about the priesthood. I spent long stretches of time thinking about it on the tranquil little bridge over the creek near our cottage. I finally decided that I wanted to live the missionary life. When I told Pop, he was so very, very pleased. Hugging me tightly, he said, "Your mother is crying tears of joy." In the spring of 1964, Sister George Mary proctored the entrance exam for Maryknoll Junior Seminary in Clark Summit, Pennsylvania. About a week later, I received the good news. I passed! Pop and Esther were very proud. When I told Louie, I was surprised by his reaction.

"Man, he said, "are you really sure about this?"

7
THE ROAD TO GOD

Pop had tears in his eyes as I boarded a bus for the Maryknoll Junior Seminary in Pennsylvania. I was just 14 years old and had never spent a night away from home, except for the 40 days I spent in the hospital with Stevens-Johnson Syndrome. I felt unsettled and nervous as Pop warned me not to let go of the bag that carried my eye drops. I had four bottles of the steroids, packed in a small box. I had visited Dr. Scholz so he could show me how to deal with my ingrown eyelashes while I was away. "If you can put up with the pain for a few days," he told me, "the eyelash will grow out normally." He showed me how to pull the eyelid upward and gently move the eyelash forward. It was not the best option, he said, because there was a chance of infection, but it was the only alternative since I had no one at the seminary to pluck out the lashes. I also packed three pairs of sunglasses because the sun irritated my eyes.

The bus was crowded, but I found a window seat in the back. I did not bring anything to read or otherwise entertain myself for the four-hour trip, but in my pocket I had something better. In a little zippered pouch I carried my mother's pink, translucent rosary beads. Having them made me feel that my mother was still with me. It was a sunny day, so I enjoyed the scenery of the forest and the mountains. The song "We Shall Overcome" popped into my head. The Cathedral School was all white, but Sister George Mary had taught me the civil rights anthem and since Pop closely followed current events, I was somewhat aware of the brutal victimization of blacks in our country. So I sang it in my head to pass the time. When the bus stopped, I got my bags, followed the other passengers to the terminal and flagged a cab.

"Where to?" asked the driver. When I gave him the address in Clark Summit, he seemed to know the place and said it would cost me $10.

I was greeted by a student who checked my name off a list on his clipboard and walked me through a big building. We climbed several steps to a large dormitory with 20 bunk beds. I was so excited and scared. After putting away my clothes, I wasn't sure what to do next. So I sat on the bed wondering, "When do we eat?"

A friendly upperclassman named Jim Landsman came by and introduced himself. My dorm, he said, was for freshmen and sophomores. I asked about lunch, but he told me lunch had come and gone. He then gave me a tour of the building which included the chapel, classrooms, a huge cafeteria, a music room, kitchen, library, gym, and the sleeping area for juniors and seniors. We then toured the outside, with the seminary's basketball court, a swimming pool, a large pond, apple orchards and even a slaughterhouse. Jim said that all seminarians were assigned to work crews. "No one likes to work the slaughterhouse," he said smiling. I wrinkled my face. "So, what gets slaughtered?" I asked. "Pigs," he said. "You hit them on the head with a sledgehammer and plunge an ice pick into their jugular vein, then hang them upside down to drain the blood. Then the pig is put into a steaming vat of water to remove the hair. Then you cut the pig into parts for eating," he explained. "But don't worry," he added. "Only juniors and seniors get that job." I found the atmosphere to be friendly, and I especially got a tranquil feeling when I walked past the chapel.

Later in the afternoon, Father John Casey, the rector, addressed the freshman class. He was a no-nonsense man who wore glasses that constantly slid down his nose. I don't ever recall him smiling. I was pleased to meet three other boys in my class from Baltimore: Mike Paradise, Tom Judd and Paul LaFrance. Other students were from Ohio and New York.

The courses included academics as well as religion. Upperclassmen studied Latin and Greek. Our days began at 6 a.m. with confession, followed immediately by Mass, which was in Latin. We also sang Gregorian chants, an ancient form of Christian liturgical music that uses unison voices with no harmony. It is meant to put you in a meditative state of prayer. It certainly did for me. I actually found the chants very soothing. After a brief break, we would have breakfast at 7:30 a.m.

Frankly, I found the studies difficult and had to work hard to keep up. When we were assigned to translate Homer's *The Iliad* and *The Odyssey* from Latin to English, it took me forever, but I got it done. I looked forward to recreation time. It didn't take long for the boys to make up nicknames. We called Jose Ruiz "Diamond" after the Diamonds gang in Spanish Harlem where he was born. We called Tom Judd "Mouse" because he was short and had a cute face that looked like a mouse. Mike Paradise, who was already 6 feet 2 inches, was dubbed "Tree" and we called Paul LaFrance "Frog" for his bulging eyes. We called another boy, Ron Renfro, "Dough Boy" because he was overweight. If I was given a nickname, I never heard it.

Pop and I wrote letters to each other and he dutifully sent the very much needed bottles of eye drops. Other than learning to stand on my own, there was nothing remarkable about the semester. I went home for the Christmas holidays anticipating conversations with Pop, Esther and friends about what I had missed all these months. Pop and Esther peppered me with questions about seminary life. Esther also shared the news that she had met a young man named John Streb, whom she would marry in 1969. I also found we had moved into a new home built near our cottage on land that had been sold to Loyola College. When I saw my friend Louie, he was still skeptical about my chosen vocation. "Is the Roman collar for you?" he asked.

I wasn't really sure how to answer, but said yes.

After the holiday break, classes resumed and I spent a lot of time in the seminary chapel meditating. While praying, I told God that I loved Him. I always felt good after a visit with the Holy Lord. There were some peculiar incidents during the school year that gave me pause. In a meeting with students in the library Father Casey instructed us not to take jobs at the local supermarkets because he did not want us to have any contact with women who were not family. In class I raised a hand. "Father," I asked, "in our ministry will we not deal with females?" Instead of answering me the priest just walked out of the room. "What a rude man," I thought. Later, Jim Landsman explained that we were barred from being near women because we were going through puberty and seeing members of the opposite sex might deter us from a life of celibacy. He also asked me if I had seen copies of *Sports Illustrated* in the library. "Didn't you notice there are photographs removed with a razor blade?" he asked. "Those were the ones with women in swimsuits."

After the school year was over, Louie's question about life in the priesthood troubled me all summer, but I said nothing. I wondered if I needed to dedicate myself to God more so I would not question my beliefs. "Do I have it in me to be a missionary priest?" I asked myself. My entire life must be devoted to God. Not having relationships with women, or forgoing a family, did not even pop into my head.

Midway through the fall semester of 1965 I knocked on the door of Father John O'Connell's office. I got directly to my question. "Father, how do you define faith?"

"Faith," he answered, "Is believing in something that can not otherwise be explained." I told him I was having a hard time reconciling the Catholic dogma that Jesus Christ rose from the dead. I could not believe in so-called miracles that did not seem humanly possible. I wondered how I could teach this to other people if I was having a hard time believing it myself.

"Either you have faith or you don't," he answered perfunctorily. Before I left we prayed the "Our Father" together. As I opened the door to leave, he only said, "God bless you my son."

I found a book in the seminary library. Called *The Whiskey Priest,* it was the true story of an ordained priest who has signs of moral weakness while teaching a higher standard to his parishioners. He is very much conflicted and prays to God for direction. I read to the end and wondered if God wanted me to find the book. It was the tipping point that the vocation was not for me. I wonder now if the priests in the seminary had ever read that book. If they had, they might have banned it from the library. The book had more impact on my decision not to become a priest than any "wrong" impression I might have gotten from photos of women in swimsuits.

That very day, I called Pop collect. Holding back the tears, I told him my decision. Pop wasn't angry and instead told me he loved me and asked if I wanted to enroll in a Catholic school when I returned home. I said no. I was tired of religious courses. He was understanding. He said he would do research to find the best secular school for me.

Just before the Christmas break I told Father Casey I was leaving. He was cold. He didn't even try to talk me out of it. He just handed me the drop-out form to sign. That was it. I later learned that three seniors, six sophomores and five juniors were also dropping out. Jim Landsman was one of them. As it turned out, junior seminaries for young teenage boys were largely a failure. That was one of the Catholic Church's dirty little secrets. I had no idea how many other secrets the Church had.

As I boarded the bus home, I was singing to myself the Simon and Garfunkel hit "Homeward Bound":

I'm sitting in the railway station.
Got a ticket for my destination.
On a tour of one-night stands my suitcase and guitar in hand.
And every stop is neatly planned for a poet and a one-man band.
Homeward bound,
I wish I was,
Homeward bound,
Home where my thought's escaping,
Home where my music's playing,
Home where my love lies waiting
Silently for me.

8
A SECULAR LIFE

I returned home in search of a public high school where I would be free of the rigorous religious studies that had taken up so much of my childhood. Finally, at age 16, I would meet boys from different backgrounds, and I would be allowed—even encouraged—to meet and socialize with girls. Whatever school I chose, there would surely be no photos of women excised from magazines and no rebuke against taking a job where I might meet members of the opposite sex. I really looked forward to this new chapter in my life.

Pop and I agreed that I would consider Baltimore's two top public high schools. Baltimore Polytechnic Institute, or Poly, was known for its math and science programs. City College high school, or City, was known for its liberal arts programs. City, one of the country's oldest public schools, was nicknamed "Castle on the Hill" for its building's imposing Gothic design and its position high above 33rd Street, just down the street from the Orioles' Memorial Stadium. City was an all boys' school at the time and was the alma mater of many successful Baltimoreans, including Kurt Schmoke, a City football quarterback who went on to become a Rhodes Scholar and Baltimore's first elected African American mayor. Schmoke's political nemesis, William Donald Schaefer, was also a City College alum who became Baltimore's powerful four-term mayor, Maryland's two-term governor and state comptroller.

City's liberal arts curriculum was definitely more suited for me, so I took the entrance exam and passed. I entered the school in the middle of the 1966 school year, at a time of great civil rights struggles. Three years before, the Rev. Martin Luther King Jr. gave his famous "I have a dream" speech at the Lincoln Memorial. When I enrolled in City College I knew that the student body was predominantly African American. This would be a new experience for me. I had spent so many years at the all-white Cathedral School and at the seminary. So it was with some trepidation that I boarded the #8 bus that first day.

That protective little voice appeared again in my head, the one that told me to be cautious before I spoke to other, wealthier students at The Cathedral School. It was about this time that I gave my inner voice a name, Chilo, which is the nickname for Isidro, my given first name, the same as Pop's name. As I walked up the hilly sidewalk on campus I thought, "Wow, it really is a castle on a hill." And as I entered the big double doors of City College, Chilo told me, "Don't look scared. Just be yourself and all will be okay."

Within minutes I heard someone call my name. It was Bumper, my old secret friend from East Baltimore. He was my only black friend. We fist-bumped and he gave me a quick tour of the school and introduced me to some of his friends. As I settled into the first class of the day, I prayed, "Thank you God for Bumper."

My life was generally going well, but there was an economic gap between my friends and me. They had spending money and I did not. Pop helped me find summer jobs so I could buy the type of clothing my friends wore, what we called the "Joe College" look. First Pop got me a job at the John Work Garrett Library at Evergreen House, climbing up and down a ladder with Neatsfoot Oil, gently dusting the leather spines of what Pop called "priceless first editions" and other ancient books. I was warned not to remove them. I had no idea that I was dusting some of the rarest books in the world, including a Latin edition of the Nuremberg Chronicle from 1493 and original Audubon prints of North American birds from the 19th century.

After a few weeks the lady who ran the library arranged for me to work at the Maryland Historical Society in the Mount Vernon neighborhood near the Peabody Conservatory of Music. I caught two buses to get downtown, then walked 25 minutes to work. That summer I was introduced to yet another universe which was foreign to me, the world of gentry and genealogy. For three days each week I learned how to search records for dates and places of births and deaths. I also learned how to research genealogy to show continuous lines of descendants for the so-called "blue-blood" society. My bosses were Hester Rich and Mary Meyers, whom I called Mother Mary, the name from the Beatles mega-hit, "Let it Be." I often responded to research requests from people who wanted to join the Daughters of the American Revolution or the Society of the Ark and the Dove, which is only open to members who can prove they are descendants of Sir George Calvert or an ancestor who came over on either the Ark or the Dove, the ships that carried the first Maryland colonists from England in 1633.

I will never forget the lady who wrote asking us to prove her pure lineage for membership to the Society of the Ark and the Dove. I determined that a family member in the 1880s was hanged for the crime of horse theft. In those days, stealing a horse was a very serious crime, particularly in the wilderness, because a victim could be left to die without the horse for transportation. Apparently this news may have disqualified the woman from joining the organization. Two weeks after I wrote to her of this unfortunate discovery, Miss Rich handed me a letter addressed to

"Isidro James Cabezas." I was taken aback when I saw the envelope. I thought that she must have seen my birth certificate. How else could she know my given first name was Isidro? The letter contained a $50 check made out to me, along with a request to omit my discovery of the horse thief. I couldn't believe it. When I showed the letter and check to Mary Meyers, she said, "Some people will stoop really low and are willing to pay a bribe to get their way." It was my very first lesson in the meaning of bribery. I would, of course, eventually become well acquainted with other unscrupulous people who paid and accepted bribes—and I would put some of them in prison. That day I ripped the check into pieces and returned it to the sender.

In the fall of 1966, I joined the Sigma Kappa Phi fraternity. I heard about it from Louie Otremba. It was started by a Poly student, so most of the members were from Poly. I was one of only four members from City. As a group, we had a lot to talk about that wasn't stereotypical of partying American fraternities. As the country was in the midst of social change our generation found strength from longhair bands singing songs of protest and the misery of war. If Bob Dylan sang it, we believed it. The frat house provided a place for much discussion, especially about the Vietnam War. None of us supported President Lyndon B. Johnson. In a few years we would be eligible for the draft and that worried us, as we watched CBS news anchor Walter Cronkite receiving the daily body count from General William Westmoreland. The nation had grown weary of the Cold War theory that military support was mandatory to stop the threat of countries falling into Communist hands. As Johnson continued to send more ground troops, peace rallies sprouted up around the country.

Frankly, we also wanted our own place where we could drink beer and have parties out of our parents' earshot. One of the members saw a "for rent" sign on an old house across the street from Poly. Bob Price somehow persuaded his father to sign a $75 monthly lease for the house at 4667 Falls Road. Immediately, assignments were handed out. The most important job was building a bar in the basement so we could drink beer before we were legally allowed. Lou Otremba and Jay Stolz were the primary workers with help from others. Bob Fifield managed to get the heating system in tip-top working condition. Others cleaned and made trips to the dump. Paul Fruend, who worked at Eddie's Gourmet Shop, arranged for beer and wine to be delivered. Jim Anzalone was appointed treasurer and I was the sergeant of arms, responsible to maintain order during meetings. Mike Beatty was put in charge of the jukebox. The Friday and Saturday night dance parties were on. We were all surprised to learn how much money the bar was making. Although our members were all white, we quickly integrated our parties by inviting the attractive African American girls (and their friends) who lived next door. On Sunday mornings we would nurse our hangovers with what was known as the Red Eye Special, when Bloody Marys and mimosas were only a quarter.

In those days boys were dating by the age of 16 so we went places where we could meet girls, such as Orchard Swim Club, which had Friday night dances We also loved the novelty of Ameche's Drive-In Restaurant, owned by Baltimore Colts running back Alan Ameche, where we could drive into a parking spot next to an intercom and order food without getting out of the car. This was long before the days of drive-thru fast food restaurants like McDonald's. Waitresses and waiters brought the food to our car. We also met girls at Sunday afternoon dances in several halls in the area.

My friends and I often spoke about girls whom we would like to date, as bragging was part of the ritual of teenage boys. One Sunday I telephoned Louie.

"Hey what's up?" I asked him. "Not much man," Louie said.

"I had a date last night with Jamie," I began boasting. "Man oh man. She let me French kiss her and before I knew it I was passing second base and went right to third."

"Are you kidding me?" asked Louie, sounding incredulous.

After the chat ended, I hung up the phone and walked into the living room where Pop was reading the Sunday paper. As he lowered the *News American*, he gave me a stern look. "Do you like Jamie?"

"Yes Pop I do. She is really nice."

"Well, you just told Louie that she's a whore."

Pop's remarks slammed me like a baseball bat. He then said, "You get back on that phone and tell Louie you are a liar."

So I called Louie and told him that I had made up the story. "I didn't believe you," he said. "You're not that good looking," When I returned to the living room, Pop said, "If you ever get so lucky that a girl is willing to kiss you, never do you kiss and tell." What a life lesson that was for me. The school semester came and went without problems. The regiment of eye drops in the morning and at night became a routine. However I was sad to hear that Bumper was dropping out of school. When I asked why, he just said that his dad was gone and that he had to find a job. That was the last time I saw my friend.

In the spring of 1967, when I was 17, I met my first love, Kathy. Jay Hubbert, whom I knew from The Cathedral School, introduced me to Kathleen Ann Bausch, an attractive blonde girl my age who went to Patterson Park High School. It was a popular school and a sports powerhouse. We began to see each other right away and arranged to meet our respective parents, who approved our dating. Kathy was very pretty, easy to talk to and she laughed at all my silly jokes. She was a serious student and eager to get a job in the business world after graduation. We both loved seeing the latest movies, most of which would become classics: *A Patch of Blue, To Sir with Love, Guess Who's Coming to Dinner, The Graduate* and *In the Heat of the Night.* We were also both music lovers. In June we went to the Baltimore Civic Center where we enjoyed the Four Tops, Stevie Wonder and Ray Charles. As the year moved along, Kathy and I spoke on the phone every night and dated every Friday and Saturday night. On Sunday I was always invited to dinner at the Bausch house. As soon as I got there her brother Ronny would say, "Let's go shoot a game or two of pool." We would be gone 90 minutes. Kathy never protested.

The frat house was also a whirlwind of social activity. We had Halloween hay rides, trips to Hart-Miller Island on the Chesapeake Bay where we rented row boats, and picnics with plenty of Pabst Blue-Ribbon and Budweiser beer. Poly was well known for putting on fantastic dances and Sigma Kappa Phi was well represented. While many teens enjoyed the British Invasion, Kathy and I preferred Motown and other soul music, especially the Temptations, the Supremes, Marvin Gaye, Gladys Knight and the Pips, Otis Redding and of course James Brown and the Famous Flames. Kathy and I were falling in love. Some of the other frat members also started dating with meaning. Louie met Laura Kihn, whose brother Greg was the front man for the Greg Kihn Band, which later had a hit song called "Jeopardy."

On Christmas, 1967, I dug into my savings and bought Kathy a full-length caramel colored suede coat with a real mink collar. It was so beautiful that she would remember it 50 years later. It was the most expensive gift I'd ever bought.

In June we both graduated, but I did not bother to attend my graduation. Instead, I went to work at the historical society. I was looking forward to attending the University of Maryland in the fall with my buddies. My life was going as planned, until all hell broke loose. Kathy called a few weeks later to say she had missed her period and was pregnant. She was very happy, but I was stunned and certainly had mixed emotions. We were just 18. "Me a father?" I asked myself. "What do I know about being a parent? Where would we live? How about money? Babies are expensive. How will I go to college?"

On the phone I just said, "Oh my God. What will we do?" Kathy said, "Aren't you happy?"

"Well yes. This is so sudden," I said. I didn't tell Kathy, but deep down inside I was sad and disappointed that my plans of going to College Park were now shattered.

"It's all going to be all right," she said, naively.

Our conversation ended with the agreement that our parents needed to be told right away. We each said "I love you," and hung up.

It felt as if we were two birds lost in a windstorm. We had no clear idea what would happen next. We had no place to live. No furniture, not even a bed. I had a part time job, but that wasn't enough. Kathy needed to find a job. Pop would be home in about an hour. I wished I knew where Esther was. Oh Lord. From my bedroom I heard Pop open the front door and go into the kitchen. An hour passed and I was still sitting in the same chair, frozen with fear. How would I tell Pop? How would he react? My little inner voice was not talking to me. Where was my little voice? Finally I spoke aloud, but softly. "Chilo, Chilo, where are you? Can you hear me? Chilo, Chilo!" Finally, I heard the voice say, "Tell him that Kathy is pregnant." I summoned the courage to walk into the kitchen.

9
LIFE LESSONS

"Hola Pop. Cómo está? Might you have a couple minutes to talk?" I asked in a weak voice.

Pop looked at my face.

"What is so wrong that you look as if you have been crying?" he asked.

We went into the dining room and sat at the table. Silence.

"Well I'm waiting." Finally I had the courage to speak.

"Kathy is going to have a baby."

The room went silent again. Pop kept looking directly into my eyes. I couldn't look back, so I looked down at the table, fraught with shame. Even worse, I was guilt ridden that I was hurting Pop. He had already been through so much emotional pain.

"Do you and Kathy love each other?" Pop asked.

"Yes Pop, we do, very much." I answered.

"Have you talked about getting married?"

"We thought that we would get married after I finished college."

"Men of honor do what's right," he said. "You know that there would never be an abortion."

"Yes Pop, I do."

"Well then, you and Kathy have a lot to talk about."

I then told him Kathy was telling her parents about her pregnancy.

When it was over I thought that I had just had the hardest conversation of my life. I didn't think that I could love my father more, but now I did.

As we moved forward, I realized that the sun still rose and set, the elevators continued to go up and down and the buses ran on schedule. Pop agreed to allow us to temporarily move into the basement, which ran the length of the house but did not have a bathroom or sink. It also did not have a set of stairs inside the house. Kathy, who was a frugal young lady, took control. We bought furniture from her brother, who was getting divorced. He helped us move an entire living-room set, kitchen table and chairs as well as a bedroom set. Kathy brought a portable TV and quickly arranged our new household. We settled in and got used to going outside and up the steps to use the kitchen and bathroom. It was not a big deal for us. We were happy and in love.

On June 28, 1968, we were married in a civil ceremony in the Baltimore city courthouse.

The night before, Kathy came to me with good news. "I'm not pregnant, I just got my period."

I did not think to ask her why she was so sure she was pregnant in the first place. In those days there was no easily available pregnancy test short of going to a doctor.

I was relieved at her news, but we were both still excited about getting married.

Kathy found a job at the Union Trust Bank. On payday, she saved a small percentage of her check for an apartment. It didn't take her long to find an affordable one at 3500 Old York Road, about a mile away. I was attending the Baltimore Junior College and studying business.

While Kathy and I faced our personal challenges, the world outside was moving at full tilt with civil rights and antiwar demonstrations, riots, and assassinations of our country's leaders. These earth-shattering changes facing our country would have an even more profound effect on my future than my marriage to Kathy.

On April 4, 1968, the spring of my senior year in high school, James Earl Ray assassinated civil rights leader Martin Luther King Jr. in Memphis, Tennessee. In Baltimore, riots broke out two days later and lasted for six days, with looting and arsons in both East and West Baltimore.

Once the rioting began, all the schools were closed.

Maryland Governor Spiro T. Agnew declared a state of emergency in the city. The National Guard and state police were called in. Both city and state police were under the command of Baltimore's police commissioner, Donald Pomerleau, who had been on the job for just two years. Both Agnew and Pomerleau would loom large in my life; one would inspire my career and the other would guide it. The riots and looting left six people dead and dozens injured. Hundreds of properties were destroyed, with losses estimated at $8 to $10 million. Nearly 8,000 people were arrested.

Two months later, Robert F. Kennedy, brother to the late President John F. Kennedy, was assassinated in California while campaigning for president. I was saddened by his death because I hoped, as president, he would withdraw American troops from Vietnam. I did not like Richard Nixon, a hawk, who was running against him. Now, I knew the war would not end anytime soon and that the world would be a different place. The war would, in fact, continue for another seven years.

In late August, another national event left a profound impression on me, planting an idea in my 18-year-old head that would lead to a lifelong career in criminal justice.

Pop and I were watching CBS when the news broke in, showing riots in Chicago outside the Democratic National Convention. I watched in horror as hundreds of police officers viciously beat war protesters with large night sticks. The police, wearing blue shirts and matching helmets, bloodied hundreds of unarmed protesters with cruel blows to the head and ribs. They then dragged their limp bodies to paddy wagons. Many of the protesters looked as if they'd been knocked out cold.

"Oh my God Pop, this is so horrible," I said. He just shook his head in disbelief. Then I said, "What's it going to take to change?"

The beatings took place after President Johnson threw his support behind his vice president, Hubert Humphrey, as his successor. Humphrey had no intention of pulling troops out of Vietnam. Protests at the convention had been planned for months, with leaders of the Youth International Party (YIP, or Yippies), Jerry Rubin and Abbie Hoffman, making moves to bring thousands of antiwar demonstrators to Chicago. Chicago Mayor Richard J. Daley refused permits to allow the protesters to congregate in city parks and threatened that "law and order will be maintained." The marchers came anyway. The day before the convention, Humphrey appeared on *Meet the Press*, saying that any position by the Democrats to support unilateral withdrawal from the war would be "disastrous." Because of the bloodshed and the affront to many people's sense of order and fairness, Mayor Daley would go down as one of the nation's most callous mayors for his defense of police brutality during the riots. In the aftermath, he called the protesters "a lawless, violent group of terrorists."

The next time I spoke with Mary Meyers at the Maryland Historical Society I asked what she thought of the violence in Chicago. Like me, she was outraged. "The only way that change can be successful, is if it comes from within," she said. That night I told Kathy I would be switching my college studies at the Baltimore Junior College from business to criminal justice. I started reading detective magazines and was riveted by the articles showing how police solve real crimes. I also bought a police scanner and listened to it at night.

I became engrossed in my studies while also working at the historical society 24 hours a week. The commutes on the bus took up even more of my time. I became too tired to pay attention to my marriage. Kathy and I decided to split up. She returned home and I moved back into my old bedroom. Our parents were saddened by our separation. Since both families were devoted Catholics, they suggested that if God became more a part of our lives, all would be fine. We got back together, and on June 28, 1969, Kathy and I were married in the Church of the Most Precious Blood in Northeast Baltimore.

Like many newlyweds, we applied for credit at Levenson & Klein Furniture Store and bought a living room and bedroom set for our new apartment in Hamilton in Northeast Baltimore. In June of 1970, I graduated with an associate's degree in criminal justice from the Baltimore Junior College. In late June, I passed the written entrance test for the Baltimore City police department. I took a polygraph exam and waited for a background investigation to be completed.

The last step was to pass a physical test which included an eye exam. Naturally, that was my biggest worry. I was in good physical condition, since I enjoyed long-distance running, but I was really worried that my eyes would fail me. Four days before the scheduled examination I experimented by applying double dosages of my steroid eye drops. I was well aware that too much of the drops came with good and bad news; my eyes were less bloodshot, but my vision did not improve. Since I had yet to get my driver's license, Kathy drove me to police headquarters. As the elevator ascended to the fifth floor, I quietly prayed to God to help me. I found the room for the exam, signed in and took a seat. I anxiously waited as other applicants were called in for their exams. Then I heard my name, "James Caba, Caba." I immediately stood and said, "It's Cabezas." The aide pointed to a door. I knocked and walked in. I was surprised to see a uniformed police officer who would administer the eye test, instead of a doctor.

"Please sit on the stool and look directly ahead," he told me. I saw the eye chart on the wall.

"I want you to read line six," he told me. I read it without a problem.

"Now go to line three," he said. Again I read the letters accurately.

"That's good," he said. "You're at 20/30 vision. Let's go on." As I looked forward I saw a graphic of train tracks. From past experience I knew that I had problems with depth perception. The officer then asked, "What do you see?"

"A train track with signs on both sides," I replied.

"How many signs do you see?" he asked.

"Sir, there are six."

He then asked me to read the second sign on the left. I answered, "Reduce speed."

He then said, "Now tell me what you see on the third sign on the right side of the tracks."

The letters were blurred. My hands sweated profusely. I knew I was in trouble.

"You can take your time," he said, "but I need you to read the sign."

I leaned forward on the stool. The letters were still blurred. I closed my right eye, but that did not help. I closed the left eye. Nothing. When I realized I could not read the sign, a blast of fear ran through me like rushing water in a hurricane.

"Son," said the officer. "How much do you want to be a police officer?"
I looked directly at him.
"More than anything in the world."
He hesitated for what seemed like minutes.
Then he smiled and said, "You just passed!"

10
MY FIRST CALL TO DUTY

My first shift as a Baltimore City police officer was to begin at midnight. I didn't need to be at the district station until 11:30 p.m., but I was so excited that I got dressed more than two hours ahead of time. I put on my new blue uniform and gun belt, holstered with a six-shot revolver and 18 additional bullets, mace, handcuffs and a night stick. I hooked a clip-on tie under my collar, a safety requirement; if someone tried to strangle me with my own tie, it would just fall off. My coat, called a "reefer," had a large slit on the side so I could quickly reach through to my holster if I needed my gun. I had cleaned my police badge with soap and water and buffed it with a paper towel. I was so proud of it.

I was suited and ready for duty by 9:30. I was 21 years old.

When asked by the Baltimore Police Department why I wanted to be an officer in September 1970, I wrote this:

The reason I have chosen law enforcement as a vocation is because it is the type of occupation which provides 1. A service to the community. 2. There is reward in everyday duty (as in helping people solve trivial problems). 3. Good job security. 4. To me it is a position to be proud of. 5. Also that you are part of a team which is attempting to decrease the social injustices. I also have another strong reason, being that I would like to get into the narcotics division. I feel very strongly about the present drug problem and I would like to help stamp the present situation out. Also, police work provides both clerical and non-clerical work which coincides with my character.

For me, police work would not merely be a profession. I thought of it as a vocation or a calling, like the priesthood. Only this time, I would not have to believe in miracles.

I did still believe deeply in God, which might explain my lack of fear in choosing a vocation fraught with danger. In those days it was not uncommon for Baltimore police officers to die in the line of duty from gunshot wounds to the chest or the back. I had not even heard of a bulletproof vest, and the department would not issue them for another four years. I left the worrying to Kathy, who was full of pride, but very concerned for my safety.

Despite my lack of fear, I knew I had to be on guard at all times and I would increasingly listen to Chilo, my protective inner voice, always reminding me to be on alert and to never, ever stop thinking.

That first night came after six months in the police academy, where I graduated at the top of my class as valedictorian in February 1971. The police department had a longstanding policy that the valedictorian could select the district of his choice. I picked the Central District after a ride-along with a police officer to the George B. Murphy Homes public housing project, just west of downtown. It was home to one of the most dangerous heroin operations in the city (and decades later would be memorialized in the TV show The Wire). The officer I rode with explained that drug networks were constantly trying to protect their territory and competing with other drug organizations.

Murphy Homes consisted of four 14-story buildings housing hundreds of tenants. Below the buildings was an open courtyard where people would congregate. If an officer was called for a disturbance, he could have 30 to 40 people quickly surrounding him. Residents would watch from the upper balconies with large water guns filled with urine, ready to spray them through holes in a security fence on police as soon as they entered the courtyard. I thought, "Man, that's where I want to be, because that's where the action is." Since I was very interested in working to eradicate drugs, I was fascinated by the chance to work the Murphy Homes beat.

But it was not to be. For some unknown reason I was not allowed to choose my district and I was assigned instead to the Eastern District. In fact, being valedictorian had no perks on the job.

My first beat would be on foot patrol, from midnight to 8 a.m. on a rickety six-block area of Greenmount Avenue, which runs north-south above North Avenue. It wasn't as dangerous—or exciting—as Murphy Homes, but it would be no picnic either. Because of the dangers on my beat I knew my foot patrol assignment would overlap with a "shotgun car," a marked police car that had two officers carrying revolvers and a shotgun in the trunk.

I also knew it was the scene of a notorious crime on Christmas Eve 1964, when two brothers, Earl and Samuel Veney, robbed Luxies Liquor Store on Greenmount at 20th Street. On their way out of the holdup, Earl Veney shot Lt. Joseph T. Maskell, the first officer to arrive on the scene. One bullet hit Maskell in the neck, puncturing his left lung. A second bullet to the back punctured his right lung. Maskell would live. But another officer would not be so lucky. A few hours later, during a massive manhunt for the Veney brothers, Sgt. Jack Lee Cooper was found dead in his patrol car about a mile away, shot three times in the chest and once in the back. If he'd worn a bulletproof vest, he might have survived. As police searched for the Veney brothers, they forced their way into hundreds of homes in a ten-block radius, with no search warrants. Such illegal searches would thereafter be known among police as "Superman warrants" because police would break in doors with their shoulders, terrorizing the residents. Despite these searches and despite the FBI's manhunt, with the brothers' photos displayed on the FBI's Most Wanted list, police would not find them for three months, when they were discovered working in a zipper factory in New York.

More fresh in my mind was a shooting of two police officers in 1970 on a street in West Baltimore. After responding to a domestic disturbance, Officer Donald Sager was murdered and his partner, Stanley Sierakowski, was wounded after they returned to their squad car.

Baltimore was a deadly city back then, just as it is now. In my rookie year there would be 323 homicides. In comparison, the deadly year of 2017 would end with 342.

I believed the six months I spent at the police academy had prepared me for my new job, but of course nothing can really prepare you for such dangerous work in a police department that I would learn was far from exemplary. In hindsight, that first night on the job would teach me lessons I could never learn in a classroom or a firing range.

At the academy we were taught report writing and patrol techniques, when we could arrest and search a person, and when we could search vehicles and buildings. We learned the difference between a felony and a misdemeanor. We were also taught public relations (or how to deal with the community), driving skills and of course the "ten code"—how you communicate with the dispatcher. For instance, 10-4 acknowledges that you heard the dispatcher, 10-7 is out of service, 10-8 is in service and 10-12 is a request for back-up. Signal 13 means an officer is in distress and 10-15 means you need a paddy wagon as quickly as possible because you have an unruly crowd.

We also learned how to use our weapons—a revolver and night stick. The teachers, all veteran police officers, taught us how to respond to a call for help in a domestic violence incident; never go alone, they told us. And they taught us how to deal generally with the community. It made sense that the better relationship police officers have with the community, the better results we will have questioning witnesses. It's very important, they said, for officers to get out of their cars, regularly visit businesses and make themselves visible at all times.

Oddly, no one talked about race relations. Here we were, a mostly white police force—just two years after the race riots following the assassination of Dr. King—and no one thought to discuss how white officers should interact with residents of Baltimore's many African American communities.

Our trainee class of 50 was all-male. We had five black members. I was the only Latino.

I was very impressed with all the teachers.

They included Lt. Bishop Robinson, a very serious teacher, who stood arrow-straight and could explain very complicated legal findings in layman's terms. One of the few African Americans in a high-ranking position, he would go on to become Baltimore's police commissioner, Maryland's secretary of public safety and correctional services and head of the state's juvenile justice system.

Another teacher was Lt. William Jackson, whom I also admired. He was an American patriot who loved his country. He was in great shape, not an ounce of fat on him. He had a crew cut and his uniform was always perfectly pressed, with highly polished shoes. Even his belt buckle was polished. He was as professional as could be. Sgt. Howard Collins, another teacher, emphasized the importance of police officers identifying with the community they serve. He mentored one young trainee named Ralph Faulkner, who became a vice detective. Unfortunately Jackson, Collins and Faulkner would go on to disgrace the department just two years later.

The class adviser was Malcom "Mike" Mayo, a veteran of the force who had previous assignments in the patrol, traffic and vice units. On Tuesdays and Thursdays he invited people over to his home to review what was taught that week. At the time, one of the most popular songs on the radio was Lynn Anderson's "I Never Promised You a Rose Garden," so Mike Mayo often told us, "working in the Baltimore police department is no rose garden." I never missed one of his review sessions. Another trainee who went to those sessions was Carroll Herald, whom we all called Spanky. Spanky was very focused on his police studies, but was a loner. He would remain a loner as a vice detective who trusted no other police. By the time Spanky was a veteran detective, he was taking his vice files home every night for safekeeping—from the prying eyes of unscrupulous cops who might tip off leaders of illegal gambling syndicates.

I also became friends with another trainee named Charles Joseph Key, who had previously served in the United States Coast Guard and had participated in searches of foreign vessels carrying hidden narcotics. He had solid knowledge of topics I had studied in my criminal justice classes at the Baltimore Junior College, especially several recent Supreme Court decisions that I believed were crucial to proper police work.

One was Mapp v. Ohio, from 1961, which protects citizens from unreasonable searches and seizures. Another was Escobedo v. Illinois, when the Supreme Court ruled in 1964 that all criminal suspects have a right to legal counsel. There was also the very important Terry v. Ohio, from 1968, that allows a police officer to frisk and search a suspect if the officer has reasonable suspicion that the person has committed a crime and may be armed. As police, we just called it the "Terry Pat." Lastly, we both knew the 1966 Miranda v. Arizona decision, which requires an officer to inform a suspect that he has the right to an attorney before and during questioning.

Both Joe and I wondered why none of these cases were taught during our police academy classes. I asked Joe, "Do you find it odd that our law course is ending and there has been no instruction about Mapp, Escobedo, Miranda or Terry?

"One could say so," he answered. Joe would become a lieutenant of operations in the Central District and a well-respected expert on weapons and the use of deadly force. He would write the department's guidelines for use of weapons for the police department's quick response (SWAT) team.

After three months, only a few trainees had dropped out and the rest of us met at the firing range to pass a target test in order to be issued service revolvers. More than any other test, I was most concerned about being able to shoot straight because of my sight problems. My eyesight was 20/30 at the time, but I was having trouble with depth perception. I was immensely relieved that I shot well enough to hit within the test range, though I wasn't as good a shot as the other trainees who hit near the bullseye. That Friday, we reported to the quartermaster's unit for fitting of our new blue uniforms. My dream of becoming a Baltimore city police officer was well on its way. That afternoon I got home before Kathy. When she opened the door, there I stood in full dress uniform. She gave me a big hug and we decided to have steak dinners at the Ponderosa restaurant.

My graduation took place on February 4, 1971. It was bitter cold, but I didn't care. At ten sharp, I proudly walked onto the stage of the auditorium of the Baltimore Police Department as the class valedictorian. Pop and Kathy were there. Esther could not attend because she was with her husband, who was serving in the army in Germany. Mike Mayo helped me write my speech. As he advised me, it was brief and to the point:

Commissioner Pomerleau, command staff, dignitaries, ladies and gentlemen. My name is Jim Cabezas and I and others in the front rows are members of the graduating class 71-3. Today, we join with a sense of pride and honor the other members of the Baltimore City police department. For the last six months, we have been thoroughly taught the skills necessary to perform the task of serving and protecting the people of this city. Our instructors have provided a beacon of light in order to avoid the many minefields which lie before us. The enforcement of the law should be in the spirit of the law and not necessarily the letter of the law. As we report to our respective assignments, we do so as well trained professionals with the many skills we have learned over these past several months. Yes, we have been through a lot and we have learned a lot. Each of us has taken an oath of office to conduct ourselves in accordance with both the state and federal laws.

I concluded by asking the academy graduates to stand, turn and wave to their family and friends. As I walked off the stage, Chilo said, "You did fine because you followed the rule of be sincere, be brief and be seated."

A few days later, after I'd dressed in my new uniform two hours early, I pulled into the Eastern District parking lot. I was thrilled. I used a skeleton key to open the side door. I walked past a recreation room with pool and ping pong tables. I stopped at a crime map on the wall. I studied it for a few minutes. It was full of pins of different colors, each representing a different crime: murder, rape, burglary, auto theft, arson, assault and robbery. I identified myself to an officer named Rich Lector and told him this was my first shift. With eight other officers I filed into a room with metal chairs and waited until Lt. Michael "Mickey" Ford stood for roll call at the podium. "Have a seat gentlemen," he said. "As you know, the crime stats are off the charts. The only way to reduce this pattern is to stay as visible as possible. If I see that any one of you has taken a fixed position, there will be consequences. I know it's colder than a witch's tit, but you footmen must walk your beat." At the end of roll call Lt. Ford handed out arrest warrants of people we should look for in the Eastern District. At that point, a sergeant approached me.

"Where the fuck is your radio?" he asked.

"Sir, no one told me where to find one," I replied.

"Did they teach you how to ask a fucking question in the academy?" he shouted.

"Yes, sir," I said.

He then showed me a rack of radios and batteries, mounted on the wall. He then left me with one last admonishment:

"You heard the lieutenant. If anyone gets in on you, I will hang your ass out to dry." I knew he was talking about burglaries committed within my post.

He started to leave the room. Almost as an afterthought he also told me that shotgun car 311 would drop me at the corner of North and Greenmount avenues.

I met up with the two officers who would drive me to my first foot patrol.

Both officers had been in the force for about five years. One was about 28 years old, a short, slight man who wore black cowboy boots to make himself look taller on the job. His feet were so small, his boots looked like they belonged to a child. The other officer was about 6 feet 2 inches and was built like a middle linebacker. Before we left, one of them opened the trunk. The officer in the cowboy boots removed the shotgun and checked it to make sure it was loaded. They both knew this was my first shift as an officer, but they made no attempt to engage me in conversation during the eight minute drive to my corner. They dropped me off without a word.

11
WALKING THE MIDNIGHT SHIFT

The temperature was 26 degrees with winds blowing when my silent partners from the Eastern District dropped me off from their shotgun car. They drove away with their car heater running full blast. As I walked up Greenmount Avenue, I noted that the streets were deserted, but there were a few businesses open. Within that five-block straightaway there were five bars, a Chinese carry-out, and Luxies Liquor Store where one of the Veney brothers shot Lt. Joseph Maskell during the 1964 Christmas Eve holdup. There was also a Catholic church called St. Ann's at the corner of Greenmount and 22nd Street. Four other storefronts didn't even have signs advertising their names. Most of the buildings were two stories and some were boarded up.

It didn't take long for me to check doors of closed businesses as I walked up and down Greenmount Avenue. In all, it was a sorry-looking commercial strip. Once, I noticed car 311 pass me, but the officers did not slow down to ask how I was doing or offer to get me a cup of hot coffee in the freezing night. I thought, "Is this snub standard procedure, or am I being treated differently for unknown reasons?" At about 1 a.m. I walked into Dickler's Bar at the corner of North and Greenmount. There were only three men seated at the bar watching TV.

"Ain't nobody called you," said the barmaid.

"I just came in to say hi and introduce myself," I said.

She put her hands on her hips.

"Been here three year," she said. "They ain't no polices ever been here unless we call."

She then walked to the opposite side of the bar and never looked back.

Now that I could feel my feet again, I walked north on Greenmount and stopped at Angelo's Bar. It was closed, and so was Mickey Griffin's Lounge. The lights were on at the Blue Front Tavern, so I walked in and was surprised to see a white man in this all-black neighborhood. He was wiping down the bar. The place was empty. "Cold enough out there for you?" he said in a friendly manner. "How about a shot of whiskey to take the chill off?"

"No sir, but I appreciate the offer," I said. As he walked to the back room, he said that he would be back in a minute. He returned with a bucket and mop. I introduced myself and told him that I was the new footman.

"What's your name?" I asked. "Everybody just calls me Blue, 'cause I'm the owner, bartender, dishwasher. You name it I do it," he explained. "You know that your boys are back in the hole." he said.

"I'm not sure I follow," I answered. "It's my first day on duty."

He told me that the "hole" is a place where police officers can park their squad car outside of public view.

"I bet they're already sleeping," he said in a matter-of-fact way.

I said good night and left, walking quietly along the wall of the bar, down the driveway leading to the rear of the building. There they were in the shotgun car. Lights out! I noticed they had backed into the driveway and kept the car running so they could race out into the street if they got a call. I could see them through the windshield, slumped over. They certainly didn't see me.

For the next three hours, as I walked up and down the freezing, dark street, I pondered the police oath "to serve and protect." I was well aware that "to protect" required omnipresence: the more visible uniformed officers are, the less likely someone will try to commit a crime.

But what does it really mean "to serve?" Finally I concluded that "to serve" means that an officer should do anything to bring about a better quality of life for the community: even calling the transportation department to report malfunctioning traffic lights, contacting the telephone company to report a broken public phone, or simply assisting an elderly person carrying a heavy bag. The best way to demonstrate the true meaning of the oath "to serve," I concluded, is to become part of the community.

By 4:45 a.m. the streets came alive with citizens traveling to work. Several ladies, some wearing nurses' uniforms, crowded the corner by Dickler's waiting for a bus. I hung around thinking that someone might want to grab a purse. While I heard the police dispatcher on my radio assign calls to report crimes, there were no major assaults, robberies or shootings that night. The shotgun car 311 picked me up where they had dropped me off. They did not bother to ask about my first night on the job. And I did not mention that I'd seen them sleeping behind the Blue Front Tavern. We rode back to the district in silence. All of the sector cars were creeping closer to the station house, waiting for the dispatcher to announce 10-99, which meant the 12 a.m. to 8 a.m. shift had ended. After returning my police radio, I drove home. Kathy had already left for work. I was really hungry. When I opened the refrigerator I was delighted to find that she had prepared a plate of food with a note saying, "Love and Kisses." Tomorrow, I told myself, I would put a sandwich in my reefer for the long night ahead.

12
TO PROTECT

After my first night on the job, I wondered why my two fellow officers in the shotgun car had given me such a cold shoulder. It would not take me long to learn that their rudeness was the least nefarious of their shortcomings. One of them, I would discover, was a brutal racist against blacks. The other was a thief. I also sadly learned that the comradery and professionalism I expected from other officers simply did not exist. Instead, many had deeply rooted racial prejudice. Some were lazy and others even corrupt. Their conduct appalled and alarmed me. Frankly, I thought about quitting, but those words of Mary Meyer at the Maryland Historical Society kept ringing in my head: "Change has to come from within."

Not surprisingly, Chilo also taunted me: "What, you want to take your ball and go home? Are you not your father's son?" I knew my father would be extremely disappointed if I quit. So, with firm determination, I committed myself to move forward "to protect and to serve."

Away from my original partners, my time on the police force soon improved. Within a few days I was assigned to work with two other officers in the 311 car. Don Trezise was a square shouldered man with amazing eyesight. He could see a man putting a gun in his pocket from four blocks away. Bert Ricasa was Filipino-born. The street people called him "Pineapple," which he despised. He was physically fearless and would dive into any fight on the street. Both were aggressive police officers who took their jobs very seriously. In their late 20s, they were friendly and talkative. During the night they often picked me up so I could get warm.

Before dropping me off one night, they showed me where a heroin dealer named Jarbo sold drugs during the day from the corner of 21st Street and Greenmount Avenue.

Since I was keen on becoming a narcotics detective, I found a place to watch Jarbo without being seen. I hid on the second floor of a vacant, boarded business with a great vantage point to observe him as he walked up and down the street. I still had 20-30 eyesight, so I had no trouble seeing him. He would cleverly hide bundles of heroin, each divided into nine packets, inside an empty soda can and place the can along the street curb or by a set of steps where he had easy access. Stashing the drugs was a way to protect himself from police charging him with possession with intent to distribute, or against a thief holding him up. He only kept a small amount of drugs in his pockets. He had a steady stream of customers. They were young and old, black and white. The black customers arrived on foot, the white customers came by car. Jarbo would approach each vehicle with its window down and make a fast exchange of drugs for cash. It didn't take long for me to realize that the same buyers purchased every day—some more than once a day.

After about two weeks of observation, I decided to stop a buyer as he walked up 22nd Street in the middle of the day. I saw him buy bags of drugs from Jarbo and put them inside his black knit cap. I approached the young man, who was very, very thin, a telltale sign of a heroin addict.

"I want to talk to you," I said. "Now we can do this the hard way or the easy way."

"Why you fucking with me?" he said.

"Put your hands on the wall brother," I said. "I ain't your fucking brother!" he yelled.

Despite his foul mouth, he followed my instructions to open his palms, so I could make sure he wasn't carrying a razor blade. He then put both hands on the wall with his feet spread out, placed far away from the wall so he was off balance. My search revealed three dime bags of heroin under the cap and a small amount of marijuana in his pants pocket. I handcuffed him and told the dispatcher on my radio that I needed a 10-14, which was the ten code for the paddy wagon. Within a few minutes, I saw one of my rude partners from my first night on the beat drive by. Police policy required him to stop and assist me to prevent a crowd from gathering. He didn't stop. Luckily another car arrived to help. The paddy wagon arrived shortly after and took the man prisoner.

When I arrived at the Eastern District the desk sergeant asked,

"What did you bring me?"

"A prisoner sir," I replied.

"You dumb fuck. I am talking about something to eat. You are out there and here I am with nowhere to go. You know, a crab cake would be nice," he said. He wasn't joking.

Just then the wagon arrived at the station. I thought, "Thank you, sweet Jesus." The sergeant now would have to attend to the prisoner and would leave me alone.

By the time I submitted the drugs for analysis and completed police reports, it was time to go home. Not one person in the Eastern District said anything about my first arrest.

Thinking about the best way to capitalize on my first arrest, I searched the man's criminal history and learned that he was on probation from an arrest for heroin possession three months before.

He nevertheless was released on his own recognizance, without having to post bail, so I hunted the neighborhood for him. Four days later, I found him walking on East 20th Street. I approached him slowly.

"I know you remember me," I said. "And I know you are on probation."

"So what the fuck," he answered,

"Well I can keep you out of jail," I replied "Listen to me. If you want to stay a free man, you will go to the vacant house at 2003 Barclay Street. Walk in from the alley and I will be there.

I told him the day and time to meet me.

The conversation lasted only about 45 seconds. I walked away before anyone saw us talking.

When the day came, he was 13 minutes late, but when he walked into the vacant house, I was so happy and excited that I told myself, "don't smile." If he was willing to tell me about drug activities in the area, I told him, I would confidentially tell the assistant state's attorney about his cooperation and request that his case be placed on the stet docket. He knew that a stet meant that if he stayed out of trouble for one year his case would be dropped. That first meeting led to many more face-to-face contacts and I eventually arranged for his admittance into a drug treatment program. He told me the street names of some drug dealers and where they operated in the neighborhood.

One, named Junebug, sold heroin in the alley behind the 500 block of East North Avenue, where he would sit on the back steps of a vacant house so he could stash the drugs nearby. I discovered that it was hard to observe Junebug in the alley, so I came to work in plain clothes on my day off and paid an Arabber (someone who sells fruit from a horse drawn wagon) a few dollars so I could walk behind the horse, unseen, to observe the drug transactions.

That gave me probable cause to search him. Two days later I went back to the alley in uniform. I said, "Hey, hey, I need to talk to you. I have a picture of someone I'm looking for."

I had no picture, but I hoped my comment would keep him from running.

It worked. I searched him and found about 15 bags of heroin in a shirt pocket and arrested him.

I went back to watching Jarbo from the second-floor window of the vacant business and saw a second addict buy heroin from him. Officer Trezise arrested the man and brought him into the Eastern District station. He was about 18 years old, also very thin, with abscesses between his fingers where he shot up the drug. I did not call for a paddy wagon because I wanted to do this as quietly as possible. I was going to offer the addict a deal to become an informant and didn't want anyone in the neighborhood to know I was going to charge him with narcotics violations. As soon as

Trezise brought the man into the station, he took him into the sector room where we interrogated people.

"I've seen you many days," I told him. "Look at those hands," I said, pointing to his abscesses. "If you don't get treatment you could die from the poison."

He didn't say a word. He was stoic.

"I know you have been buying from Jarbo," I said.

He still said nothing.

"But I am willing to go to the state's attorney. If you answer my questions truthfully about Jarbo then I will ask the state's attorney, in light of your cooperation, to hold off on charging you. If you continue to cooperate, you probably won't be charged."

This was tricky because I still had to submit a report. If he did not cooperate, but told Jarbo I was asking about him, I would have to be ready to charge the drug addict. I had to write the report very carefully. Finally, the man agreed to talk.

In the station house, I found an assistant state's attorney to talk to the addict.

"This officer said you are willing to cooperate, so I will not immediately charge you," the prosecutor said.

The addict agreed to cooperate. I did my best to put him in a comfort zone. I took off the handcuffs and offered him a soda and a cigarette, which he gladly took. He eventually gave me his name, his address and described his family circumstances. Like many addicts in the community, his grandmother raised him and he had dropped out of school. He had been arrested as a juvenile several times.

Finally, I asked him, "What can you tell me about Jarbo?"

"He my cousin."

Eventually, he gave me Jarbo's real name so I could find his address.

At this point, I was being mentored by two plainclothes narcotics officers, Lorenzo Gray and Eddie Crowder. Both officers had requested their assignments and were chosen for their special talents. They were a good team; each had skills that complimented the other. Crowder had a large network of people in the Eastern District to provide him with information. I thought he had informants everywhere. Each day he checked with the desk sergeant, Gus Drakos, to find out who had been arrested and why. If he thought he could turn the arrestee into a drug informant, Crowder would pull him out of the cell in the district station and talk with him in his basement office. Crowder was the spitting image of Mohammed Ali. He walked slowly and was always smiling. When he came by he'd greet you with the saying, "What it is, what it is."

Crowder was an outstanding officer but was not particularly good at report writing. That's where Gray came in. He was excellent at writing search and seizure warrants and police reports. Gray, who joined the police department after serving as a marine in Vietnam, kept a notebook containing information from criminal informants, or CIs, with their legal names, their street names, their addresses and the information they provided about drug activity. Both Crowder and Gray were in their mid-20s, about five years older than me. They gave me excellent advice: "Always protect your next step," they said.

My next step was to go to the court commissioner as quietly as possible and get an arrest warrant charging Jarbo with drug distribution. I didn't want it known on the streets that the police department was about to arrest him because I hoped I could turn Jarbo and get him to give up the name of his heroin distributor.

I was also frankly worried that Jarbo might be paying off police officers in the Eastern District. I wondered, "How can he be out here in daylight and nobody is arresting him?" I asked my snitches, "Anybody ever hit Jarbo?"

"Oh, no. Nobody ain't ever hit Jarbo."

To be on the safe side I arranged for Jarbo to be arrested at night and brought to the Southeastern District for interrogation, instead of the Eastern District. That way no Eastern District officers would see him.

Once he was put in an interrogation room, I told him, "You will see in the statement of charges that I have already arrested two people who observed you distributing heroin. I'm not saying they did, or they didn't, but I think if I subpoenaed them in your trial they would tell the truth."

This was very tricky. If Jarbo found out the names of my informants, he could have them killed. At this point, though, he didn't know their names, which were not mentioned in charging documents.

Again, I was learning from Gray and Crowder, always protecting my next step.

"I need you to answer one question," I told him.

"If you answer me correctly, I will go talk to the state's attorney. It doesn't mean you won't be charged today. You will be charged, but whether you go to trial is another question."

He didn't say a word. He was only about 5' 7" and very overweight, which told me he wasn't using his own product. He had half a brain. He was not selling to feed his own habit; he was selling to make serious money.

I never removed his handcuffs, which were behind his back. I knew he was uncomfortable. I went around to the table behind him. I whispered in his ear, "Who is your fucking supplier." Dead silence.

Two minutes went by. I didn't ask him anything else. I'd already put all my cards on the table. Finally he gave me a head nod. Again, I went back around behind him and hoped he would not bite my ear off.

"It's Mo," he says.

"You got to tell me more. I don't know who Mo is."

He gave me a physical description and told me Mo always drove a blue Volkswagen and parked on the 2300 block of Greenmount Avenue near a vacant building. He also said that sometimes Mo brought a baby in the car and hid bags of heroin inside the baby's diaper.

Jarbo also told me he and Mo were being investigated by the federal Drug Enforcement Administration. This was news to me. How could he know more than I did about law enforcement investigating him? I thought they must be bribing someone in the police department.

I found the Volkswagen on the 2300 block of Greenmount, parked illegally. I ran the tags and found it was registered to Maurice Proctor. I ran his criminal record and discovered he'd already been arrested for drug distribution.

So now I knew from Jarbo that Maurice Proctor, at least from inference, was the biggest drug dealer in my work area. He would be my new target. I tried to think of the best way to catch him. I wondered how he got his drugs to his sellers like Jarbo and Junebug. Maybe he stashed them inside the vacant building near his parked car.

In those days if you didn't pay a parking ticket, a warrant would be issued to arrest you for failure to appear in court to pay the fine. I found his car parked illegally on a very windy day. I brought out my parking citation book and wrote him a ticket. Instead of putting it in the middle of the windshield wiper, I put it near the edge of the window so it would blow away.

Several weeks later, in rollcall, I heard that a warrant had been issued for Proctor. I told the lieutenant I would like the warrant to arrest him and he handed it to me. Now the other officers of the Eastern District knew I was looking to arrest Proctor. I soon got a call on my radio from the officer who operated the paddy wagon, telling me to meet him and his partner at 23rd and Greenmount, the block where Proctor usually sat in his car.

I knew that if I found Proctor in the car, I would have probable cause to search it after I arrested him. But I wondered why a paddy wagon driver would be out helping with an arrest. Usually, the wagon drivers were designated to pick up prisoners, not make arrests on their own. When I arrived, I was dismayed to see Proctor sitting on the steps. The paddy wagon officer and his partner had shit-eating grins on their faces. They knew I could not search the car after they had told him to get out of the

Volkswagen. And I had no expectation he would have any drugs in his pockets. I also noticed that the car was moved from its usual spot and was parked in a legal space instead. I found that odd.

"I told him not to move," said the paddy wagon driver. Proctor had no drugs on his body, so I was only able to lock him up for failing to appear to pay a traffic citation. I smelled a rat. The second officer began laughing. He laughed so hard, his whole body shook. And I knew he was laughing at me.

While I didn't catch Proctor with heroin that day, city police and the federal government would eventually catch up with him. A few years later he got a 20-year sentence after he pleaded guilty to drug distribution and possessing a .32 caliber revolver. Years later, when he was 42 years old, a federal judge gave him a life sentence plus five years for plotting the murder of an informant who was gunned down in Northwest Baltimore.

13
TO SERVE

While I was highly motivated to arrest drug dealers on my beat no matter how many obstructions some of my fellow officers put in my way, I was always on the lookout for ways to serve the community. I knew that the AME church at the corner of 22nd and Barclay streets had Sunday morning services at 10. I also knew that immediately after the service, the pastor told his parishioners, "Now go forth to serve the Lord." The congregation would then assemble outside the front door to sing spirituals. One Sunday I was slowly driving by, when I heard the group singing, "We shall overcome. We shall overcome one day, for deep in my heart, I do believe that we shall overcome." The hymn was familiar to me because I had learned it from Sister George Mary at The Cathedral School. I also remembered that Bumper sang it from time to time. I drove around the block and parked the patrol car in front of them. I got out of the car and walked behind it. I could feel every eye looking at me. I took off my hat, unbuckled my gun belt, and put them in the trunk. I turned to the congregants with a smile and approached them. "Good morning," I said. Two ladies waved. "Good Morning Officer Jim," they said softly. Much to their surprise, I then joined them in singing. Certainly, they could not have known I was a devoutly religious young man. Or that church was like a second home to me. Or that joining them in song felt quite natural. And made me happy.

After the hymns were sung, the ladies introduced me to their pastor and some of the faithful. Weeks later, one of the congregants noticed me leaving the corner store at 23rd and Barclay.

"Walk with me," she said.

I offered to carry one of her grocery bags and took it from her.

"I be knowing those jitterbugs breaking in those houses," she said, referring to drug addicts, who are now referred to as "corner boys." She kept talking until we arrived at her home, a short walk away.

By the time we got there, I had the street names of two juveniles. I also learned that they were transporting stolen goods in a shopping cart which had a bad wheel that created a distinctive clicking sound. She also gave me the address of the vacant house where stolen TVs and radios were stored for fencing later.

I was learning that the cultures of the black and white communities are a single heartbeat away from each other, but they sadly never became one community. These were families working hard to pay bills, dress their children in the newest style and live an American life that focused on education. Like the rowhouse where I grew up in East Baltimore, many of their homes had no front yards. Families decorated the sidewalks in front of their homes with old tires, painted white and carved into designs resembling open flower petals. They filled the tire wells with soil and planted flowers with small American flags. Despite the neighborhood's persistent vandalism, I never saw those planters disturbed.

As a rookie I was scheduled to work on Thanksgiving Day. It didn't upset me in the least; I had three invitations to turkey dinner from two churches and a community leader. After I accepted the community leader's offer, I knocked on his door.

"Happy Thanksgiving. Come right in," he said.

Inside there were about ten family members, who all greeted me warmly.

"I have something special for you," said the host. "Follow me."

He led me to the basement where I saw a card table and two chairs. "Be right back," he said with a smile.

When he returned he was carrying a plate, covered with collard greens. On top was a cooked pig's foot. This certainly was not a dish ever served in my Latino family, or in the homes of my white friends. I must have looked surprised.

"It's good eating. Just break the skin," he said. "Eat it." I did and found the meat to be quite tasty, but my fingers were left very sticky. Then he said, "Now you can get to the pig knuckles," Once I pulled the knuckles apart I found the meat was very tender and flavorful.

Upstairs, I was treated to a fantastic turkey dinner while the Mighty Clouds of Joy played in the background. The community leader told me the local churches were planning a large push to register citizens to vote in the next presidential election, in which George McGovern, the antiwar Democrat, was challenging President Richard Nixon, a Republican.

Despite the efforts of the neighborhood's best citizens, it was nevertheless a troubled community.

As I became acquainted with the rhythm of the streets, I found that life in the ghetto was very different from the life I had known. The word "motherfucker," for example, could be either a term of endearment or a fighting word. Some people in the hood had volcanic tempers, which were difficult to calm. Grandmothers were raising children born out of wedlock whose mothers lived on small amounts of monthly welfare payments. Some were addicts, unable to care for their children. Fathers were incarcerated or were devotees of heroin. In the early 1970s, hand guns were not as prevalent as guns are today. Hence, women often threw lye in the face of attackers as a means of self-defense. Once, when I went with plainclothes officers to search a home, I woke up the suspect's 16-year-old sister, trying not to alarm her.

I gently patted her shoulder as she slept.

"I'm a police officer. Your house is not being burglarized. You're not going to be raped. They're arresting your brother." She reached to the floor, picked up a can filled with water and lye, and threw it towards me. Luckily it missed.

It was not unusual for children to eat potato chips, a soda and a moon pie (a cake sandwich filled with marshmallow) for dinner.

I also learned that epilepsy was a common problem. Every 60 days or so, we would have to call an ambulance to attend to someone lying in the street from a seizure, which might have resulted from taking narcotics. It was essential for the officer arriving on the scene to prevent the person from choking on his tongue. We always carried bent spoons in our pockets to hold a seizure victim's tongue down.

After working on foot patrol for several months I was assigned to the 311 car with Don Trezise. I was surprised to hear that one of my rude partners from my first night—the one built like a linebacker—had suddenly resigned. He had apparently taken a job driving heavy equipment like bulldozers, backhoes and dump trucks. I asked Trezise if he was surprised to hear that the officer had quit. Trezise started laughing.

"What's so funny?" I asked.

"I guess you haven't heard," he said.

"No, I don't have a clue," I answered.

He then told me this story:

The officer had pulled over a Cadillac with New York license plates and gangster whitewall tires, the style of car well known to be owned by drug dealers. The driver was in "the Cadillac cut," meaning that the driver's seat was pulled forward near the steering wheel. He drove with two fingers on the wheel, with his shoulder leaning sideways on the console so it was hard to see his face. The officer forced the driver to open the trunk where he found a kilo (2.2 pounds) of heroin and $30,000 in cash, which was a lot of money back then. The officer kept the cash and let the driver keep the drugs. He let the dealer go without any charges. The officer's partner stayed in the car the entire time, but he must have known what was going down. Still, I was told the police department never learned about the theft; the officer was never charged with the crime of stealing the money and failing to make an arrest.

Unfortunately his partner from my first night on the beat, the one who wore little boy cowboy boots, also lacked a moral compass. One Sunday afternoon we made a business check at Cokesberry's Lounge. As we walked to the back, the bartender gave a friendly wave. As soon as we reached the bar, two glasses of draft beer were placed before us. Cowboy Boots said, "If you don't drink when you are on duty, you will never be trusted." I knew if I had a drink, he could hold it over my head because I was still on probation and drinking on the job is strictly prohibited. I pretended to take a sip explaining that I never drank—which wasn't true. His reference to the drinking, I believe, meant that I wasn't one of the boys. Before we left, my partner drank three glasses of beer. He remained distrustful of me during my entire tenure at the Eastern District.

He, like many of the white officers I worked with, was a bigot who did not hesitate to use profound obscenities or racial slurs, including the "N" word. I would tell him, "That word hurts my ears." He never acknowledged my criticism. On one occasion we were both assigned to radio car 311. As the senior officer he drove and I wrote reports. He was too lazy to adhere to the principle of omnipresence and typically selected a fixed position, inside Greenmount Cemetery, where of course, all the residents are dead— including Lincoln assassin John Wilkes Booth. He would not drive that car unless we got a call for service. His abuse of citizens was despicable. Once he parked the car at the intersection of the narrow Worsley Street and the 1900 block of Greenmount Avenue, leaving just enough space for pedestrian traffic. As an African American person walked in front of the car, he would gun the engine and break out in laughter as the pedestrian jumped. In response to my strong objection he told me, "You know what that black shit on my tires is? It is a slow walking nigger." I did not have to wonder why some police officers were called pigs.

While I worked with many honorable and fair-minded police officers, Cowboy Boots was not the only despicable racist on the force. As a result of an alarm sounding at the Samuel Gompers Elementary School at the corner of North and Broadway, I joined several other officers searching the building floor by floor. This had once been my own elementary school and was now an all-black school. When I entered the cafeteria I found a sergeant in the kitchen area. He began to laugh. "This brings back old memories," he said. "When I worked K-9, I searched a school, jerked off my dog, squirted his cum into a gallon mayonnaise jar, stirred it and put the lid back." I felt like vomiting and walked out without saying a word.

In January 1972, just before 1 a.m., I was called with my partner, Don Trezise, to the L&M Lounge on North Avenue for a holdup in progress. Two men, armed with pistols, came running out of the bar. They pulled off their masks as they fled west on the 1100 block of East North Avenue, running along the 19th-century stone wall of Greenmount Cemetery. As Don and I ran after them, the men turned and opened fire on us, but luckily missed. I was really frightened and mostly concerned that I could not accurately fire a gun at them because of my deteriorating eyesight.

We never did fire our guns and lost them as they ran up into a junkyard of old cars and then up a dark alley. We called for backup. Reinforcements arrived with emergency vehicles and bright lights, but no one could find the suspects. When Don and I went back to the bar to interview the patrons and the bartender, one man said he saw one robber's face after he pulled off his mask. Just as he was describing the holdup man, the patron looked out the window and shouted, "There he goes now! He the one who held up the bar."

The holdup man had changed his clothes and was walking across the street by the cemetery wall. Don and I raced across the street and chased the man again. This time we caught up with him in less than a minute. I thought, "Thank God there is no traffic on North Avenue." It was the middle of the night. The man, who appeared high on heroin, did not resist us. His name was David Earl Johnson and we charged him with armed holdup and assault by shooting with intent to kill two police officers. Johnson was also charged with robbing each person in the bar. It was a great success for me and my partner, but I mostly remember that we had to write 14 separate reports, one for each patron who was robbed and one for the bartender. I never learned whether the other robber was caught. That case won me my first police department commendation, a silver star that I proudly wore on my uniform, right above my shiny badge. I had been on the force for just under a year and was only 22 years old.

Nine months later I was honored as Police Officer of the Year for the Eastern District by the Sons of Italy Lodge No. 2157. In announcing the honor, the organization noted I had made more than 20 narcotics arrests in less than two years on the force. I was given a $500 savings bond, which I split with Don Trezise by giving him $250 cash. I was given the award from a stage with other honorees from different districts at a large dinner dance at Martin's West, Baltimore's large catering hall. Kathy, who was very pleased for me, attended.

Pop had a prior engagement, but he was so proud he bought ten copies of the *News American* article about my award. He gave at least three copies to coworkers at the Evergreen House. He also walked around with the plaque in his hand, showing it to everyone. The following week he took the plaque and the rest of the newspapers to a bar he frequented and passed them around.

"Look what my son did," he told them. He was so full of pride he was absolutely aglow.

On my days off, I couldn't wait to get back to the district. I found that police work, factoring out religion, was similar to the calling of a priest.

I was totally consumed with work and my continuing studies at the

University of Baltimore. I was taking courses on constitutional law, patrol techniques and abnormal psychology, one of my favorites. It helped me understand the criminal mind.

Not surprisingly, my home life was not going well. When I was not making felony arrests, I was in court testifying at trials that could last a week or more. When I was not in trial, I was taking classes and when I was not in classes, I was studying. Kathy complained that I was not paying enough attention to her. I was working nights, weekends and holidays and I told her I knew that was unfair to her.

Kathy and I had several conversations about the problem. We decided a temporary separation might prompt me to change my priorities. I had become very close friends with Bob Fifield, one of my high school fraternity brothers, who lived nearby in the Hamilton neighborhood of Northeast Baltimore. I asked him if I could move into his attic. Thankfully, he said yes and we agreed on a monthly fee. I came home and stuffed large garbage bags with clothes and small belongings. Kathy and I were both very sad. Our separation didn't last long. Within two weeks I was back home with her, though temporarily. I would move in and out of Kathy's life several times before we called it quits a few years later.

Those troubled times came shortly after the release of the popular Carole King album, *Tapestry*, with the hit song that kept playing sadly in my mind:

> *Stayed in bed all morning just to pass the time*
> *There's something wrong here, there can be no denying*
> *One of us is changing, or maybe we've just stopped trying*
>
> *And it's too late, baby, now it's too late*
> *Though we really did try to make it*
> *Something inside has died and I can't hide*
> *And I just can't fake it, Oh no no.*

14
THE VICIOUS CYCLE BEGINS

Every 28 days my work schedule switched between the midnight to 8 a.m. shift and the 8 a.m. to 4 p.m. shift.

It was hard to sleep, especially after the midnight shifts, and the sleep deprivation affected my eyes. They became even more bloodshot than usual. I began using more steroid eye drops than prescribed to alleviate the redness, even though I knew from Dr. Scholz that the steroids would create harmful effects in the long term. He had explained it to me in language I could always understand, even as a child. But now I felt I had no choice. I was very concerned a supervisor would notice the redness in my eyes and ask, "Why do you have bloodshot eyes?" He might send me for another eye test. I was constantly worried about it. I knew it could cost me my job.

My police department personnel file contained details of my bout with Stevens-Johnson Syndrome, including the information that I was taking cortisone drops, so it was no secret.

To obscure my bloodshot eyes, I wore sunglasses all the time. I had several pairs; some had very light, tannish-colored lenses that I could wear inside the district station. Luckily, no one seemed to notice my bloodshot eyes or ask why I always wore sunglasses. The sunglasses also allowed me to see better since bright light irritated my eyes.

After several months I began occasionally calling in sick with blurred vision or an eye infection. I began to worry when I had trouble seeing out of my left eye. I saw a blurry glow around traffic lights and street lights. My eye was getting milky. And it alarmed me. In late 1972, I was on the midnight shift, driving the 311 car. I was driving an officer named Charlie Leonard to his foot patrol post at the corner of Lanvale Street and Rutland Avenue when I blew a stop sign. I didn't even see it, my eye was so cloudy. Another car came through the intersection and hit me on the driver's side. There was minor damage and no one was hurt, but the accident embarrassed me and resulted in disciplinary action that deprived me of two days paid leave of absence.

It also jolted me into a painful realization: I knew I was developing a premature cataract, something you usually find in a much older person. Today, cataracts are removed with a routine, 20 minute procedure, but in those days removing a cataract was a delicate operation that required spending days in the hospital recuperating. Dr. Scholz had written about cataracts in his 1960 book:

The symptoms of this disorder may take many forms, but a gradual impairment of vision is the most common complaint of the patient with early cataract. It may be slow at first as to be unnoticed, particularly as one eye is usually affected before the other, which may remain normal. . . . The patient may enjoy good vision when the iris is widely dilated in a dimly lit room, and poor vision in the bright sunlight where the pupil is contracted. As the cloudiness covers a larger area of the lens and becomes more dense, the added interference with the passage of light rays will result in a further loss of vision.

Dr. Scholz had always told me surgery would be my last option, but I knew after the accident I could not put it off any longer, so I made an appointment to see him.

By now we were buddies. He had been my doctor since I was eight years old. Now I was 24. He had watched me grow up and was quite pleased when I became a police officer. During my appointments, he would always ask me to tell him stories of my work on the streets.

"So, how is police work?" he would ask.

"We have a big problem with armed robberies. The district is getting slammed," I'd answer.

"What's the old police saying?" he asked. "It's better to be cleared than carried?"

I corrected him: "It's better to be judged by 12 than carried by six."

By now I had total confidence in him. I appreciated the fact that he never sugarcoated bad news. He was always looking for ways to protect my vision.

In February 1973, I began what would become a vicious cycle of eye surgeries for the next 40 years. Dr. Scholz performed the surgery at the Greater Baltimore Medical Center.

I will let Dr. Scholz describe the surgery from his book:

The entry is through an incision in the edge of the cornea. Next a small hole is made in the iris, or a small section of it is removed to permit the free flow of aqueous from the posterior chamber to the anterior chamber. This prevents the light and flexible iris from being pushed into the wound by aqueous pressure from the posterior chamber. Following this procedure, the lens capsule may be cut open and the contents of the capsule removed...

The surgery took about 90 minutes. When I awoke I was hallucinating from the anesthesia.

"Don, he's got a knife, he's got a knife," I yelled.

My body was trembling, I kept opening and closing my hands into fists;

my fingers wiggled uncontrollably and I moved my head in a rapid, side-to-side motion. Two nurses came into the room and asked me what was hurting. They told me to relax, but I kept yelling, "He has a knife, Don the fucking knife, Don, Don."

Dr. Scholz soon arrived and asked "Who's Don?" but I just kept screaming. Finally, they gave me a shot of Valium and I calmed down. When I awoke there were small sand bags on each side of my head, to prevent me from moving. Thankfully they were removed about two hours later. As I lay in the bed, I remembered when my hands were gloved and tied to the bedrail when I was in Baltimore City Hospitals all those years ago with Stevens-Johnson Syndrome.

"I don't like this," I thought.

I was feeling sorry for myself, but Chilo was on my ass like white on rice.

"Stop being a baby," the voice in my head told me.

"Next week it's back to work and you will be able to see again. Be a man."

A few days later when the bandages were removed, I could indeed see much clearer.

That surgery would be the beginning of a lifetime of the indignities of extended hospital stays. I had no clue that my long medical history would include hundreds of trays of inedible, cold food. I could not tell you how many times I have eaten Salisbury steak, carrots and mashed potatoes that tasted like they came out of a box.

After that first surgery Dr. Scholz kept trying new ways to help me. There was an eyeglass and contact lens business on the first floor of his office building. One day he went downstairs and talked to staffers about me. "I have a patient who has scratching in his eyes," he told them. "I would like to try an extra-large contact lens for him." The lens was the size of a quarter and Dr. Scholz had me wear it for about ten days to see if it protected my eye from the constant scratching from the scars under my eyelids. But the large lens starved my eye of oxygen and it became extremely dry and painful. I stopped wearing it and told Dr. Scholz it didn't work.

"We will find something else to ease the problem," he said.

I was disappointed that the contact lens did not help, but I was more concerned with the aftermath of the surgery. Dr. Scholz told me that a possible side effect of cataract surgery is the creation of adhesions. And I knew that the adhesions might one day lead to a detached retina. And I knew that a detached retina could lead to blindness. A vicious cycle indeed.

15
LIFE IS SHORT—FOR SOME SHORTER THAN OTHERS

On shifts when I was driving a police car, I would slowly drive the entire work area to view the activities of the neighborhood. As I drove, it was my practice to turn my head in each direction to look down every side street and alley. That included a little-known street called Worsley Street, tucked between Greenmount Avenue and Barclay Street, and just wide enough for one car to drive through it. You could reach out of the car windows and almost touch the tiny, dilapidated rowhouses that lined the narrow sidewalks.

On July 14, 1972, on a night that sweltered from the 90-degree heat, I drove by Worsley Street at 1 a.m. Luckily a street light lit up the little block so I could see a man placing a shiny object in his waistband. I backed up the patrol car and turned into Worsley. The man turned to see the car and began running down the street. In seconds I was alongside him, my service revolver in my right hand as I steered the car with my left.

"Drop that gun, drop that fucking gun. Drop it," I yelled.

I pulled the car onto the sidewalk and saw that he was winded. He knew he was trapped; he put his hands up. I got out of the car and grabbed the gun from his waistband. It was a .32 caliber automatic handgun. I put it in my pocket. I holstered my own gun and quickly handcuffed him. I radioed for a 10-14. The paddy wagon took him to the Eastern District, where he was charged with possession of a deadly weapon and placed in a cell.

His name was George Lester Milburn, age 22.

I completed my shift and called out of service at 4 a.m., then drove to the district station. I asked the desk sergeant, Gus Drakos, if Milburn had seen a court commissioner yet. He looked at his clipboard and said bail had been set at the very small amount of $500; Milburn could be freed by putting up only $50. Apparently this lenient bail for carrying a loaded gun was set at the request of police officers who were using Milburn as an informant.

Ten days later, when I arrived at the station house for roll call, I heard shocking news: my mentor and friend, plainclothes officer Lorenzo Gray had been killed with a sawed-off shotgun. Some of the officers were angrily talking. "These motherfucking cocksuckers don't know the meaning of life," said one.

When the shift commander began roll call he said that Officer Gray and

Officer Eddie Crowder responded to a call for a holdup in progress at the Holiday Inn at 3600 East Pulaski Highway. As they chased the suspects into the kitchen, one opened fire, shooting Gray in the chest.

Then he gave us even more bad news: he said the shooter was George Lester Milburn, the man I had just arrested for carrying a deadly weapon, who had been released with a very low bail at the request of officers using him as an informant.

"Why would any officer go to bat for a person charged with possession of a loaded gun?" I asked. The commander told me that the major of the district would deal with the conduct of the officers. He said we would hear when funeral arrangements were made.

Bert Ricasa and I went to our assigned patrol car and drove to our post without saying a word. I thought to myself, "If I had not arrested Milburn and taken away his handgun, he might not have used a more powerful sawed-off shotgun, and Lorenzo might still be alive."

This was my first experience with a fellow officer being killed in the line of duty. I would come to learn that whenever we lost one of our own, the district station would become very, very quiet. The officers would be in a sad, somber mood. There was none of the typical dark cop humor we were so used to. Naturally, we became more concerned about the danger of the job and reflective on the human condition. In the case of Lorenzo Gray's murder, some officers were very angry and frustrated, since the killer had just been let out of jail on a gun charge. To mourn him we were issued little black elastic ribbons that we put around our police badges. The station house was draped with a large black cloth. Of course, the flag was lowered to half-mast.

The day before Gray's funeral all city police cars kept their lights on during the day shift in his memory. More than 400 officers attended the funeral, many from other Maryland jurisdictions and several from as far away as Delaware, New Jersey and Pennsylvania. The Baltimore *Sun* noted that Gray had raised several siblings after his mother died. I had never been to a police funeral and was struck by the haunting sound of the bagpipe playing in the distance. As an honor guard of police officers sounded a 21-gun salute, Chilo told me, "Lorenzo is now in perfect peace."

The pastor in his eulogy called Gray a man of "devotion to duty." The six pallbearers were his fellow members of the Narcotics Squad. Governor Marvin Mandel and Police Commissioner Donald Pomerleau attended.

The Sun quoted the governor as saying there should be more cooperation between police and citizens to prevent police killings in the future.

"People should let the police know if they see someone carrying a dangerous weapon," said the governor. Obviously he did not know I had in fact arrested Milburn for that very crime just before he killed Officer Gray. The prior arrest, followed by his release from jail, would not become public for another five days when *The Sun* reported it, as well as a June charge for carrying a knife.

I attended the Milburn hearing where he pleaded guilty to first-degree murder and was pleased when he was sentenced to life in prison. The large ceremonial courtroom on the second floor of the city's circuit courthouse was packed with uniform officers. It would be a long time before I got over the murder.

Six weeks later, on September 9, 1972, Cowboy Boots and I were working the day shift. At 1:10 we heard officer Mike DeHaven shout to the dispatcher, "Signal 13, man with a gun." He and his partner John Neubauer gave chase, but lost the suspect in the rear of the 900 block of North Dallas Street. Backup units responded, including Sgt. Darrell R. Duggins and Officer Joseph J. Kaczynski. "We are less than two minutes away," I told Cowboy Boots. Though he was driving, I activated the lights and siren. Cowboy Boots immediately turned the emergency equipment off and kept driving in the opposite direction.

"What are you doing?"

"They don't need us," he said.

I was really angry at him. How can you not go to the aid of another officer?

I later learned that the officers began searching the vacant houses. Sgt. Duggins and Officer Kaczynski spotted the suspect in one of the houses. As they approached, the suspect shot Sgt. Duggins in the shoulder and ran onto the roof. Sgt. Duggins, though growing faint, tried to reload his service revolver when Officer Kaczynski grabbed the man in a bear hug to stop him. The gunman broke away and began shooting, hitting Officer Kaczynski in the chest. The 20-minute fight stopped when Officer Gary Mitchell and Officer DeHaven finally shot the suspect, Herbert Lee Malone, who was pronounced dead on arrival at Johns Hopkins Hospital. He had an extensive criminal history for assault and robbery.

As the news unfolded, I thought, "Good Lord, it's only been six weeks since Lorenzo Gray was shot and killed." Chilo said, "Life is short, but some lives are shorter than others."

As the work day came to an end, I thought about Cowboy Boots and his spineless act.

"How bad can it get?" I thought. "I work with an officer who is not only a bigot, but also a coward."

I was grateful that the officers shot that day recovered from their injuries and returned to duty.

The day of the shooting I got a call from Pop, concerned for my safety. I told him I was fine and would be over in a day or two.

When I got to his house on the Evergreen grounds for dinner, he told me, "I'm not sure police work is your best career option."

I told him I could not imagine doing anything else.

"But someone has declared open season to shoot cops," he said.

I then asked him, "Pop, if you could pick any of the following, which would you choose: fame, good health or riches?"

"None of those," said Pop. "The best thing for an honorable man is to make a new friend and the worst is to lose one."

"Right," I said. I understood that he believed there is nothing better than friendship. And I couldn't agree more. Pop was my best friend.

After dinner he said, "You are in the hands of God. May He bless you."

"Thank you," I said. "Perhaps it is God who keeps me safe. I know it's not wisdom. Maybe it's fear because fear brings up my guard."

I could tell that nothing I said alleviated his apprehension. Neither of us could know that it wasn't *my* safety we had to worry about.

16
A SOUL WOUNDED

Every Christmas Pop and I went to midnight Mass at the beautiful Cathedral of Mary Our Queen, which was so large it seated 2,000 people. On Christmas 1972, the church was packed with congregants dressed in their very best. The mood was joyful. Once the grand organ played and the magnificent choir began singing, the cardinal and priests began their procession to the Holy Alter. The 90-minute Mass ended with the choir singing a resounding rendition of the Hallelujah chorus from Handel's Messiah.

I was in a very happy mood. Kathy and I were still trying to put our marriage back together. Since we were both sentimental by nature, we loved spending the holidays together.

Before Mass, Pop told me he was hosting a New Year's party for several of his Latino friends from Washington. He really enjoyed these gatherings of close friends who would spend the night in his small house on the Evergreen estate. His parties were always festive. At midday the ladies would start cooking a 20-pound turkey, surrounded by green peppers and whole onions and stuffed with Cuban pork. For dessert they would make a creamy ambrosia with coconut and tangerines. The men smoked Cuban cigars and sipped Chilean wines. Pop said he needed to buy a new stereo to listen to Spanish records by Xavier Cugat and Desi Arnaz.

"I have two days off. I'll drive you," I told him.

"No. I'll call a cab. That way I can take my time and maybe stop at the Three J's Tavern and the Tic Toc Show Bar."

"Okay," I said, "but it would not be any bother for me to drive you," I said.

Pop insisted he would be fine taking a cab.

I was always concerned that he carried too much cash with him.

"I know you don't use credit cards, so please be careful anytime you have a large amount of cash in your pocket," I said.

Although there would be no white Christmas that year, I was glad Kathy and I were together. She went to morning Mass with her mother at the Church of the Most Precious Blood in Northeast Baltimore, while I waited eagerly with her dad for her brother and his wife to bring the homemade eggnog. We enjoyed a ham dinner and later exchanged gifts. At any dinner at Kathy's family home, there might be drama, but not on this day. I did not know it then, but it would be the last Christmas I would spend with Kathy and her family.

I was back at work on December 28, working the 4 p.m. to midnight shift. Normally the shotgun car 311 was a two-man unit, but not on this day. Since so many officers were off for the holidays I was on my own. As usual, I drove to my assigned work area to get a sense of the neighborhood. I knew holidays could bring out violence in people, perhaps because of excessive drinking, so I was on alert to any hostile behavior. The temperature wasn't particularly cold. As I chatted with some people in the neighborhood I received a strange call from the dispatcher. He said, "311, 311." When I responded he said, "4545 North Charles Street for a call."

As I responded, "10-4" I was bewildered.

The address was not on my beat, not even in the Eastern District. It was in the Northern District. And of course I knew it was the address of the Evergreen estate where Pop lived.

"Nothing good can come of this," I thought. "Oh, God please don't let it be Pop."

I resisted activating the siren and flashing lights, but was really anxious to get there. As I turned right onto North Charles Street from Cold Spring Lane, I could see a marked police car parked so it blocked the entrance into the serene Evergreen estate. As I pulled into the driveway, I told the officer my name.

He shook his head and said, "No radio communication." His instruction provided me with a hint of relief because it might just be a bomb scare. I knew the bomb protocol required no radio communication because the transmittal might activate an explosive device. As I drove the serpentine roadway it wasn't long before I saw three police vehicles parked by Pop's duplex. My heart began to throb; this was not a bomb threat.

The door was wide open. I walked up the seven wooden steps and saw three uniformed officers milling about and talking in the dining room. They didn't see me. In a few seconds I walked past them and saw a body on the floor between the kitchen and the dining room. My body shook as if it had been hit by an earthquake. I began to lose my balance, but somehow found the strength to stay standing. I heard voices, but could not understand what they were saying.

Pop lay on the floor dead. His white shirt was saturated with blood and his face was bloodied. I screamed out, "Pop, Pop, no, Pop." I knelt down beside him. I felt a hand pulling me away. I tried to break lose, but couldn't. The officer walked me to the couch, saying, "I am so, so sorry. I knew your dad. There were times when I would drive him to Mass at St. Mary's." Another officer walked over and said, "All we know is that the neighbor heard a bang and saw a Diamond cab speed away. Homicide detectives and the crime lab have been called."

I only sat for a moment or two. I wanted to cry, but remembered Pop saying, "Never let them see you sweat."

I told the officers that I was leaving to return my police car to the Eastern District.

"Are you okay to drive?" asked one. I shook my head "yes" and left. As I drove, thoughts came cascading so fast I could not get a grip on them. Esther and Kathy had to be told, I knew, but I didn't think I could tell them without breaking down. I also wondered why the officers just let me walk into the house and had not properly secured the crime scene.

When I got back to the district station, Sgt. Drakos was standing by the open door waiting for me.

"We are all here for you," he said. "All you need to do is ask."

I thanked him and handed him the car keys and the radio.

I don't remember my drive home. By the time I got to the door tears were profusely running down my face and my body was trembling. I told Kathy the news and she began to sob uncontrollably. She and Pop really loved each other.

She tried to calm me down and held me tightly. In about a half hour I had changed into civilian clothes. "I need to take a drive and be alone," I told her.

She kissed me and said, "Please be careful driving."

Once I got in the car I had no idea where I was going.

Then I thought, "I know the way to Ocean City by heart."

I took off driving south. Before I knew it, I was yelling aloud at God, uncontrollably banging on the steering wheel.

"Where the hell were you God? Preoccupied with soliciting for more church donations?

"Pop loved you so much and you abandoned him. All that scripture about humility: 'The first shall be last and the last shall be first.'

"What the hell is that supposed to mean? And what's up with so many contradictions? You want us to turn the other cheek and at the same time you say an eye for an eye. You and all your dogma are nothing more than a big fairy tale."

Then I heard Chilo's voice in my throbbing head.

"Get a grip."

I answered the voice.

"Maybe you think this is nothing more than a wrinkle in time? I'm going to find the fucker and kill the son of a bitch. Fuck jail. I don't care."

Chilo only yelled back.

"You need to be rational."

"I don't want to be fucking rational."

My religious faith had never been so shaken. It brought me back to my conversation with a priest at the seminary.

He said, you either have faith or you don't. That night I lost my faith, and it would not return for a decade.

I so very much needed to cry. Once I reached the Old Mill Pancake House just before the Bay Bridge, I pulled into the parking lot, which was deserted. For a while I just sat shaking my head until finally I started to cry. I sobbed for a long time.

"Feeling better?" Chilo asked.

"Fuck you," I screamed. "I don't need you or anybody else to tell me how to lead my life."

"You have never talked to me that way," Chilo answered. "Don't you know I am your best friend?"

I then started crying all over again. I realized that Chilo was Pop. The voice of conscience had been Pop all along.

"Pop, I love you. Please forgive me," I said.

"You are my only son," he answered. "I will always love you."

Then his voice left me with this advice:

"Don't hate the shooter. If you do, he will win."

As I drove home, I no longer wanted to know who killed Pop. The hunger to find his murderer would come much later.

When I got back to the apartment, Kathy said that her mom and dad were shocked by the horrible news and expressed condolences. It was almost midnight. I told Kathy, "I feel totally spent, but sleep won't come easily."

"Do you want me to fix you a bourbon, or a bite to eat?" she asked.

"Just the bourbon. I think I will try to sleep on the sofa," I said.

I sat down and looked up at the Christmas tree. There was a large blue ball that Pop had given us with a picture of the Nativity on it and writing that read, "O Holy Night."

"Yeah right," I thought. I began to think how my life had changed for the worse.

"Who would have wanted Pop dead and why? Was the killer someone he knew?" I asked myself. I remembered seeing two six-ounce glasses at the crime scene alongside a bottle of Old Forester bourbon sitting on the kitchen counter right above the cabinet where he kept his liquor. Since Pop was a fastidious man, there was no way that he would have left dirty glasses before leaving his home to go buy the stereo. It struck me that perhaps he invited another cab passenger in for a holiday drink. But two people in one taxi from downtown Baltimore wasn't lining up. It had to be the cab driver. Perhaps the motive was nothing more than robbery. All his cash was gone when police arrived, and there was no evidence that he bought a stereo.

Sleep seemed to be avoiding me. My mind was spinning, with my disjointed thoughts moving from memories of Pop to questions about the homicide.

I found myself looking down on Patterson Park where my friends and I had enjoyed so much fun as children. But something was horribly wrong. The entire park was scorched. Where there had once been beautiful trees and long stretches of well-cut grass, there was nothing more than smoldering earth. All of the beautiful trees of my childhood were charred splinters. I could see white fires burning every acre. The large swimming pool, the fishing pond and even the ball fields were gone. There were no fire trucks, police or any other first responders. Suddenly Kathy was shaking me.

"You're having a nightmare," she said.

"You were asking, 'where are the children'?"

As I sat up I wondered what the dream meant.

"Some shrink would probably have a field day," I thought.

After my dream I realized I had not told Esther. I could barely bring myself to dial her number. When I finally called her, she had already found out from one of her husband's friends. We both cried and shared our wonderful memories of Pop, a man who came to this country to become a proud American citizen, to raise a family to the highest moral standards, to nurse his son through a devastating illness, only to lose his wife to a brain tumor and be left to raise two children on his own. Before we hung up I told Esther I would handle the funeral arrangements.

Pop never got to have his New Year's party. He never ate his turkey or sipped his Chilean wine. He never listened to his favorite Spanish music. Instead we gathered at the Cathedral to honor his life. The Mass was celebrated by Father Joseph Whalen. There was no eulogy; it wasn't the custom at the time. The commander of the Eastern District arranged for a motorcycle escort to the Oak Lawn Cemetery. As the service ended, I thought, "Here is a fair man who was cheerful in all weather, who never shirked a task." I pledged to live my life by his example.

17
AN OATH BROKEN

Several years before Pop's murder, when I was still at City College high school, I attended the funeral of a classmate's grandmother. When someone you love dies, the minister told us, "The best thing to do is walk away." As the pall bearers lowered the casket into the grave, he said, "You all can now turn and walk."

While I was still in a state of despair, I knew I had to walk away and get back to work. My fellow officers continued to offer condolences, which I appreciated. Yes, Pop was physically gone, but his words would always be with me. I hoped my work in the Eastern District could give some relief from my thoughts of his murder.

The homicide investigation was assigned to a sergeant with a great reputation and two veteran homicide detectives. I was dismayed to learn from my father's neighbor, who was the one who reported hearing the gunshot and saw the cab speed away, that casts of the tire tracks left behind—that could be matched to the tire treads of the cab—were not taken in a timely manner. With rain a few days after the murder presumably wearing away the tracks, a mold taken later would be useless.

In defense of the department, there were 330 murders to solve in Baltimore in 1972. I knew that the goal of homicide investigators was to work toward a quick arrest. I had hoped the case would get some priority, since I was a fellow officer, but there would be none. I already knew the crime scene might have been compromised because it had not been properly secured—allowing me to walk in unnoticed. I had little hope there would be an arrest within 48 hours. And as the weeks went by, I also knew that the chances of solving the murder diminished significantly.

Before any Baltimore City police officer can pin a badge or holster a service revolver, he or she must take this oath of office:

I swear or affirm that I will support the Constitution of the United States and I will be faithful and bear true allegiance to the State of Maryland and support the Constitution and the laws thereof and I will to the best of my skill and judgment diligently and faithfully without partiality or prejudice execute the office of Baltimore Police Department according to the Constitution and laws of this State.

I had taken this oath to heart when I joined the police department. I was troubled by the obstruction of justice by the two officers who prevented me from arresting drug dealer Maurice Proctor. When I spoke to my mentors, Gray and Crowder, they told me that most heroin dealers abided by a code not to sell to addicts under 18 years old, but Proctor had no such code.

"How does anyone get anything accomplished, when your fellow officer is a traitor?" I wondered.

A week or two after I returned from bereavement leave, Don Trezise and I were working the 311 car.

"Have you ever wondered why the sergeant orders you to gas his car at the Fallsway pumping station?" he asked.

"No, not really," I answered. "Why the question?"

"You know they think you're a rat?" he said.

I had suspected for months that other officers thought I was spying on them for the police department. Commissioner Pomerleau was known for his internal spying operation. Perhaps they were suspicious as to how I ended up in the Eastern District when I had requested to work in the Central District. But I was not sent to spy (at least not yet) and I never learned why I was sent to the Eastern.

From my first day of work, it seemed that getting the cold shoulder was just part of the rookie experience. However, as time went by, it was more a feeling of being shunned. I did not understand why I would be ostracized. About six months after I arrived in the Eastern District, while traveling to the Circuit Court, I had a very odd conversation with a plainclothes officer who suspected me of being a rat. He also intimated that he was taking bribes.

"You know I have six kids don't you?" he asked.

"No, I didn't know," I said.

"And my wife doesn't work," he added.

"The word around the district is that you're a spy."

"What do you mean?" I asked.

"That you're a rat placed here to snitch about officers on the pad."

"What are you talking about? I'm not here to do anything but patrol the streets," I said.

"Hope you're not lying," he said, adding, "It's not a lot of money."

I told Trezise I didn't care if people thought I was a rat.

Then, as always, he explained some facts of Eastern District police life to me.

"Always around Christmas and Easter, after shopping hours, they send you to get gas," he said. "While you are down there, they place a small fire cracker on the door of the Sear's department store [at the corner of North Avenue and Harford Road] to set off the alarm. Once the private security officer arrives to investigate, he unlocks the doors. That's when they go to town. One police officer will go with the private security guy to keep an eye on him, while two others steal whatever they want to take." They usually stole children's clothing, small appliances and expensive tools. In fact, they often took orders in advance from other police.

"Those cocksuckers will burn one day," I said.

He then told me another story about a sergeant who owned an antique shop. He would break into vacant houses to steal crown molding, brass and other collectables and haul them away in a police paddy wagon. I wondered what would happen if I came upon such a burglary. I would have to arrest my fellow officer if I caught him in the act. How awkward would that be?

I went straight home after the shift. I wondered what I should do about the corruption.

Was it not my duty to notify the Internal Investigation Division of the Baltimore Police Department of criminal activity by its own officers? I knew it was a delicate decision: internal investigators had a less than stellar reputation for protecting their sources. I had heard about word leaking out when officers snitched on others in the department. The next time the police snitch needed backup in a dangerous situation, no one came to his aid.

This was the same year that the film *Serpico*, starring Al Pacino, came out. Based on a true story about New York City police officer Frank Serpico, it shows what happens when he reports corruption of fellow officers who take payoffs from criminals. After his superiors fail to investigate, Serpico is left in harm's way by other officers and he is shot in the face by a drug dealer. The assault would never have occurred if his partner had not purposefully shirked his duty to protect him.

On the morning of January 27, 1973, I was home eating breakfast when WFBR radio station's DJ interrupted The Box Tops' popular song "The Letter" for breaking news. A federal grand jury had returned indictments charging six Baltimore City police detectives and two former detectives with taking bribes from three different illegal lotteries. Such "numbers" businesses were very lucrative in the years before the Maryland lottery was established.

"Wow. What is happening with this department?" I asked myself. I knew firsthand about corruption in my own Eastern District, but that paled in comparison with an FBI investigation using wiretaps to collect evidence. I did not get the newspaper delivered, but my neighbor did. I found *The Sun* still lying on the sidewalk, so I ran out of the house to take a quick look. I read that police commissioner Donald D. Pomerleau—who had come to Baltimore to reform the police department six years before—had contacted federal authorities to initiate a probe of the department's vice unit, which was supposed to ferret out illegal gambling.

The article quoted the commissioner as saying, "A dishonest police officer is something extremely repulsive."

I was both excited to hear that something was being done about police corruption and troubled as I read the names of those indicted. I stopped reading when I saw the name of Ralph Faulkner, age 23. I didn't want to believe it. I thought, "Ralph, how could that be?" When I was training in the academy, Ralph was the assigned trainee under the supervision of Sgt. Howard Collins. The realization that I personally knew one of the arrested made the bad news even worse. (A month later I would learn that Sgt. Collins was demoted after investigators discovered that he was also involved in the bribery case.)

When I arrived at the district station for my shift, the rec room was buzzing about the investigation.

I said to a fellow officer, "The investigation is ongoing. Another shoe has to fall."

"Those motherfuckers," he said angrily

"Who are you talking about?" I asked.

"The fucking Feds. They don't have any idea of what we deal with every day here in the ghetto. Fuck them."

His abrasive comments brought to mind advice I received shortly after starting on the force in the Eastern District, working on a largely white police force in predominantly black neighborhoods. "Don't ever think that any of those we protect are your friends. They'll backstab you in a New York minute." Even as a rookie, I knew this was a warped, counterproductive attitude toward public safety and crime control that would only create a feeling of isolation. How stupid is that? I thought. Here we were, just a few years after the riots following the King assassination, and we were taught nothing in the academy about race relations. Instead, it was us against them. Now I knew why other officers didn't make routine business checks—unless it was a white-owned business. It seemed to me that the root of corruption within the department came from a lack of respect—and even a disdain—for the very community we had taken an oath to protect. No matter how hard the police department tried to clean up corruption, I knew that racial prejudice would linger.

The newspaper reported that the investigators were so concerned about "leaks" which could derail the probe that they destroyed typewriter ribbons used during their final investigation. This reminded me of the advice I got from officers Gray and Crowder: always protect the next step of your investigation. In addition to the gambling bribes, the article mentioned at the very end—almost as an afterthought—that Commissioner Pomerleau refused to comment about an investigation into 1,250 missing bags of heroin from police headquarters. It was common knowledge in the department that there was missing heroin from the evidence room. Even more chilling was the news that the bribery investigation was ongoing. There were sure to be more indictments of police officers.

I found some solace in the knowledge that Commissioner Pomerleau had started the probe. I knew before his appointment by Governor Marvin Mandel that the department was in the dark ages. Police reports were written on what was called a "95 Form," which was nothing more than a lined piece of paper that required an officer to write only "To" and "From" and a date. Officers frequently folded their 95 Forms and placed them under their hats. They would keep them for about two weeks. If the sergeant asked for the report, the officer would hand it over. If not, he would throw it away. Officers also verbally informed their sergeants of crimes or arrests. The sergeants then decided whether or not to tell the lieutenants. Consequently, statistics were totally inaccurate.

There was little, if any, regard for constitutional rights. The department had flagrantly disregarded the law in 1964 when officers illegally broke into hundreds of houses occupied by black families, searching for the notorious Veney brothers who had murdered one officer and wounded another. Police called the around-the-clock raids "Superman warrants" because the cops, without any search and seizure warrants, just busted open the doors with their shoulders, like Superman.

There was no adherence to a chain of command. Promotional exam answers could be bought for $500. I also learned that most officers only had an eighth-grade education; police jobs could be purchased by paying a city councilman or a state senator. If an officer wanted to drink on duty, have at it. In the days before police radios, there were call boxes located throughout the district. Inside each box was a telephone—and often a pint of whiskey.

In his attempt to modernize the department, Pomerleau hired retired FBI agents and assigned them to a division which reported directly to him. Four of them were assigned to internal affairs to investigate complaints against police for criminal misconduct. He promulgated three types of reports: crimes against persons, crimes against property and miscellaneous reports. Additionally, he established an inspectional service division, which had carte blanche to thoroughly inspect police facilities and vehicles looking for violations of police rules. The division also had a section for the sole purpose of collecting intelligence information. This section targeted outlaw organizations such as motorcycle gangs, hate groups and large gambling and narcotics syndicates. Pomerleau made it well known that any members of the department who filed a false report would be fired immediately. He believed in the principle, "If you don't inspect, don't expect."

On June 14, 1973, the other shoe fell. New federal indictments were announced, even more disturbing than the January indictments; now police commanders were charged with taking bribes from gambling operations. Five lieutenants, six sergeants and three patrolmen were charged with protecting a large illegal gambling organization which operated within the Diamond Cab Company located in the Western District. One of those indicted was Lt. William Jackson, the clean-cut, high-quality instructor from my academy class. I had really respected him.

Among the gamblers named in the indictment was Carroll T. Glorioso, who ran a $7.5 million gambling operation. He was once married to Blaze Starr, the nationally known stripper who owned the Two O'clock Club, located in the infamous Baltimore red-light district known as The Block. I didn't know much about The Block then, but I would come to know it intimately as a deep undercover covert. Another gambler charged was William I. Klemkowski, whom I would later meet while working on The Block. Apparently the bribes were so routine that the money was picked up weekly by a "bag man'"—a former officer—who took it to the Western District police station, where it was doled out in the parking lot and the men's room.

I was just 23 years old. In my two-and-a-half years on the police force I had watched two fellow officers obstruct justice by preventing my arrest of a heroin dealer. I'd heard about a cop stealing drug money and letting a major drug dealer go without arrest. I'd learned about cops burglarizing houses and transporting stolen antiques in a paddy wagon. I'd been wrongly suspected of being an internal spy. I was kept from observing a burglary— by police officers—of a major department store. I'd seen cops sleeping and drinking on the job. I had lost trust in fellow officers I had respected who were accepting bribes—even one who was my academy instructor. And I saw racism at every turn. I thought I'd seen—or at least heard—it all.

That was, until October 10, 1973.

I was in the state's attorney's office in the city circuit courthouse on North Calvert Street discussing a search warrant with a prosecutor. The office was buzzing with word of what was going on across the street in the U.S. District Courthouse. They said the vice president of the United States, Spiro T. Agnew, a former Maryland governor and Baltimore County executive, was in a federal courtroom on the fifth floor—as a defendant. He was pleading "no contest" to charges of tax evasion. That meant that he did not plead guilty but still admitted the government had enough evidence to convict him. I would learn that the federal government had laid out an elaborate case against him of accepting kickbacks from consulting engineers for government work in no-bid contracts, dating back ten years. He was sentenced to three years' probation and fined $10,000. He then resigned as vice president. The news took my breath away. It really got me thinking, "What skills must you have to conduct such a complicated investigation?" I had no clue. But that day a kernel of an idea entered my head: maybe one day I would have the acumen to work a case against a corrupt elected official.

18
GOT TO GET OUT OF THIS PLACE

I was desperate to get out of the Eastern District. Pop and I had an ongoing conversation about it in the months before his murder. He wanted me to stand pat and I wanted to get out.

"I could apply to the Federal Drug Enforcement Administration," I told him. "I'm thinking that with my associate's college degree and two years of quality police service, coupled with the fact that I'm fluent in Spanish, I would be a very good candidate."

Pop did not disagree, but warned, "You will surely be sent to either Bogotá, Columbia, or to El Salvador."

"Is that so bad?" I asked.

"I have no doubt that you are street smart," he said, "but you have no idea what it would be like to enforce drug laws in Third World countries. You would be street stupid. You think there is a corruption problem in the Baltimore Police Department? Well, in Third World countries bribery is part of the culture from the very top to the last rung on the ladder. Drug cartels won't think twice about killing anyone, even American law enforcement officers." I was sure he knew what he was talking about. He'd once worked for one of the most corrupt dictators in Central America.

"Okay Pop. I surrender," I told him.

"Just keep your ear to the ground. Something will come along," he told me.

Now that he was gone I was on my own to sort out my problems and look for a way out of the Eastern District.

I was driving patrol one day when I heard unit 324 call the dispatcher for backup in the rear of a schoolyard, where he found a man bleeding from several stab wounds. The officer requested an ambo to the rear of the 900 block of East Biddle Street. Since I heard no other car responding, I went to back him up. When I got there, I met Officer Wayne Carneal, a college classmate of mine. He was standing over an elderly man splayed face down on the ground. Some of his clothing had been cut off and his throat had been severed. His body had too many wounds to count. Blood was splattered all over the playground.

"Wayne, you know this guy?" I asked.

"He lives around here, but I never had any troubles with him," he said.

"Evidently, somebody did," I said.

Wayne told me that homicide and the crime lab were on their way.

While we waited I asked him what he thought of the recent indictments of police for taking bribes from gambling operations.

"Those pieces of shit," he said of the indicted cops. "They should be hung by their balls."

I was not surprised by Wayne's response. I already knew him as an officer dedicated to quality policing. He had made several felony arrests, including an armed robbery charge.

"Hey," I said, "Have you heard any rumors that the department is thinking about creating units to supplement patrols and emphasize police–community relations?"

"No, but I can make a call to a friend who works in the personnel division," he said.

"Please let me know," I said. "I really need to get out of this district."

As I started to walk to my car, I asked, "Are you going to be alright here?"

"Sure, I'm not afraid of any ghost," he answered.

Later that day, my sergeant told me a new footman was being assigned to our sector. His name was Frank Whitby. "You are his training officer," the sergeant told me. "I understand that he is very aggressive. Take the time to teach him how we do things around here. I don't need a problem child."

As soon as I was introduced to Frank, I could see that he was probably a gym rat who pumped a lot of iron. When we shook hands I felt that his was the size of a catcher's mitt. His chest had to expand 50 inches. He stood about 5 feet 10 inches and was nothing but muscle. Frank was also young, just 21 years old. He certainly was friendly enough, but he struck me as a military guy. Experience taught me that wasn't necessarily a good thing; military men came with their own set of rules, which didn't always mix well with inner-city policing. They could be obstinate and come with preconceived notions.

I told him he was assigned to a foot post and described the area it covered. I said there would be lots of drunks, people having epileptic seizures (probably from taking illegal drugs), burglaries and many cases of domestic violence to contend with. I also mentioned that the shift we relieved had a bully for a foot-patrol officer who liked to provoke the folks in the community. By the time we got to our assignments, I told him, the people we protect would not be feeling any love for the cops.

He just smiled confidently.

"I can roll with the best of them," he said.

As we worked the shift, I watched Frank walk out onto the middle of the 2300 block of Greenmount Avenue during rush-hour traffic for no apparent reason. "What the hell is he doing?" I thought in alarm. "He is going to get hit." I watched cars swerve so they wouldn't slam into him. Horns honked. Passengers yelled, "Get out of the street you dumb shit."

Frank pointed at a random car. "Pull over, pull over!" he screamed.

I watched, anxious, as he approached the driver's side of the vehicle in a manner that put him directly in front of the driver. "Oh no," I thought. "If this guy wants to shoot Frank, he has an easy target." Frank barked at him, "License and registration." The driver complied and asked, "Why did you stop me?" Frank did not answer, but moved to the sidewalk and called the dispatcher to request a warrant check. He got his response ten minutes later; the driver was not wanted. Meanwhile, the driver's car was parked in the street, blocking traffic. Finally, Frank told the driver, "Get the hell out of here."

The next day I ripped him a new one.

"Are you out of your goofy mind? The stunt you pulled yesterday could have gotten you killed," I said. "There is no way you could have known the driver's state of mind or whether he was a nut bag on the run."

"I had everything under control," said the overconfident Frank.

"Bullshit. No you didn't. The idea here is that we work an honest eight and go home safely."

He was defiant. "I went home and drank a beer," he said.

"You could have approached the car from the rear so your body would be positioned parallel to the door frame. That way if he wanted to shoot you, he would need to turn and point the gun over his left shoulder, giving you enough time to escape."

"Anything else?" he asked impatiently.

"Yes, safety first."

As I walked out of the station house, I thought, "I hope he doesn't become a statistic."

I worked with him for four months and unfortunately concluded that he was not coachable.

I was now living with my old high school fraternity buddy, Bob Fifield. The phone rang one day and Bob yelled from the kitchen, "Wayne is on the phone for you." Wayne told me he had spoken to his friend in personnel. Commissioner Pomerleau had authorized three new units of officers to be called Crime Control Teams, paid with a federal grant. Each team would be assigned to two police districts, to augment patrol in high crime areas and devote special attention to police–community relations. According to Wayne, an announcement would be made in a week or so. It sounded like it would be right up my alley. I told Wayne, "I've had enough of the ABCs of the Eastern."

"What do you mean?" he asked.

"A for aggressive conduct which is without merit; B for brutal behavior, both verbal and physical, by prejudiced officers; and C for corruption, big and small."

I hung up and walked out of the kitchen, humming the 1965 monster hit by the Animals, "We Gotta Get out of This Place."

Less than a week later, I submitted a transfer request and it was granted. I was assigned to the Crime Control Team, working out of the Northern District.

Before I left the Eastern District, I said goodbye to community and religious leaders and thanked many who treated me so kindly, especially Pastor Bolinda, a church leader. I promised to come back to visit, but never did. That is something I regret to this day.

In my new job on the crime control team, I was thrilled to learn that Don Trezise, Wayne Carneal and another officer named Charlie Walas were also transferred.

My assignment began in July of 1973. We had six officers in our unit with one sergeant and one lieutenant. I was especially pleased to be working with Charlie Walas, who had worked for the Drug Strike Force and had a reputation as a no-nonsense cop with an outstanding knowledge of policing. He knew how to conduct narcotics investigations that were far more sophisticated than any of the drug arrests I'd made. I had a great interest in learning from him. He was also well known for his odd humor. He loved playing pranks. We had a lieutenant who routinely brought a half dozen hard boiled eggs for lunch. Charlie replaced two of the hard boiled eggs with raw eggs. What a mess! Another time, we found our office secretary in tears because she left her new puppy tied up at home when she went to work, and discovered he'd hung himself. When Charlie heard the news, he asked her, "Did he leave a note?"

Charlie stood 6 feet tall and had a slender build. His hairline receded and his face was slightly marked from acne. He was the first officer to be given the title of "Police Agent," a designation awarded to any officer who had a four-year college degree. It didn't seem to bother anybody that his degree from the University of Baltimore was in transportation, not criminal justice

The assignment to the Crime Control Team certainly was better for my eyes, since we did not work a midnight shift. The regimen of eye drops twice a day continued and I continued to wear sunglasses all the time, because the light made it harder to see well. But I knew the wolf was at the door. I would soon need another cataract surgery, since my right eye was becoming more blurred every day. I thought I should take annual vacation leave instead of medical leave when the time came, so I wouldn't alert the department to my deteriorating eye condition

Under Charlie's direction, we wrote our first search and seizure warrant for narcotics violations. On October 23, 1973, at 10 p.m. we raided the home of Larry Gillette, at 3106 North Calvert Street in the Charles Village neighborhood. Our search found marijuana and Top smoking papers for rolling joints. In the basement, we found an unusually large amount of camera equipment that looked brand new. We also found pay stubs from Paramount Photo Supplies, in the 3100 block of Greenmount Avenue, where Gillette worked. I said, "Charlie, there must be a couple of thousands of dollars' worth of camera stuff here." That was a lot of money in those days. "Shouldn't we confiscate it?"

Wayne asked the same question.

Charlie replied, "You're right, but there isn't enough evidence to grab it. Remember this: what you think or believe in your heart doesn't amount to a pile of shit. The only thing that counts is what can be proven in a court of law in accordance with the rules of evidence." Gillette was arrested and charged with simple possession of a controlled dangerous substance.

The next morning Charlie, Wayne and I were at the camera store as soon as it opened. After asking a series of questions to the owner, who made an inventory check, we learned that the items we saw were indeed stolen. Gillette had been pilfering from his employer. Now we had probable cause to execute another search warrant. Charlie was a veteran at writing search and seizure warrants, so for him it was just another day at the office. But Wayne and I were pretty excited to execute two warrants in as many days. As a result, $5,728 of camera equipment was recovered. Gillette was charged—and convicted—of felony theft.

By now I had learned that the Baltimore Police Department—and probably all metropolitan departments—is divided into two unofficial groups. There are the Goofs who do most of the work. They believe that they work in a profession and do their very best to serve the community without prejudice. The other group is the Humps. They are lazy, incompetent and sometimes corrupt. They have little respect for the citizens they took an oath to protect and serve. My motto is, "Never let a Hump get in front of a Goof."

Even in the select Crime Control Team there was more than one Hump. The worst was a 6-foot-4 officer who weighed at least 250. Secretly I called him Tree. He was an alcoholic and a man without a backbone. On the 2800 block of Greenmount Avenue there was a bar and lounge called Tattersall's, which got large crowds during the weekends. We got a call for a bar fight one night. The Crime Control Team responded and found that several fights had broken out at once. While Wayne Carneal tried to handcuff a disorderly customer, he looked up to see Tree standing in the doorway, doing nothing to help. When Tree saw what was happening, he left without assisting. Word that he had shirked his duty spread like wildfire. The next time Charlie Walas saw the drunken coward he let him have it. "What a gutless bastard you are. The next time I find you sleeping on duty, I'm going to put superglue in your eyes."

On East 36th Street in the Ednor Gardens community, there was a small grocery store owned and operated by a Native American called Rosie. He was very well liked because of his outgoing personality and his willingness to teach anyone who was interested about Native American customs. Rosie was a soft touch who allowed customers to buy on credit. The store had a beer and wine license, so Tree took full advantage of Rosie's generosity. Tree would park his patrol car two or three blocks away and walk to the store. It was not unusual for Tree to stay at Rosie's for three hours, drinking Rosie's free beer. Tree knew that Rosie was too kind to drop a dime on him.

Our unit was working a 6 p.m. to 2 a.m. shift when we got a call for shots fired in the parking lot of Memorial Stadium, where the Orioles and Colts played. Charlie and I responded to find Tree shooting his service revolver into the air from the car window. Charlie got out of our car and approached him. "You stupid son of a bitch," he said. "You are nothing but a snot-slinging drunk. The best thing you can do is resign. If you don't, tomorrow I will get a warrant for your dumb ass and lock you up." Charlie and I then discussed whether we should arrest Tree on the spot for driving while intoxicated. After some back and forth, we decided it would be an embarrassment to the unit if we charged him. Soon after the shooting incident, Charlie and I were greatly relieved to learn that Tree did indeed submit his resignation. We were now a police unit with one less Hump. As for the Goofs, Charlie Walas was one of the best I ever worked with. He became a lasting friend and confidante. We would work together, on and off, for the next 15 years.

19
ANOTHER BROTHER GONE

The spring of 1974 saw our spirits lifted at the Crime Control Team, now that we had rid ourselves of Tree, our drunken, trigger-happy colleague. Our good mood changed on April 6 when we heard another colleague had been gravely wounded in the line of duty. This one hit me to the core. It was Frank Whitby, whom I trained on patrol in the Eastern District. I had worried he would not take my "safety first" advice to heart. He was shot while responding to a call about a man shooting a gun in the air on East Lanvale Street. The officer entered the house and was immediately shot in the stomach by a man who stood at the end of a hallway. Frank, though seriously wounded, was able to push his partner out the door to safety. He lay in an intensive care ward at Johns Hopkins Hospital for 29 days, receiving more than 100 pints of blood, donated by fellow officers and civilians. He had seven operations. If he'd worn a bulletproof vest, he might not have been so seriously wounded, but bulletproof vests would not be issued to Baltimore police for another year.

I believed I had failed Frank as his training officer and was consumed with guilt. If I'd done a better job at teaching him about safety, perhaps he might not have been shot.

Six weeks after Frank's shooting I prepared for my second cataract surgery, in my right eye.

I wondered how many more operations there would be in my future. It's a good thing I didn't know the answer. "Life can really suck," I thought. I was feeling sorry for myself, but not for long. The memory of Frank's shooting would pop into my mind and make me feel guilty for feeling sorry for myself.

On April 24, Charlie Walas drove me to the Greater Baltimore Medical Center at 5 a.m. Within 30 minutes, I was in a chilly, brightly lit operating room where I disrobed and put on a surgical gown, complete with the indignity of baring my ass. The head nurse introduced herself. She said, "My name is Mary and today I will be taking good care of you." Even in an embarrassing surgical gown I put on my best sense of humor.

"Mary, might you have a husband name Joseph and a son who walks on water?" She smiled and asked if I needed to use the rest room. I said yes. Once I was out, she walked me to the operating table and instructed me to jump on. As I did, someone covered me with a warm blanket. I thought to myself, "Thank you Jesus." She then began asking about 20 questions, which had already been asked and answered. As she was finishing, Dr.

Scholz arrived. As always I was happy to see him. I had such tremendous confidence in him, I knew without a doubt that after the surgery I would have normal eyesight.

"Which eye are we doing this morning?" he asked.

"The right this time," I answered. He shook his head in agreement and marked an "X" on the right side of my forehead. The anesthesiologist introduced herself and explained that the IV line, which she inserted on the top of my left hand, had a mild sedative.

"Will I feel any pain?" I asked.

"Not a thing." Then it was lights out.

Two hours later, I was awake in a single room. My eye was patched and I was very thirsty. When a nurse finally visited, she said that Dr. Scholz would be in the next morning. She helped me drink a small cup of ginger ale and I soon fell back to sleep.

As promised, Dr. Scholz came into my room early in the morning and told me that all went well. He would be sending me home with two antibiotic drops to prevent infection. He also gave me a warning. "Many surgeries have been ruined because patients could not keep their hands away from the operated eye. Don't try to peek to see how your vision has improved. The rule is to place no hand higher than the cheek bone and no lower than the eyebrow."

Before he left he said he wanted to see me in about seven days.

I spent three days in the hospital. When they removed the bandage I could already see the improvement. Once again, I had 20/30 vision in each eye. I was sent home with my eye bandaged and extra gauze, as well as a protective shield to wear over it to bed to make sure I didn't touch it in my sleep.

Of course, I also knew that my clear eyesight might be temporary; premature cataract surgeries could result in premature retina detachments. But I'd had enough else to worry about lately. My concerns about detached retinas would have to wait for another day.

On May 5, we got the sad news that Officer Frank Whitby died of an infection from his gunshot wound. "Oh my God, Don," I said to Trezise. "It isn't even two years since we lost Lorenzo." Don grimly shook his head and walked away. When I got home, I dropped onto the sofa and was thankful to find no one home. I didn't feel like talking to anyone. I knew that Frank had a wife who fortunately was very close to her family, though I also knew her life would forever be changed. I very much missed talking with Pop. I really needed him. After a while, I thought if Pop were alive, he would tell me, "No one knows when death will come so try to live every day with a smile in your heart." I got off of the sofa and went about my routine, but I could not escape the news of Frank's death. All three local TV news programs led with coverage of his murder.

That night sleep did not come easily. Frank was still on my mind. Once again, the front doors of the Eastern District would be draped in black cloth, black ribbons would be distributed to place on every badge of every police officer and another member of the force would be laid to rest. One thousand of us attended Frank's funeral on May 8, some arriving from West Virginia and Washington, D.C. Others came representing state and federal law enforcement agencies. Commissioner Pomerleau was there, along with Governor Marvin Mandel, Mayor William Donald Schaefer and other city officials. Frank's widow, hysterical with grief, had to be helped from the funeral home. I thought, "He who wipes the tears of a widow will be held in high esteem." When officers arrived at the gravesite, they formed long lines saluting Frank's coffin as a bugler played taps. He was 22 years old.

I went to my car and waited until everyone was gone before I walked back to the gravesite. "Good Lord Frank," I said aloud. "We are down to this. I hope you are in perfect peace." I wanted to say a prayer on bended knee, but could not bring myself to do it. Instead, I looked up to the sky. It seemed that no matter the reason, death was always around.

"God, are you really there?" I said before I walked away.

Frank's killer, Luke James, was convicted the following February and sentenced to life in prison. He would later argue unsuccessfully that he did not get a fair trial because he suffered from alcohol-induced amnesia when he shot Officer Whitby.

One day I received a call from Joe Key, who graduated with me from the academy. He was now assigned to the Intelligence Unit. He mentioned another classmate of ours who was working on a Crime Control Team.

"Do you remember him?" Joe asked me.

"Yes, I see him all the time. What about him?"

"We have information that he is smoking joints while on duty. We need your help," said Joe.

"What do you want from me?"

"The next time you see him, get near enough to tell if he has been smoking marijuana. You should be able to smell it."

The following week I saw the officer walking down the side steps of the Northern District.

"Hey, got a second? I have a photo I want to show you," I said.

I pulled out a surveillance picture of a robbery suspect. "Do you know anything about this guy? We think he has hit three places, always with a gun."

"No idea," he said.

A few minutes later I called Joe and told him the pungent odor of grass was obvious. That was the last time I saw my fellow member of the Crime Control Team. Three days later, Joe called to say that I had given him the probable cause to search. The effort resulted in the confiscation of two joints found in the officer's shirt pocket. The seizure led to his immediate resignation. Joe complimented me, but I didn't feel good about what I had done.

I always believed in the unwritten code that you should never rat on a fellow officer. I hoped I would never be asked to do it again.

In June the news was full of reports that the Baltimore City government was having a very difficult time reaching labor contracts with city employees, especially the police union. I had reluctantly joined the Baltimore police union because membership provided legal services if I ever needed it. I certainly thought that unions were necessary when sweatshops existed, but I was not so sure they were needed in modern-day America. By July the sanitation workers were on strike. Garbage was piling up in the summer heat and the citizens were demanding an immediate resolution.

Simultaneously, members of the police union of the American Federation of State, County and Municipal Employees were in a showdown with the city's labor negotiators over pay raises. The union had rejected the city's standard offer of a 6 percent raise. Any increase above 6 percent would have required the city to match the extra raise to its other unions— the teachers, firefighters and the sanitation workers already on strike. Union members threatened to take job actions that would slow down the force and prevent police from keeping the peace. They might "work to rule," for example by writing police reports about pennies found on the curb or writing parking tickets if cars were parked an inch too far from the curb. The union's negotiator, Thomas Rapanotti, threatened to call a strike, even though it would be illegal.

I believed police should never abandon their oath to protect the public.

On July 3, Rapanotti played hardball by stating that no one should rule out the possibility of a strike. Tempers among officers flared. I believed the vast majority of officers did not understand the difference between a legal and illegal strike. I felt strongly that union leaders should have explained to members that we had no legal authority to walk out.

On July 5, the union rejected the offer made by the city; Mayor William Donald Schafer warned not to expect a better offer. The union represented 1,800 members of the 2,800-strong police force. Union leaders gave instructions for officers to begin working to the letter of the law. Officers began calling out of service to write reports of found property like discarded washing machines, broken bikes, old truck tires and other worthless items. Some officers used paddy wagons to transport the junk to the evidence room. The auto storage yard on Pulaski Highway was packed with abandoned vehicles that officers had towed. Cops brought dictionaries to the district stations, determined to fill out reports without any misspellings. They took fixed positions, refusing to move unless they got a call for service. They stopped making business checks. Some called in sick. We dubbed their malady the "Blue Flu."

On July 10, the union called for a strike vote by its members. I remember taking a count of my fellow officers on the Crime Control Team, who were unanimous in their decision not to walk. I was sent to the union hall with the "no" votes. Bringing in votes for fellow officers was weird enough. But on July 11, when I walked into the union hall at 305 West Madison Street to cast my vote—well within the time allotted to cast a ballot—I was told the vote was over and that the union was already on strike. "That can't be fucking right," I yelled. "Not all the votes are in."

The officer I yelled at ignored my protest and told me to take a picket sign. I walked out in disgust. The official notice came at 8 p.m. and immediately hundreds of police walked off their jobs. As word spread through the city, looting began and fires were set. The Southwestern District had about 85 percent of its members on strike. The Western District followed and only five officers reported for the 12 a.m. to 8 a.m. shift at the Southeastern District. In the Eastern District, only one officer, Frank Hoyt, the son of union president George Hoyt, walked out. The next day there were picket lines at each police station. Wayne Carneal and I arrived at the Northern at the same time. We saw the picket line manned by officers we knew and once respected. I watched officers pushing and spitting on each other.

As we crossed the line we were called traitors, pussies, and fucking queers. Two officers tossed small wads of paper at us. It seemed that the projectiles had to have something inside in order to travel such distances. I walked over to one on the ground. When I opened it, I found small stones inside. That really made me blistering mad. Our entire unit reported for duty. It made me feel proud. I thought to myself, "This is crazy. What about the people we swore to protect?"

Just then Wayne said, "I can't stand this shit. I'm quitting."

True to his word, he resigned the very next day. At the time, he had a four-year-old daughter and a stay-at-home wife.

Meanwhile, in a three-block area of Central District there was looting in stores and vacant buildings were set ablaze. On the east side, looters busted store windows and hauled off televisions and furniture. Looters broke into pharmacies. Groups of juveniles roamed the street. They pulled fire alarms, then pelted firefighters with rocks when they arrived. Four men were arrested while looting a gun store. People were robbed, some needing medical treatment. At the Western District, while 50 officers picketed the station house, looters raided liquor stores two blocks away. By morning the media reported that some owners were guarding their businesses with shotguns and family dogs. The fire department reported that 185 firefighters were on the streets battling fires set in vacant buildings and dumpsters.

Ten minutes after I got home on that first day the phone rang. It was Joe Key. He said the police commissioner needed eyes and ears on ground zero.

"What do you mean?" I asked.

"We need to know everything the strikers will do next," he said.

"Are you asking me to spy on fellow officers?"

"Yes. There is no one else we trust for such an assignment. Look, the city is in trouble," he said. "Not only will innocent citizens get hurt, but there'll be untold losses to the business community. The strike's made national news."

I did not answer for a long time, but then said, "Okay." I had been unjustly called a spy for the police department before. But now I was actually agreeing to become one.

I didn't like the thought of becoming an informant, but I understood the need.

I was very conflicted. I remembered Pop telling me there would be times I'd have to dig deep for courage to do the right thing. I wondered about my future in the department. Who would want to work with me? I'm not sure that I would want to work with myself.

20
AM I MY BROTHER'S KEEPER?

"It can't get any worse than this," I thought. Brother against brother, one betraying the other. I started thinking the strike was analogous to the Civil War. Could I be the brother who would commit the inconceivable act of providing information to the enemy? Dear God, that is exactly what I am doing. I kept thinking, "There has to be a better way." It is simply impossible for a civilian to understand the close relationship between police partners. It is a bond tightly woven through the shared experiences of treachery, danger, fear and the relief of safety. Officers spend eight hours a shift in the close confinement of a patrol car, exchanging more personal information than they share with their spouses. They confess to extra-marital affairs, illness, financial distress and chatter about sports. One cop may even secretly co-sign a loan for another, so an officer's family won't know of his financial woes.

After I agreed to spy on my brothers in the union I learned on the second day of the strike that there would be a meeting in a suite of the Lord Baltimore Hotel downtown. I got the room number, knocked on the door and was invited in. Two of the strike leaders were there, but no union officers. The purpose of the meeting was to plan strategy for the next step, but there was no organization or any game plan. All I found was disorganization. It was a rudderless ship. Cops sat on every piece of furniture, while others sat on the floor. Most wore their guns. I heard Pop talking to me: "Take it slow and don't ask any questions." No one had command of the meeting. Some officers had taken a food run, while others just watched TV. Cigarette smoke filled the room. One yelled out, "Somebody open a window."

No sooner had he said it, when someone else followed up: "And throw out that fucking piece-of-shit commissioner." Ed Crowder and I saw each other, but we did not speak. I was aware that Ed was now assigned to the intel unit, which told me that he must also be spying. I stayed for about two hours. By then some of the strikers were starting to think that there would be no more negotiations. The mood was doom and gloom.

I left the meeting and drove several miles east to make sure I wasn't being followed. I crossed the city line into Baltimore County. On Dundalk Avenue I found a pay phone and called Joe Key to report what I'd heard, even the comment about throwing Commissioner Pomerleau out the window, which I noted was a joke. I told him I would return to the hotel later. When I got back to the hotel, many cops had left the room. Those who remained were saying, "If the strike turns to shit, guys will be fired left and right." I noticed that Ed was still in the room, but not talking with anyone. Three hours later I left to go home. My frat buddies were full of questions and I was surprised to learn that they too were divided over the strike. I, of course, did not tell them I was spying on the union. It made me feel very isolated. I worried that I had be extraordinarily careful about what I told them. It was a new feeling for me, not to be forthcoming with my closest friends. I did not know it then, but it was a feeling I would have to get used to.

Later that evening, I called Wayne. He wasn't able to say much, since his wife was nearby. I did learn that he had told her of his resignation and she was very upset. We agreed to talk in a few days.

On the morning of the third day of the strike, I was back at the Lord Baltimore. When I walked in, some cops were screaming, "We have a motherfucking spy who is reporting everything we say." I walked over to an officer I knew from the academy.

"What the hell is up?" I asked.

"A sergeant from the homicide unit just left. He and his partner were asking who wanted to toss the commissioner out of the window."

"Jesus Christ, that's not good," I said. The commissioner must have taken their joke seriously. I listened while other officers bitched about some cops who promised to strike, but did not walk.

Meanwhile, public officials worried about public safety. The Maryland State Police were already patrolling the streets. Governor Mandel, Mayor Schafer and Commissioner Pomerleau were considering activating the National Guard. By the third day of the strike a judge began leveling daily $35,000 fines on Rapanotti and the union. On the fourth day, the strike ended with the union agreeing to accept the original raise offered, though the city agreed to further boost salaries in the second year of the contract. Pomerleau was unforgiving toward the strikers. He fired 91 probationary officers and suspended 24 others. Another 25 resigned. In *The Sun*, Pomerleau said, "There will be no general amnesty as long as I am police commissioner."

We were left disheartened, some even embarrassed that fellow officers would even think of going on strike.

The day the strike ended, I called Wayne.

"Is your wife still mad?" I asked.

"Yeah, I have to find work really fast. I submitted an application for a sales job with Proctor & Gamble and some others."

Our conversation ended with a brief discussion about what might happen to the Crime Control Teams. We had no idea, but two weeks later we learned the commissioner had disbanded them and sent the team officers to replace cops who lost their jobs over the strike.

Later that day, Joe Key called to say that I had been re-assigned to the Southwestern District. This was the district with the most strikers; Pomerleau was concerned about more possible job actions. I would be working with the desk sergeant filling out paperwork and meeting with walk-in complainants wanting to report crimes, most of them domestic.

But I was also given instructions to learn who had been involved in planning job actions during the strike and if any more were being planned for the future. I would hear nothing of the sort.

I was not pleased to hear what Joe had to say. It was very unsettling to think I was still expected to be a rat. I began reviewing all of the information I gave to the Intelligence Unit. I did find some peace in the realization that my reports had been about problems and not specific people. Still, I fell into a funk. I thought to myself, "There is no getting out of this short of resignation."

I walked to my closet to look at the blue uniform. I said out loud, "Pop, Pop, Pop, what am I going to do?"

I heard no words of advice. I thought about driving to the corner bar, but didn't. I had long practiced the philosophy that liquor was not the lantern which would lead me to wisdom. That night I was in such a bad mood, I could barely stand myself. I went to bed early just to toss and stare at the ceiling.

21
A HALF TRUTH IS A WHOLE LIE

In late 1974 I turned in my uniform, my badge, my service revolver and my riot gear. I left my post at the Southwestern District without saying goodbye to anyone. I did not even call Charlie Walas or Wayne Carneal. I said nothing to my old fraternity friends. I went to see Esther just before Christmas and told her I was quitting the police force and would be looking for a new job. I needed a change, I said. I tried to be as convincing as possible. My sister didn't believe a word, but, thankfully, she didn't call me a liar. If anyone else asked, I let it be known that I had resigned. My personnel records, though, mentioned nothing of the kind. Instead, someone typed, "10-25-74: Transferred to Personnel Division Casualty Section," the designation usually given to someone with a serious medical problem. This lie, I knew, was for my own safety.

My unexpected odyssey began a few weeks before. I was working the midnight to 8 a.m. shift at the Southwestern District when I answered a phone call.

"Southwest can I help you?" I said.

"I'm Joe Key's sergeant and we have another assignment for you."

In a flash of panic I hung up without saying a word. My mind immediately went into high gear.

"What the fuck!" I thought. "Can anyone be that stupid to call me here? Jesus Christ, I must be working for goddamn idiots."

Here I was in the Southwestern District station, the heart of the police strike and its aftermath, sent by the department's Intelligence Unit to spy once again on my fellow officers to find out if they were planning more disruptive job actions.

And now I'm getting a phone call in the same station house from the sergeant at the Intelligence Unit. What if any other officers heard the caller? They would certainly wonder why a sergeant from the Intelligence Unit was calling me. Thank God this was years before the invention of caller ID.

I felt my face flush. Worried that the desk sergeant might ask if something was wrong, I told him I was running to the rest room and would be right back. I threw cold water on my face and dried it with a paper towel. I looked into the mirror and thought,

"What have I gotten into? Have I become a victim of my own virtue?"

As soon as my shift ended I went home and dialed Joe Key's number. I was surprised to learn that Joe was unaware of the call. He apologized and said he would get back to me after talking with the sergeant. I told Joe I'd hung up without speaking because I had no idea who was calling and I worried it was a trap. Joe said he understood. Thirty minutes later Joe confirmed that the caller was indeed his sergeant. Joe then told me he was being replaced as my contact by his sergeant. I had known Joe since our academy days, so I spoke to him candidly.

"Does this mean that I now have an idiot as my new handler?"

Joe said it was out of his hands and thanked me for my service to his unit. That was the last time I spoke with Joe for many years.

Three days later, I received a call at home. It was the sergeant. He said he would like to meet me and propose a new assignment.

"What might you have in mind?" I asked.

"I would prefer to tell you in person."

He suggested that we meet several miles outside Baltimore at the Blue Bell Restaurant on Bel Air Road at Route 152 in Harford County.

I hesitantly agreed.

"How will I know you?" I asked

He asked what kind of car I drove and said he would find me.

"A baby blue Pinto hatchback," I answered.

Before he hung up he told me the Blue Bell had the best crab cakes in town.

A week later I drove out to the Blue Bell and met a middle-aged, overweight man with eye glasses. He wore gray pants and a blue shirt with polka dots. He introduced himself and said, "You're going to love these crab cakes."

As we walked across the parking lot, I thought, "I find nothing impressive about this guy; he seems more interested in eating than anything else."

The restaurant was empty, since it was just after the lunch rush. He pointed to a booth in the corner. After the server brought menus, he said, "Order what you want, the treat is on me. I suggest the crab cakes."

"Wow," I thought. "What's up with these crab cakes?"

When the crab cake platters came, he just started eating.

Exasperated, I asked, "So what is on your mind?"

He only said, "Enjoy the crab cakes and then we can talk."

"Is he trying to piss me off?" I wondered. "What an annoying man."

When he asked for a dessert menu, I almost walked out.

He ordered a piece of cheesecake with fresh strawberries on top.

After a half hour, he finally got to it. He explained that the Baltimore Police Department's Inspectional Services Division (ISD), as well as the FBI, had collected information indicating that the Philadelphia Bruno mob family, headed by Angelo Bruno, intended to expand their territory into Baltimore City.

When I asked, "How do you know this?" He just said, "I can't tell you. It's on a need-to-know basis and you don't need to know."

He further explained that Commissioner Pomerleau wanted verification one way or another. "That's your new assignment. You will officially resign and turn in all of your police-issued equipment."

"I'm not sure I'm getting what you are saying," I said. "You want me to quit, give back my badge, gun, uniform and riot gear?"

"You got it," he said. His tone of voice was so casual you'd think he'd just asked me to show up in court over a parking ticket.

He didn't acknowledge that he was assigning me to a potentially dangerous job. He didn't even say why I'd been chosen for the job.

He just waved to the server and ordered another piece of cheesecake.

I was absolutely stunned by his lack of guidance.

I said, "And what could I possibly do to confirm that the mob is coming to town?"

"Hang around and learn what you can."

"Hang around where?" I asked.

"You know. Go to The Block and keep your ear to the ground," he said, referring to the three-block red-light district known simply as The Block. It was on East Baltimore Street, oddly situated behind police headquarters.

"You can also go to Little Italy and have something to eat at one of the places, but there won't be any crab cakes."

"If I agree, how long will the assignment last?"

"You don't have an option," he said sternly. "If you want a job in this department, you will agree. No one tells the commissioner 'No.'"

I was not happy with the conversation. I was perplexed about my assignment, as well as his lack of direction.

"When do you need an answer?" I asked.

"Right away."

It was now my turn to get stern.

"No matter who wants what, you are not getting an answer today." He just shrugged.

After he ordered a crab cake to go and paid the check I was off in my Pinto, headed down Belair Road back to Baltimore.

On the way home, it struck me that the sergeant didn't do or say anything to instill confidence. This was certainly not a good omen, since he would be my contact person as I searched for the mafia in Baltimore.

Not surprisingly, I wished Pop were still alive to provide guidance. His unsolved murder weighed heavily on my mind. It had now been two years since his death without an arrest. In February of 1975 *The Sun* wrote an article quoting the homicide detective, James Ozazewski, claiming that police had no suspects after interviewing 200 of the 357 Diamond cabdrivers working in the city the night Pop was killed. The article did not say if molds were taken of the tire tracks, or if they were trying to match them to tires on taxi cabs.

When I got home I put on a Simon and Garfunkel record and played "Bridge over Troubled Water" and tried to weigh the pros and cons. I thought I should feel good that Commissioner Pomerleau believed that I had the street smarts for the assignment. I kept thinking, "This is crazy. How am I going to infiltrate?" I didn't know a single person who worked on The Block. And how many dinners could I eat in Little Italy? Still, the more I thought about it, the more intriguing the assignment seemed.

One positive thought was my eyesight, for once. After my last cataract surgery I developed an infection, but it was now cleared up. I had pretty good eyesight in both eyes now. If I chose not to take the assignment, I could quit the city police force and apply to the Baltimore County Police Department. I was confident I would pass their eye test.

I got a piece of paper and drew a line down the center. I labeled "Good Things" and "Bad Things" on either side of the line, but I was so exhausted I didn't write a word.

Instead, I drank two beers and went to bed.

The more I thought about it, I became intrigued by the assignment, despite the fact that my supervisor would be little help. I would be left to my own devices and imagination. I would be completely self-reliant. And since it was a criminal area foreign to the Baltimore Police Department, they would have to believe what I told them. They could not even set my work hours. I would have the freedom to move as I saw fit. I would be creating my own job and be completely independent. The position would be the complete opposite of the semi-military role of a patrolman.

I had a second meeting at the Blue Bell with the sergeant, whom I will call Sgt. Crab. I told him I agreed to take the assignment. Sgt. Crab instructed me to turn in reports on plain paper, rather than standard police reports.

I was to call the ISD office every day to speak with him. "And what do I do with the written reports?" I asked.

"You will give them to me whenever we meet. And you should also bring me a report explaining how much money you paid out in expenses and where you spent it."

"Are you telling me that you won't be paying my expenses up front?"

"That's right," he said. He smiled in a devilish way.

"That's totally fucking wrong," I said as I raised my voice.

"You're going to have to live with that," he said.

The only good news he gave me was about my paycheck. He would cash my check and bring the money to me every other week. To make sure we were not seen together in Baltimore City, he would arrange to meet me each week far from the city. Not surprisingly he chose the Blue Bell Restaurant. I was to meet him in the empty parking lot early in the morning before it opened. He made no pretense that the police department would have my back while I worked. He made no mention of having me wear a wire for my protection, so police could listen in on my conversations and come to my aid if they heard trouble. Uniform cops on the beat at The Block would not know my true identity.

Even though I had to turn in my service revolver, he did say I had the option of carrying a concealed gun, a 2-inch .38 Smith and Wesson revolver. I would eventually choose not to carry the gun. I decided it might give me a false sense of security. Instead, I chose to live by one rule: You can never stop thinking.

Before our meeting ended, Sgt. Crab told me never to use my name when calling his office.

"When you call the office tell the secretary that you are number 232 calling."

I immediately thought of the Johnny Rivers hit song, "Secret Agent Man," from 1966:

> There's a man who leads a life of danger
> To everyone he meets he stays a stranger
> With every move he makes another chance he takes
> Odds are he won't live to see tomorrow
> Secret agent man, secret agent man
> They've given you a number and taken away your name...

As I walked into police headquarters to turn in my uniform, badge and revolver I thought I never imagined at the academy that I would be taking on any assignment like this; it certainly would be better if I had more insight into the job.

The next morning, while lying in bed, I thought I needed a cover story if anyone asked why I left the department. I decided to tell people I was accused of taking bribes. I knew this might not be too believable, since I had been police officer of the year, but I also thought a mobster might feel comfortable with an ex-cop who was accused of taking bribes.

I also needed another cover story while hanging out on The Block. Who would I pretend to be?

I decided to visit the Baltimore City Liquor Board to read the directory of licensees. I thought it would be difficult, but the directory identified bars, liquor stores and restaurants by streets. I checked the 500, 400 and 300 blocks of East Baltimore Street where the show bars and strip clubs were located. While it seemed unfair to the Italian community, which had made so many significant contributions to our country, I had to be logical. I knew I needed to identify the Italians who owned show bars on The Block. It just made sense that if the Bruno crime family was actually trying to take control of illegal money-making schemes in Baltimore, they would not be reaching out to the Irish, German, Polish or Greek criminals.

Two days later I visited the Maryland Room in the Enoch Pratt Library. In college I found it was a great resource for preparing research papers. I found several filing cabinets full of newspaper clippings, where I read articles about Baltimore's Block. To my surprise, it was internationally known. The stories were passed on by sailors who brought cargo to Baltimore's harbor and visited The Block's prostitutes. The articles were written in a positive light without any mention of criminal activity.

Although disappointed, I now had the addresses of the Flamingo Show Bar, owned by Samuel Manafo Sr., 500 East Baltimore Street; the Doll House, owned by Samuel Manafo Jr., 416 East Baltimore Street; the 408 Club, owned by Joseph Manafo Sr., 406 East Baltimore Street; the Plaza Show Bar, owned by Joseph Manafo Jr., 402 East Baltimore Street; and the Block Show Bar, owned by Thomas Bruno, 417 East Baltimore Street. I wondered if the Baltimore Bruno was related to the Philadelphia Bruno. Then I dismissed the thought; Bruno is a common name.

I realized I could no longer live with my old fraternity friends and tell them a lie that I was no longer on the police force. I have a deep dislike for liars. Now I would be living a lie. I decided rather than lie to so many frat brothers, I would drop out of sight, take a powder and move out of the apartment I was sharing with Bob Fifield as well as Louie Otremba, who had recently moved in. I was lucky to find an apartment in an isolated building on Ritter Avenue in Northeast Baltimore. I didn't need a moving van because I had no furniture. Since I only had clothes, a radio and books it took me ten minutes to pack. Before I left, I wrote a brief note: "Bob and Lou, need to take care of a situation. Will be in touch." In the envelope I placed a check for the December rent.

Of all the unknowns, perhaps the biggest question was how long I would work as a deep undercover covert. Sgt. Crab never told me. I went into the year 1975 having absolutely no idea how long I had to live this lie. If anyone told me I would not resurface for another three years, I would have thought "there is no way."

But that is what happened. For the next three years I would not ride in a police car or step foot in a police station or have any direct contact with my fellow officers. I would give up all my cherished friendships with my old fraternity buddies and learn the dismal habits of living life alone. I would spend my work days with bartenders, drug-addicted prostitutes, strippers and gamblers and learn the jargon of these sad degenerates. I would grow my hair and a Fu Manchu mustache. People I met would only know me as Jim the taxi cab driver.

22
LIVING A LIE TO FIND THE TRUTH

The truth is not always easy to find. Some people are very accomplished liars. That's how their minds work. Even when the truth will do, they still insist on lying. The fabrications can reach several levels deep. In some situations investigators must travel to hell and back searching for what is real and what is not. Ironically, I was about to live a lie so I could determine the truth. And to find it, this former seminarian—once banned from peeking at *Sports Illustrated*'s swimsuit photos—was about to jump into the devil's trough, Baltimore's many dens of depravity where men threw money at naked dancers.

I had studied organized crime at the Baltimore Junior College and the prospect of investigating it on The Block fascinated me. I knew these bars and clubs were the most likely places the mob would begin controlling Baltimore's many shady enterprises, from bookmaking, sports betting and drug rings to legal liquor licenses, trash hauling agreements and even construction contracts.

If the mafia were to come to town, they would push aside the top Baltimore bookmakers and drug dealers, for example, and place trusted associates from other cities in charge. Since these enterprises produced large amounts of cash, the mafia would never trust the locals to work with them and turn in all the money. They would keep Baltimore people for just enough time to learn the territory. Then the mob bosses would push them out with a threat of bodily harm. If the mob wanted to gain control of Baltimore's lucrative illegal video gambling machines, found in hundreds of bars and earning millions of untaxed dollars, they would expect kickbacks from the machine owners. They would come to Baltimore and say, "We're now in charge. If you want to keep a minor percent of the revenue you can. Otherwise, we have ways to deal with you."

In a mafia-controlled town you can't get a liquor license unless you go through the mob. Inspectors of all sorts, as well as cops, are on the "pad" receiving mob bribes on a routine basis. The mob also tries to influence contracts for construction and sanitation work, no matter if they are using public or private funds.

Though I knew The Block was the most likely place to look for these mob connections, I didn't go there right away. I wanted a little time to get comfortable in my new role. I began visiting two bars about a mile away on the west side of downtown Baltimore, where the dancers (called go-go dancers) did not strip and there were fewer prostitutes. In fact, Pop had once taken me to the Tic Toc Club at Eutaw and Lombard Streets. I jokingly called it the "exciting and intimate" Tic Toc. So I had a little familiarity with the place. I figured an officer working undercover and doing surveillance might naturally feel paranoid, but would not want to project that image. I figured I could practice at the Tic Toc.

It was a brisk, sunny day when I opened the door and stepped into the darkened club.

"Whoa, I can't see," I said. It must have taken me 30 seconds before my eyes adjusted. There were five men seated at the front bar. The lady bartender had a sour look on her face. Later I learned her name was Margaret. She called all her customers by the same name: asshole. I walked to the rear of the joint toward the stage. I grabbed a stool and ordered a beer which cost $1.50. That was a lot in those days. I thought, "At these prices, I won't be getting drunk."

In about five minutes, I heard a voice over my right shoulder. "Hey partner." To my amazement, it was former Southwestern District patrolman Larry Gross, a union official who was terminated after the strike. He was friendly enough, so I told him I had quit the force. "This whole frigging thing about the strike has left me with a sour taste. I don't want to be around them," I lied.

Larry was now the bar manager. I wondered how he got that job. "Larry, I know you can pull a rabbit out of your ass, but how did you pull this one off?"

He laughed and said, "Well the district orders meals for the prisoners and I was the guy who had the pickup detail." He didn't have to tell me that the meals were purchased at the Ambassador restaurant next door, so that was his connection. "I get it now. You felt it was your duty to catch a dance or two," I said with a smile.

"Who could blame me?" he answered. "Pauline was always glad to have a uniformed officer stop by from time to time." I didn't know who Pauline was, but did not ask. My guess was that she was the owner.

Two minutes after Larry walked away, a tall overweight dancer approached me. She placed her hand on my right knee and said, "Hey handsome, want some company? You could buy me a drink and I'll make you feel special."

"Is that right?" I answered.

I wasn't at all nervous. This is what I had expected.

"Yes Honey," she said and ran her hand up my leg. "So who am I talking to?" I asked.

"Everyone calls me Dee Dee, because my bra size is a double D."

When she told me that her drink would cost $10, I said maybe next time. She kissed my cheek and walked to another customer. I stayed for 90 minutes and had similar conversations with four other dancers. And so, my new life was on its way. I was learning to be the great pretender.

As the early days went by I was concerned that I was not always working a 40-hour week. Sgt. Crab didn't seem to have a problem with the schedule, and he said absolutely nothing I could label as direction. "I'm nothing more than a leaf drifting in the wind," I told myself.

As my visits to the Tic Toc increased to three times a week, I just posed as an ordinary customer, with no particular cover story. I would get there around 10 p.m. Larry introduced me to Pauline Schwartz, the owner, who, to my surprise, was well educated and claimed to have a degree in art history. Before relocating to the Baltimore area, she and her husband, now deceased, operated two show bars in Boston's red-light district known as the Combat Zone.

I thought that was very interesting. Maybe they had mob connections. I wondered how someone who was in the Boston game had come to Baltimore. Eventually Larry introduced me to another former police officer who was fired after the strike. His name was Howard Glashoff and he often hung out at the Tic Toc. I was thankful that he did not ask me why I left the BPD or what I was doing hanging out at the club. I found him to be a very funny, engaging man with a keen intellect. I was delighted years later when we reconnected and worked together in law enforcement. Howard, in fact, would become my best friend.

Larry Gross did not last long as the night bar manager and was replaced by John Rosati People called him "Fat John," though not to his face. He resembled the character called Poncho in the TV series *The Cisco Kid*.

I was learning that I had to become more than just a customer if I was going to gather in-depth information. On a bone-chilling night, I finally got my chance when the phone rang at midnight at the Tic Toc. It was someone from the Harem Club, a block away, shouting, "Get down here fast. Bar fight!"

John Hanson, a bartender who was called Little John, jumped the bar. Fat John was moving slower than a fat cow, so I thought, "At last an opportunity to gain some credibility." I joined the run to the Harem. When we arrived, we slammed the door open and found a big guy fighting with an elderly bartender and another man. The fight didn't last more than a few minutes. The big guy said, "Okay I give up you cocksuckers." Before he left, he paid his bar bill. I said, "What no tip?"

They all chuckled, except for the soon-to-be-ejected troublemaker. "Fuck you!" said the big guy as he walked out. Before we left, I was introduced to Paul Balton, the Harem's owner, who said, "I owe you a drink." I could not have asked for more. I guessed correctly that Balton was not his real name. I later learned his real name was Paul Francis Battaglia, a good Italian name.

I also learned why the managers of the Harem called the Tic Toc, instead of the cops. Calling the cops was the last option to resolve a problem in a Baltimore bar. Any police report would go to the city's liquor board, placed permanently in the bar's file and could lead to a suspended or revoked license.

So I began a new routine: two nights at the Tic Toc and two nights at the Harem. Balton was in his mid-20s, stood 6 feet 3 inches, loved to talk sports and had a remarkable memory of sports statistics. While I was a big fan of the Baltimore Colts, I had limited knowledge about the other teams. I bought *Sports Illustrated* and other sports magazines to become more familiar with the NFL. It was part of my work plan to find common denominators, so I would not engage in forced conversation that might give me away. The next part of the plan was to look for vehicles with Pennsylvania plates. Of course, I hoped to get to know Balton well enough to learn if the Philly mob was leaning on him.

As a regular at both bars, I learned that Pauline had a silent partner named Jerry Green. It was mere luck that one night he arrived at the Tic Toc parking lot just as I did, which gave me the opportunity to memorize his tag number. A week later, Sgt. Crab told me that his real last name was Greenbaum. As time went on, I learned that he took frequent trips to Miami. I overheard Greenbaum telling Little John about moving cash between Baltimore and Miami. I could not tell which direction the money went or if it was for drugs or just to be laundered.

In my new assignment I had to teach myself how to remember what I heard by association. I could not write anything down, and did not even use a hidden tape recorder. It was too risky. If I heard a piece of useful information, I had to remember that I heard it from a particular bartender. Then I had to remember the name of the bar where I heard it, not to mention what crime was discussed. I always made it appear like I was just having a casual conversation, but my mind was working a mile a minute so I would not forget. As soon as I got home, I wrote it all down. Then I repeated it to my handler over the phone. At the time, I had no idea how beneficial this memory training would be for a blind man.

I gave all the information to Sgt. Crab, but he never told me if the information was of value or not. He said little when I called him each morning to make my verbal reports. When I met him in person every other week, he handed me my pay as I handed him my expense report. He never once asked about my personal wellbeing, or indicated how I was doing on my assignment. Our meeting lasted just a few minutes and left me feeling disappointed with his lack of communication or instruction. If he'd just directed me in some way, I thought, it might point me in the right direction for my next move.

On Christmas Eve, Pauline brought a large platter of food to the club for staffers and customers. One of the dancers looked like Olive Oyl, Popeye's girlfriend, but had a stage name of Miki. Why it wasn't Olive was beyond me. That night, as a customer bought her drinks, she started singing to the melody of "Silent Night," "Come to me, Come to me. Your face looks like cum to me." I thought, "Here we go. Another fight." The guy just laughed and bought her another $10 drink. Go figure. How life can change, I thought. Just two years ago, Pop and I were spending Christmas Eve at the beautiful Cathedral enjoying midnight Mass and listening to "Ave Maria."

When business slowed Pauline told the dancers to go topless on their second dance out of three. Fat John, who frequently reeked from smoking a joint, had an odd accent which I could not identify. Another slow night, I asked Little John, "What is Fat John's accent?"

"That fat fuck is from the Bronx. He had it made but he fucked it up."

"What did he do?" I asked.

"The stupid motherfucker stole 30 G's from the boys controlling the gambling rackets on the New York waterfront. As a favor to his father, a mob associate, the boys promised not to kill the dumb shit and here he is."

Little John was such a bull-shitter. I wasn't sure if he was making up the story, but if it was true I thought, "Now this is interesting. Two transplants, one from Boston and one from New York, who may have had connections to mobsters from two different cities, end up at the Tic Toc." I didn't know what to make of it, especially since neither came from Philly, where the mob I was looking for was based.

After a few months Paul Balton hired two new bartenders. One was Ronnie Smuck, a bully with a long criminal record. The other was Dave Dykes, who would sadly meet an untimely death. Smuck, who frequently squeezed 10-pound hand grips or rubber balls to strengthen his hands and forearms, thought that he was a badass. One night I watched him angrily grab a dancer's breast and squeeze until it squirted blood. He spoke like a Damon Runyon character and used sports metaphors in his speech. He once told a drunken customer, "Take a ball four," which meant "take a walk." When a customer walked in, Smuck's greeting was "How are you batting them out," his way of asking "how are you?" As for Dave Dykes (whose real last name was Shiner), he wore thick, darkly tinted glasses. He was a happy guy full of nervous energy and told silly anecdotes. "Today for lunch," he'd say, "I ordered turtle soup and I told them to make it snappy."

Another corny favorite: "I was going to visit my sister in Jersey, but my arms were too tired to fly." He would always flap his arms as he told the story. Both Dykes and Smuck were degenerate gamblers. Dykes had such bad luck that Balton would ask him how he wagered and bet the opposite. Dave once actually bet on a horse named Miss Reverse. After I got to know Dykes better, he confided to me that Smuck killed a guy while carrying out a contract in Reisterstown. I reported what I heard, but the murder wouldn't be solved for another 29 years when Smuck was finally convicted and sent to prison for ten years.

One day at the Harem Club I watched a customer I didn't know taking photos of the strippers with an old-fashioned Graflex Speed Graphic camera with a large flash bulb. It was the kind of camera old press photographers used in the 1950s. Balton told me the photographer's name was Samuel Gorn, a wealthy developer who built the Horizon House apartment building on North Calvert Street, best known as the home to one of the city's finest restaurants, The Prime Rib. Gorn was an unimposing man, hardly noticeable among the cast of characters at the Harem. He was in his mid-50s, average height, slender build with graying hair. He always wore a suit. Gorn was a peculiar patron, since his only purpose for visiting the Harem Club was to pursue his hobby of photographing the dancers while they were on stage. Balton, who told me that Gorn printed his own photos, allowed the developer to instruct the strippers to pose for him. Luckily I was already learning how very important it is for a criminal investigator to have a good memory. I would meet Gorn several years later, under more trying circumstances, and remind him about his old hobby.

I was finally ready to visit The Block and look more closely for organized crime.

I drove across downtown long after nightfall, parked near the 400 block of East Baltimore Street and walked to Pollack Johnny's, a famous Block restaurant known for its Polish sausages. I ordered one with mustard and chili and looked out the window, watching the carnival rhythm unfold on the very busy street. I didn't stay long on that first visit, but walked away with some familiarity. I would work my plan, which wasn't much, of becoming a regular at the show bars owned by Italians. I promised myself to always be careful not to ask questions about illegal conduct. I could only imagine what would happen if I was discovered by any of these Block employees.

I now felt confident enough to visit The Block on a daily basis. At least I had learned the bar routine. Dancers would dance to three songs. On the first dance, they kept their bikinis on. On the second, the tops came off and on the third, the dancers wore no clothes and would lay on the stage simulating sex acts. When they were done, they would ask every customer, "Honey, are you tipping the dancers?" Customers typically gave them a dollar. Each time a customer bought a dancer a drink, she would get a swizzle stick which she turned in to the bartender at closing time. For every stick, she would get $3. Most had regular cab drivers to take them home, or wherever they were going. I thought, perhaps I could become a cab driver. It would be a good cover and I could get to know the women better. Maybe they would trust me enough to tell me about other illegal activities that did not involve the sex trade.

23
THE J. EDGAR HOOVER OF BALTIMORE

I had never met Commissioner Pomerleau, even though it seemed he had personally steered my career for several years, persuading me to spy on my fellow officers during the police strike, following up at the Southwestern district and checking out the FBI's tip about the mafia coming to Baltimore. He was like the Wizard of Oz, the man behind the curtain, controlling my professional life. I was grateful that he had modernized the department when he arrived in 1966, made sure officers filed accurate reports, collected crime statistics in a new research department, and had proper training. He rooted out corruption in our ranks, getting the FBI to investigate numerous police officers and commanders for taking bribes from gambling rings, which led to their conviction.

But there was another side to Pomerleau. To him information was power, and he craved any information that would make him the most powerful man in the Baltimore region. In the early 1970s Pomerleau began to emulate J. Edgar Hoover, following in the footsteps of the infamous FBI director who illegally eavesdropped on public figures like Martin Luther King Jr. and used the information he collected against them. Pomerleau began to spy on everyone, from elected officials to political groups to the tame city school board, thereby violating many citizens' civil rights.

In essence, Pomerleau "Hooverized" the Baltimore Police Department by creating an illegal spy agency inside the Inspectional Services Division, or ISD. He held his cards very close to his vest; his operation was so secretive that most officers and commanders in the BPD knew nothing about it. I certainly had never heard of it. Other than knowing I was put in the uncomfortable position of spying on the police strikers, I had no clue how far the commissioner went to violate private citizens' rights without first seeking court-ordered searches or wiretaps. In fact, Maryland law would never have allowed him to obtain such wiretap orders because he had no evidence that any of the people he was spying on had committed a crime.

In late 1974 the department went into a tailspin over the public revelation of widespread illegal surveillance by Pomerleau's covert unit inside ISD. The news came in a series of articles in The News American by reporters Michael Olesker and Joe Nawrozki.

Their explosive stories detailed how Pomerleau ordered ISD (the same division where I worked under Sgt. Crab) to spy on journalists and numerous black politicians, including U.S. congressman Parren Mitchell, state senator Clarence Mitchell III and even the city's top prosecutor, State's Attorney Milton B. Allen. Pomerleau's spies compiled dossiers on leaders of the women's liberation movement, black members of the Baltimore City Council and several prominent black ministers. "Our function in ISD was keeping tabs on anything that might embarrass the commissioner," one police source told the reporters. "The unit is used for political means, not crime," he said.

The News American's first article was indicative of how far Pomerleau went to break the very laws he was hired to enforce. An ISD secret operative named Leonard Jenoff infiltrated the law offices of a defense attorney representing Liddie Jones, one of Baltimore's biggest heroin dealers. Jenoff, working directly for the police commissioner, apparently had access to the defense attorney's files and witnesses, one of whom fled to New York after being warned not to testify in defense of the drug dealer. This was stunning news. I have never since heard of any illegal police activity that came close to this level of violating a citizen's right to a fair trial or the sacred attorney-client privilege.

Jenoff also infiltrated the reelection campaign of Congressman Mitchell, posing as a volunteer. The reporters quoted a suspicious Mitchell: "This becomes part of what many of us in the black community have suspected for a long time, that information is being kept on certain people."

Mitchell, of course, was correct. Nearly two decades later, Olesker, by then a columnist for the Baltimore Sun, wrote this memory of a conversation he had with Pomerleau, who at first denied the surveillance. Pomerleau told Olesker:

"I know you've been told we're collecting personal information on . . ." and he named several prominent politicians. "Forget it," he said. "We're not doing that."

"Wait a minute," Olesker said. "Are you telling me you're not collecting personal information on any politicians?"

"And here is precisely what Donald Pomerleau replied," wrote Olesker. "'Just the blacks. Just the blacks. Just the blacks.'"

One of those 1974 News American articles hit especially close to home for me. It provided great detail on the infiltration of the police union during the strike, by officers sent by ISD to spy on the strikers.

"That effort, according to sources, included 24-hour tails on police union leaders, photographing of all strikers, infiltrating of contract negotiations and surveillance of strikers for at least three weeks after the strike was over," said the article.

"We worked on nothing but the strikers throughout the walkout and for three or four weeks after the strike ended," said one policeman who was in ISD during the strike.

I was not named in the article, but Eddie Crowder was mentioned. Former policeman Howard Glashoff, who once worked for ISD, told the reporters, "I'm positive ISD infiltrated the contract negotiations because Lt. Donald Woods of ISD told me personally that he sent patrolman Edward Crowder in.

"Crowder never left the office the whole time we were in negotiation. After the strike was over, he told the whole story to ISD—who was in on the negotiations, what their roles were.

"He was even there when the phony threat was made on the commissioner's life," continued Glashoff, apparently referring to the strikers' joke I heard about wanting to throw Pomerleau out the window.

"Either Crowder reported it back as a real threat, or the room was bugged, but everybody knew it was a joke," said the article. "Pomerleau briefly considered pressing action for conspiracy to assassinate him, but that action was later dropped."

Another article ran on the front page with a blaring headline, "Pomerleau Admits Getting Spy Reports on Newsmen." The commissioner readily acknowledged to *News American* editors that his police department spied on reporters as they were preparing their articles and kept dossiers on several local reporters.

In those days the city's police department was under the control of the governor, not the mayor, and Governor Mandel oddly muted his criticism of Pomerleau. So did Mayor Schaefer, who went on to become the state's most powerful politician. Subsequent grand jury and state senate investigations resulted in no criminal charges—or even a slap on the wrist for Pomerleau. A year after the *News American*'s revelations, a state senate committee released a 157-page report on Pomerleau's abuses of power. In response, Mayor Schaefer had this to say: "He's doing a fine job." In fact, I would eventually learn that the revelations and investigations did nothing to stop Pomerleau from his illegal spying. He would continue his activities for at least three years.

I always wondered what dirt the commissioner had dug up on Mandel and Schaefer to keep them quiet.

At the time of the news accounts I had only been working as a deep covert for a few months, but my supervisor was upset by the revelations and worried I might be subpoenaed to testify before a grand jury investigating the illegal surveillance.

"I think it's best that you take a two week sabbatical," he told me.

I was surprised. "Why do I need to do that?" I asked him.

"You don't know what I know," said Sgt. Crab.

"What I do know is that I haven't committed any crimes," I told him.

"How weird is this," I thought. "They have all this sophisticated electronic equipment to spy on absolutely innocent people and I have nothing to spy on dozens of people committing crimes around me every night. I'm a cop who doesn't even carry a gun."

Nevertheless, I followed orders to get out of town. I knew someone whose parents owned a condo in Ft. Lauderdale, so I went down to Florida and spent a few weeks there alone.

24
NOT ALL STRIPPERS ARE PROSTITUTES AND NOT ALL PROSTITUTES ARE STRIPPERS

After several months I settled into my lonely little Ritter Avenue apartment, where I never had a visitor. After I fled Bob Fifield's apartment I bought a few pieces of new furniture and a record player. Since my Ford Pinto was on its last legs, I traded it in for a new red Mustang with a white vinyl top. I would leave the apartment every night at 9 to start my work shift on The Block. As I said, I took nothing that would identify me as a cop. No police ID, no hidden tape recorder or wire, and no gun that might give me a false sense of confidence. I relied solely on my wits.

I looked nothing like the patrolman I had been the previous year. I wore a red leather jacket that came to my waist and a pair of black jeans with white tennis shoes. My naturally curly dark brown hair had grown long and I now had a well-trimmed beard.

I parked the car on Custom House Avenue which was home to three strip joints, just around the corner from The Block. As I turned the corner onto East Baltimore Street, I could see the reflections on the wet blacktop of the neon signs and advertisements for the various show bars. The atmosphere made me feel like I was at a raunchy carnival. Every single joint had a doorman, better known as a barker, soliciting business. In those days they were all white men. The owners would not hire anyone of color and even made sure—with the help of an East Baltimore city councilman—that the African American sanitation workers employed by the city were finished picking up the trash by early morning so no white customers would see them. Some of the barkers wore tuxedo shirts and others wore colorful T-shirts. One read: "If nobody talks, everybody walks." Another read: "You're not here to be sober." Some of the barkers solicited patrons with jingles. The doorman of the Block Show Bar sang out, "Gentlemen, Gentlemen, Gentlemen, if you got the money we've got the honey. Step right in, no cover, no minimum."

One night I entered the Gayety Show Bar. It was very dark and the music was incredibly loud. A dancer was on stage shaking every body part that moved. While watching the stripper, I heard a female voice. "Hey Jimmy!" It was Cabaret Kay, from the Harem. Everybody called her CK. She was a stunningly attractive lady who had long black hair and a body that made men stop and look. "CK, how the hell are you?" I asked. "I wondered where you went after leaving the Harem."

"I needed a change. You know, the same old guys with the same old shit," she said. Then she leaned her body against mine and said, "You have to buy me a drink. You know, for old time sake." I told her, "We have a deal as long as you don't guzzle."

We talked for about ten minutes. She told me about the bar's owner, Eddie Kaplan. She said, "Eddie is really a great guy. He sold his taxi cab to buy this club." I wondered if I could get to know Eddie to find out if the Philly mob had made any contact with him or other bar owners. I watched eight dancers take a turn to do their set of three dances. After CK got off the stage, she came over and said, "How about another drink. I really need the money. My rent is due at the end of the week." I bought her one more and she agreed to introduce me to Eddie. By the time he came over it was almost closing time. CK asked if I could give her a ride home so she could save cab fare.

She lived in an apartment building in Mount Vernon across the street from the Maryland Historical Society, where I worked in high school researching genealogy for descendants of our country's founders who wanted to join the Daughters of the American Revolution. I shook my head just thinking how I'd gone from dealing with blue bloods to guttersnipes.

Before CK got out of my Mustang, she said, "Come and see me tomorrow." I said, "I can't afford you." She answered with a smile and said, "You never know baby." As I drove home, I wondered if Sgt. Crab had any idea how big my expense account would be.

The next night, I walked into the Flamingo Show Bar and walked right out when I saw the bartender. He was one of the federally indicted Baltimore vice officers who took bribes from the numbers rackets. He might recognize me. If he had, I would have to come up with another phony cover story. I heard Pop say, "Be sure to watch your step and move slowly. You are not in a hurry."

The next stop was the Block Show Bar owned by Thomas Bruno. On the bar was a bucket with a bottle of champagne available for $250. An announcer was at the microphone, introducing each dancer as she stepped on stage. People called him Nappy because his full name was Napoleon. He had a gravely smoker's voice as he barked, "Just back from Paris, it's the beautiful long-legged Cheri Nicole." When the stripper didn't appear onstage, he turned to another dancer, not knowing that the microphone was still open.

"Where is the fucking cunt? She's just coming from Dundalk" (a working-class neighborhood as far from Paris as you can get). The other dancer ignored him and took the stage in Cheri's place. I ordered a beer and leaned against the wall. The bar was standing-room only. This gave me the opportunity to make some observations. Not all of the dancers were attractive. At least two appeared under the influence of heroin. They were very thin and sickly looking. One was in the nod. Her head would fall to her chest until she pulled herself awake. The whole time she was masturbating her customer with her hand.

The only reason there was sexual conduct at the bar was that the two back rooms were full.

Sex was for sale at every bar. And although prostitution was illegal, I never once saw police make an arrest. Likewise for the drug dealers, loan sharks and bookmakers. As long as the drug addicts were inside the bars, shooting up between their toes or fingers, behind their knees or even in the armpits where the track marks were less noticeable, they were never busted, even though a beat cop was assigned to The Block around the clock. I did, however, learn that the foot patrolmen were given a case of beer and a bottle of hard liquor of their choice every Christmas and on their birthdays.

In return, bar owners expected them to convince customers alleging theft by dancers or bartenders not to report the crimes. The cops would notice a customer's wedding band and say, "Hey, you might not want to report this so your wife won't find out."

I, of course, reported all these crimes to Sgt. Crab. Although I did provide evidence that helped solve many crimes, I never once heard of any sweeping busts for drugs, prostitution, illegal gambling or loansharking during the entire three years I worked as a covert.

Nevertheless, the job was not without humor. I particularly enjoyed learning the dancers' stage names. There was Ginger Ale, Windy Summers, Misty London, Candy Bar and my favorite I-need A-man. Other names were more sexual, such as Do Me, One Suck Low, Destiny Blew and Pussy Galore.

While I was sad to see so many drug- and alcohol-addicted dancers and prostitutes, I did meet some who were neither. In September I met a dancer who called herself Morticia. She was working on a college degree. Her grandparents, she told me, owned and operated a funeral home in Hagerstown in Western Maryland. She planned to become a certified mortician like them.

Another dancer who was sober asked me for a drink one night. I said, "What's your name darling?" She laughed and said, "My name *is* Darling." Trying to blend in, I said, "I'm not usually this pushy, but time is short. What does it cost to go to the back?" She answered, "That's not my game. I dance, get my money and hit the road. Are you buying?"

I bought her a drink and learned that she was working her way through college. Weeks later she graduated and I never saw her again on the street. Many years later I walked into an animal hospital with a friend who had a sick dog. The dancer who called herself "Darling" was the veterinarian. She said, "You look familiar. What's your name?" I smiled and said, "It's Jim and you might be remembering me from a different world."

She smiled like she recognized me and said, "Well Jim, how may I help?"

While the economy was in a downturn during the early 1970s, there was no shortage of customers with bundles of money to spend. Baltimore's port was the unloading destination for hundreds of cargo ships. Many of the merchant marines had not been off of the ships for months. The Block had the perfect formula: men with thousands to spend and the availability of dozens of prostitutes to sell them what they wanted. It was common for the ship workers to spend a thousand a night.

The payment protocol for the sex trade workers was simple: Each dancer was paid $70 per seven-hour shift, plus $3 for every $10 drink purchased for her. If a customer bought a dancer a $250 bottle of champagne, she received $50. If a dancer didn't walk out at the end of a shift with at least $400, it was a bad night. The bartenders were paid $70 for each shift plus tips. It was common for bartenders to walk out with about $700 a night. The doormen were paid $35 for each shift plus a dollar for every drink sold to dancers. The bartender was expected to pay the doormen 5 percent of generated tips. Two show bars had a VIP room on the second floor for sex. The cost was $1,000 per hour. This entitled the customer his choice of two dancers and all he wanted to drink. The dancers were paid $150 each, plus tips. Typically, professional ballplayers were the ones who leased the rooms. Occasionally a Baltimore Orioles, Colts or Bullets player would be seen, but mostly they were out-of-town players.

One night a dancer was found lying on the dressing room floor at the Block Show Bar. She had overdosed, but no one called an ambulance. The doorman drove her to the hospital, instead. I thought, "She could have died. Maybe she did." Here was another example of strip bars not wanting any negative reports filed with the Liquor Board. It was unsettling that no one seemed upset by the overdose. Maybe it was such a common occurrence. Here was more confirmation that the dancers had no value unless they were making money for the bars.

The Block was known as a place where a man could buy any kind of kinky sex. One customer who showed up at the Block Show Bar each month would buy several cocktails and a bottle of champagne for a dancer. Once they were in the back room he would ask her to beat him with a hairbrush while he masturbated. One time the dancer forgot her hairbrush, so the bartender, who was Dykes, told her, "Don't worry. I'll be right back." In a minute he returned with a large push broom and unscrewed the handle. That night the dancer received an extra tip of $100.

One night I visited the men's room when a dancer barged in and began feeding quarters into the condom machine. Another man, assuming she was about to have sex with a customer, asked, "What does this guy have, two dicks?" She replied, "No baby, I'm doing a double bubble." A double bubble, I learned, was a street term for anal and vaginal sex at the same time.

The strippers referred to themselves as adult entertainers. They were in total denial of the obvious. They were prostitutes selling their bodies for the almighty dollar. Most would agree to conduct any sexual act, even with animals, if the price was right. Dancers had no problems taking the stage to perform cunnilingus with each other, while the customer watched. Typically, the sex act was requested by a customer and the dancers were paid $40 each.

Not all but certainly the vast majority of dancers were "heroin whores." Many went to the "pusher man" for more drugs as soon as they were paid. Knowing that long-term use would create scarring called tracks, addicts would inject in between fingers, genitals, behind knees and in armpits. During these years crack cocaine had yet to hit Baltimore. So the heavy drug of choice was heroin. Another popular drug was methamphetamine, which was snorted, known on the street as crystal meth, crank or meth. Anyone under the influence was easy to spot. I watched them move their teeth from side to side, making a grinding sound. They frequently scratched their skin. The other major hard drug was phencyclidine, which was smoked, known on the street as PCP, flakes or greens. The Pagan Outlaw Motorcycle Club controlled the meth and PCP sales. The gang also supplied "biker chicks," prostituting them to clubs for a price. Back in the 1970s there were no black drug dealers on The Block.

The dancers lasted for only about five years. They either died of overdoses or the drugs so ravaged their good looks that bar owners would no longer find them profitable. No owner would hire a sickly stripper.

I learned that the majority of the dancers were sexually molested in their early teens, typically by a family member or the boyfriend of the mother or aunt. So they were emotionally damaged even before they stepped on The Block. They lacked self-esteem and were starved for attention. How very sad, I thought, that most of them had not experienced real love in their lives.

A few years later, in 1977, I would be reminded of this endless cycle of drugs and prostitution when the Eagles came out with the song "Hotel California."

Mirrors on the ceiling
The pink champagne on ice
And she said "We are all just prisoners here, of our own device"
And in the master's chambers,
They gathered for the feast
They stab it with their steely knives,
But they just can't kill the beast

Last thing I remember, I was
Running for the door
I had to find the passage back
To the place I was before
"Relax," said the night man,
"We are programmed to receive.
You can check-out any time you like,
But you can never leave!"

Each day as dawn was breaking I would end another work shift as the rest of Baltimore came to life. Many police officers go home to fix a drink at the end of a shift. Since I had been drinking for several hours, alcohol was the last thing I wanted. I was lucky I'd been able to get home without being stopped by a cop for driving under the influence.

When I got home I would decompress by listening to Gregorian chants that always put me in a meditative mood since my junior seminary days. I also went to the record store at the Rotunda shopping center and bought opera recordings: *Madame Butterfly*, Mozart's *Requiem* and *La Boheme*. The music cleared my mind and erased the offensive behavior I saw on The Block. There were times when I just went home and took a very long hot shower. There was no amount of soap and water that could wash away the depravity I'd seen and heard.

25
SPEAKING IN A FOREIGN TONGUE

I finally applied to the Maryland Public Service Commission for a license to drive a cab. Three weeks later I was driving a Royal taxi transporting workers of the sex trade. To my surprise, they were excellent tippers. In particular, I concentrated on driving dancers who worked at the Block Show Bar owned and operated by Tommy Bruno. I thought that I could finally walk into the joint with a reasonable expectation that a dancer who was one of my regular passengers would ask for a drink. Of course, I hoped she would introduce me to Tommy Bruno, who in turn might mention a mob connection. Now I had a new identity to give me a legitimate reason to be there. I was also discovering that I needed to learn a whole new language in this unconventional world.

This lexicon certainly wasn't written down in any dictionary, I began to memorize the terms until they became second nature to me.

Here is my brief dictionary of The Block street slang. My apologies for the offensive nature of these definitions.

5-O: cops

8 ball: eight ounces of a narcotic

9: 9-millimeter handgun

Bitch club: men who wish they were part of an outlaw motorcycle gang

Body wire: a concealed microphone worn by a police officer or informant which transmits oral communication for recording purposes

Bookmaker: person who accepts illegal bets on sporting events and lotteries

C note: $100

Cherry bomb: the largest bottle of champagne, costing $1,000

Coke or snow: cocaine

Crib: place to live

Dime bag: $10 worth of a narcotic

Dump: the weekly emptying of cash from illegal video gambling machines

Farmer: police officer who plants drugs on a suspect

Fire bug: arsonist

Fix: shot of a narcotic

G note: $1,000

G string: garment which consists of a very narrow piece of cloth covering a woman's genitals

Get even day: on Tuesdays, after Monday night football, bookmakers and their clients settle up accounts over that week's games.

GJ: grand jury

Hamilton: $10 bill

Hit or raid: execution of a search and seizure warrant

Horse, H, or smack: heroin

Hot shot: overdose given intentionally without the user's knowledge

Jackson: $20 bill

Jug: bottle of methadone

Jump-out unit: police officers who jump out of cars in hopes of arresting drug dealers

Knockers: narcotics detectives

Lid: small container of marijuana

Line: illegal wager on a baseball game

Look out: person attempting to spot police

Meth: methamphetamine

Missile: high-quality heroin

Mud: Mexican heroin

OD: drug overdose

Odds or spread: the margin of points needed to win a bet on a football or basketball game

On the nod: under the influence of heroin

One percenter: the 1 percent of motorcycle riders who belong to outlaw motorcycle gangs (based on a congressional hearing that 99 percent of motorcycle riders are law abiding citizens, while the rest are outlaws)

Over and under: amount of points made by both teams in a football or basketball game

Oz: an ounce of a narcotic

Piece: handgun

Pimp: man who controls prostitutes, arranging "dates" and then taking part of the money

Pop or shooter: shot of alcohol

Ring: amount of money made by the bar during a work shift

Runner: person who is paid to purchase food, tampons, drugs or any other item for a bartender or dancer. A runner is not the doorman.

Saturday night special: cheap handgun

Shit face: a drunk person

Skin popping: heroin user who does not want to inject into a vein. These addicts are typically new to the game, often called weekend addicts.

Spike: hypodermic needle

Spoon: miniature spoon used to snort cocaine or to heat heroin

Structuring or laundering: hiding money

Sugar daddy: man paying for a woman's living expenses

Tester: volunteer heroin addict willing to be injected by a new drug supply to determine the quality. Many a tester has died as a result.

THC: active ingredient in marijuana

Tourniquet: shoestring, belt, tie or scarf used to locate veins to inject narcotics

Turning a trick: act of prostitution

Vigors or juice: amount of interest charged for an illegal loan

Covert: A deep, long-term undercover investigator who works alone and is not known to other police officers. He or she will have one handler with whom to communicate. Some will work with an alias name and have a driver's license, credit cards, apartment and phone in the name of the alias. Others will have no such cover. A covert is different from a plainclothes officer who can continue to walk into any police facility. A covert needs to have an above-average IQ and be able to be extemporaneous at any time with anyone. He or she must be able to have credibility whether in the role of a custodian or executive. The life of a covert is a lonely and dangerous one. If the covert is fluent in another language, it's a plus.

26
THE POLISH CONNECTION

One early morning the phone rang as I was trying to relax to Gregorian chants. It was Sgt. Crab.

"What do you know about the waterfront?" he asked.

"It's a movie with Marlon Brando," I said. I thought everybody had seen *On the Waterfront*, the classic 1954 crime drama.

Sgt. Crag was clueless. "What? I don't follow."

"It was an attempt at levity," I told him. He did not laugh.

Finally he explained that he wanted to meet the next day to discuss a new assignment. I thought, "I hope it gets me off The Block."

When I arrived at the Blue Bell Restaurant, I saw his car, but he was not at the wheel. Three minutes later, he walked out of the restaurant carrying two food containers. I guessed that one was a crab cake platter and the other was an entire cheesecake topped with fresh strawberries.

"Get in the car," he said, placing the food containers in the back seat.

"I don't know how you can do it, but the boss wants to know if Tony Scotto has strong-armed his way into the docks."

"Which docks are you talking about?" I asked.

"You know. The Dundalk Marine Terminal and the Seagirt Marine Terminal," in Southeast Baltimore.

"Do you mean where the cargo ships are unloaded?" I asked. Now it was my turn to be clueless.

"That's right," he said.

"Wow, you're talking about stevedores." They are a hard-drinking group of guys who would prefer to fight rather than getting laid.

"Who is this guy Tony Scotto?" I asked.

I was astonished by what he told me. The Baltimore FBI field office had received word from the New York FBI office that a member of the Gambino crime family had sent Anthony M. Scotto, a mobster and Brooklyn International Longshoreman's Association officer, to take control of the Baltimore dock business. According to Sgt. Crab, Scotto was president of the Brooklyn ILA Local 1814. In 1969, Scotto had been the subject of several federal and local investigations as a suspected "Capo," or captain, of the Carlo Gambino mafia family in New York, though no charges had been filed against him.

"If this guy is a captain of a La Costa Nostra family, why aren't the Feds doing the investigation?" I asked.

"That's not your concern," my boss answered.

"Well, how do you suggest that I verify?" I asked in an angry tone.

"That's not my problem. It's yours," he said. Not surprisingly, he didn't even bother to tell me to be careful.

"That's bullshit. Look, other than watching Marlon Brando in the movie, I have no idea what happens on the waterfront."

Before I got out of the car, Sgt. Crab said weakly, "Look, you know, do what you usually do. Hang around."

As I walked to my car, I thought, "That's easy for you to say."

I went home and thought about Pop's advice: "Plan your work and work your plan." I ate some leftover pizza and left for a noon appointment with Dr. Scholz. As always, the waiting room was packed, but I didn't mind waiting a bit. I'd spent many hours in that room over the last 18 years as the good doctor saved my eyes. I was relieved that his exam showed both eyes had stabilized. While driving home, I kept asking myself about my new assignment.

"What to do, what to do, what to do?"

I decided to head to the Maryland Room of the Enoch Pratt Library, always a good place to begin. I found several articles that grabbed my attention. *The News American* published a story about the Airport Bar and Grill on Riverview Avenue near the Seagirt Marine Terminal. The story described the hard life working the docks. I found it most interesting that the three people interviewed all had Polish names. Another article reported that about 80 percent of the dock workers were Polish, and that the coveted jobs were handed down from generation to generation. The rest of the workers were from the black community.

Now a plan was starting to come together. I would become a customer at the Airport Bar and Grill. I also needed to hang around the Polish community. I wasn't sure exactly how I would do that. I began to wonder, "Where are the Feds?" I thought that the Baltimore FBI office should have at least two agents detailed to illegal union activities. Maybe I was just being sent on a wild goose chase by Commissioner Pomerleau, who wanted to shove it in the faces of the Feds. But that didn't make sense, since the FBI supposedly generated the tip.

I was also bothered that Sgt. Crab could not, or would not, give me any information about Scotto. Crab and I had a very strange relationship. I certainly didn't trust him.

Finally, after much thought, I realized the answer to infiltrating the Polish community was right in front of my face: the Baltimore Polish community was deeply Catholic. I would just drive around the Locust Point and Fells Point neighborhoods to find a Polish Catholic church. I found one, St. Stanislaus, on South Ann Street in Fells Point. It was only about a dozen blocks from where I'd grown up in East Baltimore, but I had never known it was there.

I wondered, "Is this God's way of getting me back?" I had not been to church since the day my father was murdered. I called the church's rectory and learned that the Mass was celebrated in the Polish language at 11 a.m. I would mumble my way through it in the hopes of meeting church attendees who were stevedores. It was a long shot, but it was my best option.

So I returned to the Catholic Church. I was very pleased that there was a fellowship after Mass, in the basement. They served coffee and the most delicious Polish strudel with apples and peaches. On the third Sunday, I met a young man named Joe Kempa. What a break. He and his four brothers worked on the waterfront. I pretended to be a college student writing a paper about the history of Polish families immigrating to Baltimore. Why Joe was so very talkative and friendly, I didn't know. He invited me to join him and his brothers at the monthly dance at the Polish Home on South Broadway in Fells Point.

I couldn't wait. In the meantime, I found the Airport Bar and Grill one morning at 7 a.m. There were only two customers at the bar, in addition to a lady having her gallon bottle filled with draft beer. The bartender was a surly old man who sat as he read the paper. I only stayed for 15 minutes, but noticed the sign noting opening time was at 5 a.m.

When I arrived on my next visit just after 5 a.m. the place was packed with men on their way to the work at the waterfront. I was amazed at the amount of clothing they wore. Their outer wear looked like ski-jumping suits. One said, "That fucking wind will rip us a new asshole today."

When it was his turn to order he asked for one pint of Rock and Rye whiskey and three codfish cakes—known as coddies—with mustard and crackers. It seemed as if every worker ordered a pint or a half pint of something alcoholic to drink. I thought, "The alcohol must keep them warm. No wonder that stevedores are a hard-drinking bunch." I tried to get into a conversation, but their cold shoulders were as frigid as the blowing wind. Maybe it was because I ordered coffee and an egg sandwich or that I just looked out of place. When I left, I thought, "This is a dead end." The radio was set to WCBM. The DJ announced the song "Roses Are Red (My Love)" by the Polish Prince, Bobby Vinton. On the way home, I stopped at the music store and bought his album, which was very good.

I also tried to find out about a connection between the docks and Tony Scotto at a bar in South Baltimore called the French Quarters, on Fort Avenue near Ft. McHenry in Locust Point. I remembered that William Irving Klemkowski had been indicted for running a gambling operation that involved bribes to city police commanders and vice detectives. I also knew he controlled all the illegal gambling at the nearby Locust Point Marine Terminal. Surely, he would have heard if Tony Scotto or his associates had been to Baltimore.

When I walked into the bar I was wearing the clip-on Public Service Commission ID card that permitted me to operate a cab. The place was a lot more presentable than the strip clubs on The Block. The two barmaids were dressed in tuxedo shirts, complete with red bow ties and black miniskirts. They were very friendly. One was named Jezebel. The other called herself Cleopatra. I ordered lunch and saw Klemkowski sitting a few bar stools away.

I told Cleo, "If you ever need a cab, I'm your man."

"Are you flirting with me?" she asked.

"Can you blame me? You're a very attractive lady," I said.

"How long have you been driving a cab?" she asked.

I could tell Klemkowski was listening, so I didn't even need to draw him into a conversation.

"Not too long," I said. "I was a cop for about two years, but got fired. Some asshole claimed that I was on the pad," I answered, loud enough for Klemkowski to hear me.

That's when he turned to me. He might have suspected a fired cop would sympathize with him.

"Jesus Christ, when I got indicted, I read the indictment. It said, 'The United States of America versus William I. Klemkowski.' I thought, 'That's the whole fucking country against me.'" I laughed and introduced myself. Despite several conversations with him, he offered no information confirming that Scotto (or the Philly mob) were in Baltimore. Klemkowski was known as one of the city's most colorful criminals. In one of the many federal cases when he was convicted of running large betting operations, a police officer described Klemkowski as one of the nicest guys you could ever meet who single-handedly corrupted the vice squad of the Baltimore Police Department.

Apparently, not everybody thought he was so nice. In 1989 he was found in his car outside his home with a single bullet to the back of his head.

I knew I could never ask a leading question about the mob or Tony Scotto. I had already learned that if you want to be credible you have to be believable. I had a practice: I would only claim to have been somewhere no one could prove I hadn't been. I would not say I had been to a certain bar, for example, at a certain time when I knew somebody could easily say, "I was there, but didn't see you." As a covert I always needed to use my imagination to get to the heart of a matter without giving himself away. For example, while working on The Block, I was very interested to find out who was controlling the loansharking business. I went to the Villa Nova Show Bar one night, knowing that the bartender was always in the hole, or in debt, because of his bad gambling bets. Surely he knew the loan sharks. Before leaving home, I placed a thick wad of medical tape over my chin. I walked in around ten and grabbed a bar stool. As if on cue, the bartender said, "What the fuck happened to you?"

"My shark doesn't have a sense of humor," I said.

"You need a shot of whiskey. It's on me," he said.

After serving other customers, he came back and asked me, "Who is your loan shark?"

"I got a Greek guy from the Ponca Bird Inn," I said.

"Fuck that guy. You should go see Mutzie. He is a reasonable guy. Tell him I sent you."

There I had it. Sam Manafo, known as Mutzie, the owner of the Flamingo, was the man. Now all I needed was to find out if Manafo was getting heat from the Bruno family in Philly.

When I arrived at the Polish Home, Joe Kempa was waiting for me outside. The dance was on the second floor and it was packed. For the $5 admission I got a draft beer and a buffet dinner. Joe introduced me to several men, some of whom had dates. One of the men was named Bill. I had no clue how valuable he would be in solving my problem. The Polish band had an accordion player who really got into the music. One of the ladies tried to teach me how to dance the polka. I had a great time.

As I began talking to Kempa's friend's, I remembered how I engaged Klemkowski in conversation and how I learned Mutzie was a loan shark. Again, I needed to use my imagination.

Joe Kempa introduced me to Bill, who would turn out to be a wealth of information. While introducing us, Joe told Bill's sad story of being kicked out of the ILA as a union officer. Bill had attended a national ILA conference in Miami. A Maryland container company paid the cost of a leased car for him, a violation of union rules. As a result, Bill was banned as a union officer for life. Joe said it was a real shame his friend was banned because of "Mickey Mouse charges." Bill, he said, had negotiated good wages for the members.

I thought, "This is perfect. I can easily dovetail on this conversation."

As casually as I could say it, I asked, "What about those other stories about the New York people taking control?"

"That never happened," Bill said. "The FBI got it all wrong."

He told me that Tony Scotto never came to town, but sent two minions instead. They pressured the heads of two of the largest container companies to pay the mob so they could continue operating on Baltimore's waterfront. The proposal was rejected by the companies, but there was no fall out. To this day I do not know why there were no repercussions against the Baltimore dock companies for refusing to pay off the mafia. Scotto stayed in New York and was convicted a few years later of extorting more than $200,000 from Brooklyn's waterfront companies. He did five years in federal prison for labor racketeering.

27
STATUE OF A FOOL

The human condition, with few exceptions, demands interaction with others who can be trusted, respected, admired and loved. I had learned that the lonely life of a deep covert is simply not conducive to the human condition.

After almost three years living this solitary life, I was reduced to a nonentity by my own police department. When I called ISD, I still couldn't use my name. Instead, I identified myself with the code number 232 that Sgt. Crab gave me. Then he had the bright idea to change the number to 237. "That's ridiculous," I said. "The people answering the phone in ISD will know me from my voice, whether I tell them I'm 232 or 237."

Life had become unbearable. I had very few honest interactions with anyone. Sgt. Crab didn't count. I was having difficulty sleeping. Classical music and Gregorian chants no longer relaxed me. I stared at the ceiling, wishing I could resurface and go back to a normal life. My disjointed thoughts ping-ponged from my persistent eye problems to the fact that my own police department had not solved my father's murder. Since I had shut out all my friends, I had become a 27-year-old man with no healthy, meaningful relationships. I had not even had a date with a woman in years.

"I'm in really a dark place," I thought. "Something has to change."

After spending my nights pretending to be friends with prostitutes, drug addicts, loan sharks and gamblers, I had a powerful yearning to socialize with respectable people.

I happened to meet a very attractive young lady named Diane Rose Kushner, who called herself Dee. She had a nice personality and was easy to talk to. She only knew that I drove a Royal Cab to earn my living.

We agreed to meet at a country-and-western bar on Pulaski Highway. Since it had been so long since my last date, I was nervous. When she walked in ten minutes after I arrived, she attracted many looks from the other customers. She was strikingly beautiful with blonde, shoulder-length hair and hazel eyes. She stood 5 foot 3 and was very well proportioned.

I found her to be a cautious person who didn't want to disclose much about her personal life. I found that peculiar, but who was I to judge her for keeping secrets when I was introducing myself to her as someone I was not?

I did learn that she was a single mother with two small children and worked at Eddie's Supermarket on Philadelphia Road in the Rosedale area of Baltimore County. We had a good time dancing to songs by Waylon Jennings, Willie Nelson and Johnny Cash. I noticed that she was a heavy drinker. She always ordered whiskey and water with lemon in a tall glass.

She had so many refills that, by the end of the evening, her glass was full of lemons. Two hours later, we kissed each other on the cheek and said goodbye. She seemed to have a hard time hearing me. Perhaps, I thought, it was nothing more than the loud music. I left feeling very conflicted over not being able to tell her my real identity. No matter that I had good intentions, I was still an imposter.

On our second date, Dee agreed to have dinner with me at Karson's Inn in Dundalk. "If I'm picking you up," I said, "I need your address." She declined to tell me and said she would meet me at the restaurant's bar instead. She was already sitting at the bar when I arrived. We gave each other a friendly hug and she seemed glad to see me. We ordered delicious surf and turf. I noticed that she favored her right ear, so I thought she had a hearing problem in her left ear. It also struck me that she might be a bit paranoid. She declined to share any personal information about herself. When I became concerned that she would be driving and drinking I asked if she had taken a cab or driven. "Hey." She said, "I got here, didn't I?"

On the way home, I asked myself what I was getting into. What was crystal clear was that she had my full attention. Despite her secrecy, I really enjoyed her company.

I knew the perils of developing a personal relationship with a woman whom I could not level with about the simplest things. If she just asked how my day went, I would have to lie.

Here's just one glaring example:

One Sunday I drove my Mustang to pick up Duchess, a stripper from the Block Show Bar, to take her to Tommy Bruno's beach party at Rocky Point State Park.

She was a natural beauty with dark brown curly hair and a beautiful face with green eyes and the ideal body for a stripper. She was very open and forthcoming and had a great sense of humor.

I was still trying to figure out if Bruno had heard from the Philly mob. I thought that if I could become his trusted friend, he would open up and give me more information.

I believe this was the only moment in my covert life when I thought I might get seriously hurt, if not killed. I knocked on the door of the house where Duchess lived with her brother on East Fayette Street.

A young man opened the door, dressed in a leather vest, a T-shirt, jeans and black leather motorcycle boots. He also had tattoos on his fingers that I knew to be jailhouse tats favored by prisoners.

His eyes were completely dilated. He was on something, I thought, but I had no idea what it was. In my friendliest voice I said, "Hi. I'm Jim. I'm here to pick up Duchess. We're going swimming." He let me in and I sat on the couch. From upstairs I heard Duchess shouting down to me, "I'm almost finished. I'll be right down." Her brother had a patch on his vest that said, "1%" with a circle around it. I had no idea what it meant, but I thought it was odd. I would later learn that the "1%" referred to the 1 percent of motorcycle riders who were violent criminals. That meant Duchess's brother was probably a member of an outlaw motorcycle gang. Suddenly he jumped on the couch next to me, landing on his knees. He pulled out a four inch dirk knife and shot the dagger blade out against my neck. "How do I know you're not a fucking cop?" he asked. He followed up with several cuss words. He was very, very angry. I could smell him, he was so close.

I knew I could not appear wimpy in a situation like this. Duchess came down the stairs, dressed in blue flip-flops, white hot pants and a red bikini top. She yelled at her brother to leave me alone. Finally, after several seconds he pulled the knife away.

"Well, he's going to do flakes," he said in a hostile tone.

I knew he was referring to PCP, or phencyclidine. It is the active ingredient that veterinarians use to anesthetize horses. He wanted me to smoke a joint of it. I knew this was the drug of choice of the outlaw Pagan's Motorcycle Club.

"Fuck you," I said. "I'm not doing that."

I had heard many stories of people smoking flakes: they hallucinate and can develop the strength of five people.

I quickly made up a believable story.

"The last time I did flakes," I told him in a defiant voice, "I hallucinated so bad that I ended up in the emergency room and got charged with assaulting a cop."

Duchess came to my defense. "Hey get off of him, get out of here."

Finally, her brother went out the door, crossed the street and walked into a former hardware store. I later learned it was the Pagan's clubhouse.

The beach party had a much friendlier atmosphere with picnic tables set up with all kinds of food. Tommy Bruno brought two kegs of beer and we all played softball. He was very friendly with me, but I couldn't find any reason to bring up the question about the Philly crime family.

Since Sgt. Crab had given me no background about Angelo Bruno, who headed the Philly crime family, I drove to Philadelphia one day to visit the public library and research the mob boss. I found a treasure trove of information. He was born in Sicily on May 21, 1910, and emigrated to Philadelphia with his family. He became the boss of the mafia family in 1959 and soon was dubbed "The Gentle Don" for his practice of using reconciliation, rather than violence, against his adversaries. Bruno was a close associate of Carlo Gambino, the Don of the New York family. In the early '60s, he went to prison for three years for refusing to testify at a federal grand jury.

On our third date, Dee gave me her address on Choptank Road in Middle River. Her small home was on a waterfront property. The house had living quarters on the first floor with the kitchen in the basement, a common Baltimore setup. I noticed the house was spotless. Outside there was a 15-foot pier. In time she introduced me to her children. Joey was six, Diana was seven. The children were very polite and well behaved. Dee also had a large, playful German shepherd named Shannon who was at least 80 pounds. Not long after we met she took a job working in the pharmacy department of the Giant Supermarket on Stemmers Run Road and Eastern Boulevard.

As she began to trust me more, she invited me to spend time with her children. I quickly began to fall in love with Joey and Diana. I found I could most be myself with young children, who didn't care to know my grown-up problems, but only how well I treated them. It was a special relationship for me after the years of isolation.

It was such a pleasure to watch Joey on the pier while he fished with a pole and net. Whenever he could, he would fish from dawn to dusk. He would get so excited with each little fish he snagged, whether it was a perch, a sunfish or even the occasional eel. As soon as he reeled in his catch, he would run to the porch where I sat watching him.

"Do I get a prize?" he'd ask.

"Yes you do," I answered, as I handed him a little ribbon from a bag of prizes I'd bought at a five and dime store.

We put all the fish in a tub of water so they would not die. At the end of each day, we tossed them back into the river.

Diana was not as welcoming with me and I frankly found her to be distant, even though I tried to befriend her. My relationship with Dee was blossoming and I was starting to feel human again. Still, I knew the big lie was unavoidable, unless I could resurface. I couldn't pretend to be a Royal Cab driver forever.

She took me to meet her parents and siblings on Bradford Street in East Baltimore not far from where I grew up. The family had moved there from Pottstown, Pennsylvania, where her father had worked as a coal miner. By the time I met him, he was suffering from black lung disease and had become a heavy drinker. Dee's mother barely said a word, choosing to keep her opinions to herself about any subject the family discussed. Their home was dilapidated with peeling paint and missing linoleum floor tiles. None of the torn furniture matched.

Dee had two brothers, Johnny and Steve, and a sister named Sue. When I learned that Sue was a stripper on Baltimore's Block, I thought, "What a small world" and made it a point not to ever be in her company.

Johnny had already lost a son to a heart problem; the loss sent him right to the bottle. He lived with his parents. Steve was a house painter who was sentenced to two years after his third DWI.

"Wow, can a family be more dysfunctional?" I thought. "Pop would not be pleased with my choices."

Dee had not said a word about Joey and Diana's father and I had seen no evidence that he was around. After dating for about three months, Dee finally told me about him after the bars closed one night. She was drunk and her words slurred. The father of her children was a man named Elmer Scaggs, known as J.R. She had been with him since she was 15. She had their first child at 17. Scaggs had recently begun a life sentence in a Maryland prison for first-degree murder. He was convicted of killing a delicatessen owner in the Patterson Park neighborhood on Christmas Eve, 1973. He was also convicted of robbery after police found $14,000 in cash he stole from the deli owner, an elderly woman. Dee told me that Scaggs was a Vietnam veteran who returned with a heroin addiction, though I could never prove this. His brother had married Dee's sister, Sue, and shortly died of a heroin overdose.

As bad as it was, Dee was hard at work, totally committed to ensuring that her children would live a better life. I admired her for her dedication. But the truth is that I really fell more in love with Joey and Diana than with Dee. I was not sure that Dee and I would have remained a couple without the kids because I really wanted a family.

During the next meeting with Sgt. Crab, I told him I wanted out.

"Boss, I'm burned out," I told him, adding that I wanted to resurface and take the exam to become a sergeant. I hoped to go up the police department's promotional ladder and focus on narcotics investigations. I figured I had certainly paid my dues.

"I don't have the authority to make such a decision," he answered.

"Who does?" I asked.

"I don't know," he answered.

I was blistering mad when I left.

A week later, I received a call from Sgt. Crab's supervisor. He invited me to his home in the Frankford area of Northeast Baltimore. When I knocked on the door, I got a warm welcome. The lieutenant offered me a cocktail, which I declined. Then came the snow job.

"Jim, you are a true credit to our police department and you do your name proud," he said.

"Thank you sir."

"I certainly understand you wishing to be promoted," he added.

I was waiting to hear if he would let me resurface.

Instead he said, "I suggest that when the exam is given next, you wear a wig." That was it. He didn't even say "no" to my face.

I could feel my face reddening and said, "Thank you sir. I think that will do just fine."

As soon as I was in my car, I started to yell. "Jesus fucking Christ. I am working for morons! How can anyone be that fucking stupid?"

When I calmed down, I thought, "Maybe they are not as stupid as I thought. They don't really care whether I am angry or not, or whether my life is coming unraveled. Their goal is to keep me under for as long as possible." I never wore a wig, but instead waited many years to take the test, which I passed.

That Friday, Dee and I went to Club Stabile's on Eastern Avenue in Highlandtown. According to Dee, the country singer Ray Price, was to appear. He wasn't there, but I did hear a song called "Statue of a Fool," by the composer Jan Crutchfield. It hit home for me and left a lasting impression:

Somewhere there should be, for all the world to see
A statue of a fool made of stone
An image of a man who let love slip through his hand
And then let him stand there all alone
So, build a statue and, oh, build it high
So the world can see
And inscribe, "The World's Greatest Fool"
And name it after me

28
TO HELL AND BACK

Shortly after Sgt. Crab and his lieutenant turned down my request to resurface, I was walking downtown and ran into Paul Balton, the owner of the Harem Club, and his wife. He seemed pleased to see me and invited me to join them for dinner at Connolly's seafood restaurant on the edge of the Inner Harbor. After we talked about sports I asked about his club. He said business was going great. He made no mention of any outside forces causing him troubles. He also ordered an expensive bottle of wine. When it came time to pay I said, "What do I owe you?"

His answer was chilling.

"Just take care of me and my club," he said.

That could only mean one thing, I thought. He believed I was still a cop.

My desperate need to resurface for my own sanity was just amplified by the knowledge that a club owner knew my true purpose and I could now be in danger.

While I considered my next move to extricate myself from my assignment, I dutifully continued my covert activities uncovering crimes. I knew an insurance claims adjuster who played high stakes poker every week above the Villa Nova Show Bar. I heard that one particular game was rigged against him; before the night was over he had borrowed $30,000 from a loan shark to pay his debt. Of course, he then had to find a way to repay the debt. Although I was never able to verify this account, I did confirm that the insurance adjuster came up with an illegal scheme—whether to pay off the debt or simply enrich himself—that I would call the "slip and fall case."

Since he worked for an insurance company that covered accidents at local department stores like K-Mart, Montgomery Ward and Sears, he recruited about a dozen Block workers, including bartenders, doormen and strippers, to assist him in his scheme. He sent them in pairs to the stores. The first person took a cup of soda and placed it on the floor just under a rack of clothing. Before walking away, the person kicked over the soda, then reported to a sales clerk that there was liquid on the floor, creating a hazard. The second person would come in a few minutes later, purposely slip on the floor and pretend to be injured.

Each "distressed victim" filed a claim for the "injury." The insurance company, under the direction of the adjuster, paid out a settlement. He had the sole authority in his company to sign claims checks up to $5,000, so he did not need to consult his superiors before paying out numerous claims. He then split the money with the "injured" person. After I reported the "slip and fall" scheme, the criminal investigation was handled by the U.S. Attorney's Office because the insurance company was from out of state. It was prosecuted by Assistant U.S. Attorney Stuart O. Simms, who later went on to become Baltimore City's state's attorney. The culprits were all charged with mail fraud because the U.S. mail was used to send them money. Several were convicted and sentenced to federal prison terms, including Dave Dykes, the corny joking bartender.

I was hanging out one day at the Gayety Show Bar. I knew the owner, Eddie Kaplan, pretty well. He was a very nice man. When I walked in I noticed he had no doorman, which was very peculiar. His long time doorman was called Socks, though his real name was Walter Fisher. I noticed that Eddie looked troubled.

"Eddie, is everything alright?" I asked.

"We had a sailor in here last night. He spent a lot of money. I'm not sure what happened, but one of the girls told me the sailor was invited to a party and got into a van with my doorman, Socks, and Tiny, the doorman at The Jewel Box." We soon discovered that the sailor was actually a 23-year-old Coast Guardsman from San Juan, Puerto Rico named Ricky Hull. He had stopped off at The Block for a good time while waiting for his ship to depart for Greenland. He had cashed $592 in government paychecks, a lot of money in those days, so someone in the bar must have seen the money and thought he was easy prey. He was bludgeoned to death and his body was dumped out of the van. Socks and Tiny were charged with the murder.

By the time of my next meeting with Sgt. Crab, I knew that Socks and Tiny had already been arrested. When I saw Sgt. Crab pull onto the parking lot for our biweekly visit, I thought to myself, "The genius has arrived. I ought to buy a wig and stick it up his fat ass."

"You know the murder of the Coast Guard guy had to involve a third person," I told him. He seemed unconcerned.

"There are already two people charged with the killing. Why is there a need to look for a third?" he said.

"Well, the two guys arrested were doormen who don't go into the club, except to take a leak. How would they know that the Coast Guardsman cashed nearly $600 in checks just before leaving the club?" I said. "There had to be a third person inside who knew he had so much money."

He seemed to care less about uncovering the whole truth about the murder.

"Look, don't worry about it," he said. "Maybe one of the other two will cooperate."

"Maybe, but I doubt it," I said. "I think one of them had a stripper girlfriend who told the doormen about the money. Don't we owe it to the family to be thorough in our investigation?" I could not persuade him to see my point.

"Don't go around asking questions. It's way too risky," he ordered.

On the way home, I committed myself to checking things out, despite his orders.

The next time I saw Eddie, I said, "I guess you were questioned by the homicide guys."

"Oh yeah," he said. "So far they have been here twice. They wanted to know if Sock's girlfriend worked here."

"That's interesting," I said. "Do you know why they asked that question?"

"They thought she had given him the information about cashing the checks," Eddie said.

"That makes sense. Does she still work for you?" I asked.

"No. She overdosed two days after Socks was arrested. Now she's tits up," he said. It was a typically crude description that meant she had died.

For their part in the murder Socks got a life sentence and Tiny got 45 years.

By the summer of 1977 I had developed a strong emotional feeling for Dee and the children, but I discovered, to my dismay, that Dee was unable to control her spending habits and was purchasing record albums, magazines and other items she could not afford. She finally admitted to me that she was buried in debt. She had no sense of money management and had no budget to match her spending with her income. I considered asking her to marry me, but was unsure if I could take on the challenge.

As in any crisis, I wondered what advice Pop would give me. The decision weighed heavily on my mind. After an hour of contemplation and seven beers, I remembered Pop had once told me, "Whenever you have an opportunity to carry out an act of kindness, you should just do it."

First, I needed a plan. I decided to look for a home without telling Dee. I found a house to rent in the Middlesex area of Baltimore County, just a ten-minute walk from an elementary school. The house had three bedrooms, a clubhouse basement, a very small kitchen and a nice yard with a parking pad. My plan also included a promise from Dee that I would handle all money coming in and out of our household. She agreed to everything.

We got married in a Protestant church on Philadelphia Road. Joey wore a suit and Diana wore a pretty little dress. I wore a blue blazer. Dee was dressed up, though not in a traditional wedding gown. Since I was still living an isolated life without friends, the only other person attending was the minister. After the wedding we went on a family vacation to Luray Caverns in Virginia.

It felt absolutely wonderful to visit the Blue Ridge Mountains, seeing nature and wildlife with my new family. Joey and Diana were so excited to see a small bear from an overlook platform after we stopped to take in the view. It warmed my heart as I watched Dee smiling from ear to ear. We stayed in a motel for four days in Front Royal, Virginia. Joey and I were developing a close father-son relationship, but Diana remained distant to me.

When it came time to leave, all our bags were packed. "I can take the suitcase," said Joey, who was all of six years old.

"Are you sure you're strong enough to handle it? It's rather heavy," I said.

"I'm stronger than I look," said the little boy.

I watched him drag the bag over to the car. It must have weighed more than Joey.

Dee, Diana and I followed him. When we got to the car, Joey was sobbing.

"Oh my God! Why are you crying?" asked Dee.

He didn't answer, so she walked over to hug him.

"Nothing can be so wrong that you are crying crocodile tears," she told him.

Between whimpers he told her what was wrong: "I locked the keys in the trunk."

I gave him a big smile and did my best imitation of the cartoon character, Yogi Bear.

"Hey, hey, hey who is smarter than the average bear?" I pulled out my wallet and removed my spare car key. As soon as he saw the extra key, Joey jumped into my arms. He really warmed my heart.

"This is how life should be," I thought to myself.

Three days after we returned, there were more tears, with everybody sobbing. Dee was hemorrhaging early one morning before the kids went to school. I called 911 and the ambo thankfully arrived in about three minutes. Dee was transported to the emergency room of Franklin Square Hospital.

The children and I waited for what seemed to be a very long time. I sat between them in the waiting room with my arms around them. Diana kept asking, "Is Mom going to die?" I said no, it's not that serious. At last, a doctor came out to explain that she had an ectopic pregnancy and was undergoing surgery. I told the kids that Mom had a blood vessel which ruptured and that she would be home soon. I drove them to Stemmers Run Elementary School. After telling the staff what happened, Diana and Joey went to their respective classrooms.

I sat in the car for several minutes to collect my thoughts. I drove home, gathered the bed sheets, saturated with blood, and threw them in the trash so the children wouldn't see them. For the next five days, we ate peanut butter and grape jam sandwiches, Oodles of Noodles and pizza. When Dee came home we picked up our lives together as a new family.

She never asked any questions about my work as a cab driver or how much money I made. She never suspected I was anyone different from the man I presented to her, so I was able to continue living the Big Lie. Still, I could not keep my secret for much longer. The frightening experience of her ectopic pregnancy made me realize that I loved her more than I'd thought. I needed to find the right moment to break the news to her.

I had saved some money and began to secretly look for a house to buy. Once I had a contract in hand, I figured, I would tell Dee that I was a member of the Baltimore Police Department. It was a Saturday. We had taken the kids to the Mt. Carmel Church carnival. While Diana and Joey were on a thrill ride, I told Dee the truth.

"I need to tell you something, but before I do I owe you an apology because I have told you a big lie."

"What is this big lie?" she asked.

"I am actually a Baltimore police officer. I have been working in a very deep undercover assignment. Driving a cab gave me some cover," I told her.

She was incredulous. I wasn't surprised that she didn't believe me.

"Show me your badge," she said.

"I don't have one because of my undercover role."

"Sure, right!" she said.

The ride was coming to an end and the kids were about to come off.

I quickly told her, "Look, I have requested to be resurfaced from my assignment. As soon as that happens, I will get all of my equipment back. Then you will see not only my badge, but my uniform, my gun belt and riot gear."

She still didn't believe me.

"You know what they say," she told me. "When I see it, I'll believe it."

I understood that as an intelligence officer on a deep covert assignment I was responsible for reporting all sorts of crimes—from illegal sports betting to insurance scams, drug dealing and murder—that would be distributed to other police units for investigations. But those crimes had nothing to do with the Bruno crime family coming to Baltimore to shake down business owners and government officials.

For three years I befriended as many bar owners, bartenders, doormen, strippers, drug dealers, gamblers and loan sharks as I could, searching for some small indication from our conversations that there was an out-of-town mob controlling the vending or video gambling machines, the liquor licenses, the prostitution business or the drug dealers who fed the strippers' habits.

Despite all of my efforts at infiltrating the areas where the mob would most likely go—the red-light district, the waterfront and various ethnic communities—I did not establish a scintilla of evidence to support the

FBI's information. I thought, "They were wrong about Tony Scotto. So why should the Feds be right about the Bruno crime family?"

For a long time I worried, "How difficult will it be to prove a negative?"

After I heard the city was using eminent domain to purchase some of the Block properties, I asked Tommy Bruno, whom I had befriended, if he had heard the "landscape was changing on The Block." I kept my inquiry vague enough so he might use the opening to tell me about any new mafia connections. But he said all was well and nothing was new. I decided to submit a report outlining everything I had done, listing every place I had visited and many of the business owners I had met, including Bruno. I cynically wondered if the ISD division kept me in my covert assignment because they thought of me as a human firehouse. "If the alarm rings," they must assume, "we have Cabezas in place to put out the fire."

In the end I did prove a negative. To this day I believe no mafia has ever been able to control Baltimore's home-grown criminal organizations because our city is a "rat town," a place where criminals can't be trusted with each other's secrets. It is also a rest town, a place where mafia associates in trouble for violating a mob code of conduct can find a safe haven. In fact, Baltimore's old nickname of "Mobtown" comes, not from any mafia connection, but from a bleak period in the city's history in the 1850s when it was inundated with street killings, political violence and police shootings.

Finally, I decided to pull out all the stops to get out of my covert assignment. Wasn't it enough that I had gone without a friend for three years, including fellow officers like Charlie Walas and Wayne Carneal, not to mention my fraternity brothers (boy, I really missed them), lied to my sister—and then my new wife? I had risked my life with no weapon and no backup and was nearly gutted by a dagger-wielding motorcycle Pagan high on PCP. I had passed along evidence to various crimes and worked for an ignorant supervisor who never once asked about my safety. And I had proven the FBI was wrong about the mafia.

I told Sgt. Crab if he did not allow me to resurface, I would call Roger Twigg, the Baltimore Sun's veteran police reporter. "I'll tell Twigg everything I've been doing," I said. I figured it was my best move. I wanted to hit him with full force.

Well, that did the trick.

In August of 1977 I reported to the quartermaster's unit where I received my badge, service revolver, riot gear and a full set of uniforms. I was not concerned about carrying a gun again. My eyesight had been stable now for several years, though I still had problems with depth perception. I was nevertheless greatly relieved when I passed my gun qualification test shortly after resurfacing. My shots at the target were from seven yards, 15 yards, 25 yards and finally 50 yards, the most difficult.

I traded in my jeans and red leather jacket for a new dark-blue pin-stripe suit and a white starched shirt with a tie. I walked into police headquarters to a new job as a detective in ISD, just a block away from the red-light district where I'd spent my nights over the last three years.

I was nervous as I opened the mezzanine door to the elevators. I pushed the button to the eighth floor, to the ISD office, down the hall from Commissioner Pomerleau and three of his deputy commissioners. I worried that too much of the street life had rubbed off on me. I was going from rubbing elbows with guttersnipes to working for an elite unit that answered only to the commissioner. I was also concerned about resurfacing because I wondered who might know that several officers had been fired after I reported that they took petty bribes on The Block.

Shortly after I resurfaced, I ran into Gus Drakos, who had been my first desk sergeant back when I started on the midnight foot patrol in the Eastern District when I was 21. He was there for me the day my father was killed, waiting with concern in the station-house doorway for me as I returned from the scene of the murder.

"I knew you never quit," he said. "I never believed it. There's too much cop in you."

My parents, Isidro Cabezas and the former Rebecca Mendoza, in 1945, a few years before I was born

Mom with my big sister, Esther, and me in 1950. I was one year old

Esther and I wearing velvet outfits made by Mom, 1952

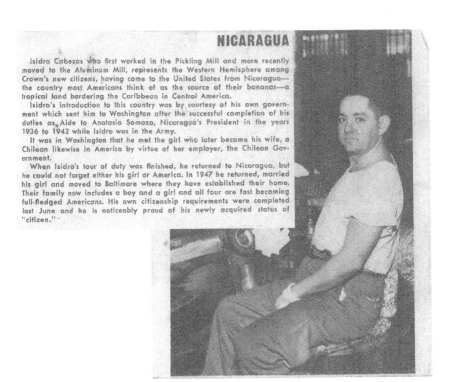

NICARAGUA

Isidro Cabezas who first worked in the Pickling Mill and more recently moved to the Aluminum Mill, represents the Western Hemisphere among Crown's new citizens, having come to the United States from Nicaragua—the country most Americans think of as the source of their bananas—a tropical land bordering the Caribbean in Central America.

Isidro's introduction to this country was by courtesy of his own government which sent him to Washington after the successful completion of his duties as Aide to Anatasio Somoza, Nicaragua's President in the years 1936 to 1942 while Isidro was in the Army.

It was in Washington that he met the girl who later became his wife, a Chilean likewise in America by virtue of her employer, the Chilean Government.

When Isidro's tour of duty was finished, he returned to Nicaragua, but he could not forget either his girl or America. In 1947 he returned, married his girl and moved to Baltimore where they have established their home. Their family now includes a boy and a girl and all four are fast becoming full-fledged Americans. His own citizenship requirements were completed last June and he is noticeably proud of his newly acquired status of "citizen."

Pop posing at a machine for the company newsletter when he worked at Crown Cork and Seal, 1953

My First Communion, 1956

At home with Mom and Pop, 1952

154

My graduation from the Cathedral School of Mary Our Queen, 1964

Lou and Laura Otrembo 1968

On the athletic field at the Maryknoll Junior Seminary in Clark Summit Pennsylvania, 1965

Here I am with Kathy, my first wife, in 1968

Pop with Kathy enjoying themselves in a dance, 1968

At home with Pop, 1970

With my three children, Joe, James and Diana, 1978

With my second wife, Dee and baby James, 1979

With Joe and James, 1981

*With the boys at James'
Confirmation, 1991*

With Laura at our wedding, 1993

The three of us, 2018

My sister Esther and I, 2018

My granddaughters, Autumn and Alexis, with James and I, 2018

A proud grandfather with the girls, 2018

With Laura on our 25th anniversary 2018

Our whole family, 2018

Visiting the Block, 2018

A portrait of me the year I published this memoir, 2018

My police graduation class, 1971, with me in the front row, far right

Commissioner Donald Pomerleau, far left, congratulating the police officers of the year for 1972; I am the third officer to the right of Pomerleau

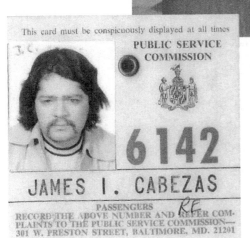

My cab driver's license when I worked as a deep covert, 1975

Sharing a drink with my best friend, Howard Glashoff in the 1980's

John P. O'Neill, my friend and colleague from the FBI, who died in the 2001 World Trade Center attack

With my good friend and colleague, Baltimore City Deputy States Attorney Mary Ann Willin, 1979

The Mayor Dixon prosecution team in 2009, from left: Bob Rohrbaugh, Mike McDonough, John Poliks and Shelly Glenn; Photo by Maximillian Franz, used by permission from The Daily Record

Emmet Davitt, the Maryland State Prosecutor and Mike McDonough, Deputy State Prosecutor, the day I accepted an award as the Fraud Fighter of the Year, 2016

29
RUNNING WITH THE BIG DOGS

I felt considerable trepidation as I used a key to open the door of the ISD office. I made my way to the reception area, where I was pleasantly greeted by the administrative staffers, Dawn Thomas and Jeanne Bell.

"Can you guess who I am?" I said with a smile.

They didn't answer.

"Well, suppose I tell you that I am 232."

They looked surprised to see me. Apparently, no one had told them I had resurfaced.

"Well at last you're in," Dawn said.

"No one has been a covert as long as you have," added Jeanne.

"You know," I said, "I was also 237."

"Yes we knew," they both said, giggling.

Of course they must have been amused at the absurdity of having my code number changed. Dawn and Jeanne were the ones who answered the phone when I called, so they knew my voice, whether I identified myself as 232 or 237. I never figured out how a new code number would protect me.

"I can just imagine what genius ordered you to change your number," said Jeanne. I didn't bother to mention that the genius's boss was the one who suggested I masquerade in a wig to take the sergeant's exam. As she rolled her eyes, a bearded man walked in and introduced himself as Sgt. Frank Napfel.

He showed me to my new desk and returned a few minutes later with a ceramic mug full of hot coffee. "The cup is gratis," he said. "You will need it around here. Lots of land mines around. Walk carefully."

He added, "I am not your supervisor. You will report to [he gave Sgt. Crab's real name]." I was really disappointed. God knows I didn't need more of the same lack of direction. He told me I would be meeting with the lieutenants. The big boss was Bernie Norton, director of ISD, a retired FBI agent who was personally selected by Commissioner Pomerleau.

I sat down at my new desk and thought, "Frank was really forthcoming." I wondered, "What land mines is he talking about?" I recalled all the newspaper articles about illegal spying by ISD. That was nearly three years ago. I assumed the illegal wiretaps and surveillance of black politicians and political groups had stopped after the grand jury and state senate investigations. Well, I was about to find out I was wrong.

As the rest of the squad arrived I was introduced. Detective John Gavrilis was especially friendly to me and explained that investigators write reports that were subsequently condensed to three by five index cards. He was showing me the file room, marked IEO (Intelligence Eyes Only) on the door, when the lieutenant, Donald Woods, walked in and greeted me warmly. He told me to come to his office at 10 a.m. for a meeting. "Yes sir," I said.

When I got into the meeting, there was Sgt. Crab.

The lieutenant did all the talking. My old supervisor didn't say a word. Woods explained that ISD had two units. One conducted inspections of police facilities to determine if the rank and file were abiding by BPD's promulgated policy. The second was the intelligence side. He emphasized that ISD only answers to the police commissioner. Each detective was assigned to collect intel about motorcycle gangs, hate groups such as the Ku Klux Klan, illegal gambling or narcotics organizations.

"Sir, what will I be doing?" I asked.

"I'm still thinking about what your job will be. You have one of those personalities which allows you to mix well with almost anyone," he answered.

When the meeting was over Sgt. Crab said, "Welcome to the unit." It was the first gracious thing he'd said to me in three years.

In one of my first few days in the ISD office I saw a detective with a gray briefcase made of hard plastic, issued to every officer in the department. As he opened it I saw it was lined with a silk-like pocket which had an elastic string to keep it tightly closed. I watched him place a wire with a microphone and a small battery pack inside the concealed pocket. He placed two thick folders inside the briefcase and pressed them against the pocket. Then he locked the briefcase. I did not see a tape recorder, so I assumed the wire and the microphone would transmit a live conversation to a recorder in a different location.

I had no idea where he was going.

"What the hell's that?" I asked another investigator.

"They take the briefcase to City Hall when the command staff meets with the mayor," he said, referring to Mayor Schaefer. "Of course, they know what was said in the meeting, but they actually want to know what was said after they leave the mayor's office," he said.

"So they bring the briefcase and purposely leave it behind," he said, in case the mayor says anything negative about the commissioner behind his back.

"Later they retrieve the briefcase, saying it was left behind by mistake."

When not in use, the briefcase was locked away in a walk-in safe inside Lt. Woods's office.

I knew it was illegal in Maryland for a law enforcement officer to tape record another person's conversation, or to listen through a live electronic eavesdropping device, unless he had a court order, obtained only after presenting a judge with strong evidence that a crime has been committed. In fact, state law required law enforcement investigators to exhaust every other investigative tool before being allowed to wiretap a phone or legally tape record a conversation. So I was certain that the scheme with the briefcase wired for sound in Mayor Schaefer's office was illegal.

I watched the detective open a little leather pouch the size of a wallet where he kept a set of small instruments I did not recognize.

"What's that?" I asked.

"They're lock picks," he said in a matter-of-fact manner.

I knew it was a violation of state law to possess a set of lock picks without approval from the Maryland State Police, even if you were a police officer. I had no idea why he possessed lock picks, but I knew they were used by thieves to break into homes and offices. I had no idea what he was going to use them for and he didn't tell me.

He told me that some ISD detectives had gone for intel training at Fort Holabird, just outside Baltimore, where the federal government's Counter Intelligence Corps (CIC) Center was headquartered. I have no idea how long the illegal spying continued, though maybe it ended when Commissioner Pomerleau retired in 1981.

The following week, ISD director Norton was summoned to Commissioner Pomerleau's office. When he returned, he met with Lt. Woods, who subsequently called me to his office.

"We have a sensitive situation," he told me.

"Last night a naval intelligence officer was in Baltimore, carrying a briefcase containing classified documents. We don't know the specifics, but somehow he became separated from the briefcase in a bar somewhere on The Block," he told me.

The commissioner received a call from a high-ranking official of the naval intelligence unit who requested an assist.

"I am authorizing a $500 withdrawal as a reward for anyone providing information that leads to the recovery of the briefcase," he said. "You need to get the briefcase back. Get started right away."

I looked at him in surprise.

"What is your problem?" he asked.

"Sir, you said that the briefcase was lost last night. The day shift won't have a clue about it." I asked, "Was the officer in uniform?"

"I'll get back to you on that," he answered. By lunchtime I was told the officer had indeed been in uniform and I was handed ten $50 bills.

Several hours later, when I knew the night shift had arrived for work, I walked just a block from headquarters, back into my old stomping grounds toward the pinks, yellows, reds and greens of the neon lights with the carnival chatter of the doormen and drunken customers, wearing my new pinstriped suit and tie.

I was hungry, so I stopped at Pollack Johnny's for a Polish sausage first. I walked down Baltimore Street like someone who had memorized every crack in the sidewalk, which I had. The doorman at the 408 Show Bar noticed me right away. His nickname was Photo because he frequented the Maryland racetracks, always standing at the photo finish line to see who won. I said, "Hey Photo how's it going?" He looked at me in my new suit. "Have you been taking a goofy pill and gotten married?" he asked.

"No not me. But listen, I have a good story for you," I said.

"The fact is I am a cop. For the last three years, I worked a deep undercover assignment right here on The Block. But you have no worries, since I didn't hurt anyone on this street." Before walking away, I handed him a $10 bill and asked him to spread the word.

My first stop was the Block Show Bar where the doorman said, "Wow! Look at you." I went directly to Tommy Bruno. I told him the same story that I'd just told Photo. Tommy said, "You know I run a clean joint." I smiled and said, "Right you are." When asked about the naval officer, he had no information to share with me. I made similar stops at the Gayety Show Bar, the Villa Nova and the Midway, the only bar on The Block that had no dancers. I said hello to Joe the doorman, a former professional boxer who fought at Madison Square Garden with his five brothers. When I went inside, Paul the bartender said, "Mother of God. What have we here?" I told my story one more time.

Then I said, "I'm on a mission to save the job of a naval officer." After hearing the story, Paul said, "There must be a reward."

"It all depends on who has what to say," I told him, sensing that he knew something. I ordered a beer. After serving other customers, he said, "Okay, what's the amount of the reward?"

"If someone can hand me the briefcase, I have $300." I expected him to ask for more, but he did not. He said, "Your next beer is on me." He walked away, but returned in about 60 seconds, carrying the prized briefcase. I shook my head when I saw a pair of handcuffs dangling from the handle, knowing that the officer had used the cuffs to make sure the briefcase was always tethered to his body. But somehow, perhaps while he was having a good time, he must have untethered himself.

The next morning I walked into the office with the briefcase in hand. I have never seen Sgt. Crab move so fast. "Is that what I think it is?" he asked me. I told him it was and he grabbed the case right out of my hands and walked into Norton's office. Not one supervisor, except for Frank

Napfel, said "Nice going."

I thought to myself, "I need to get transferred, but who would have me?" I worried that once a police officer is sent to spy on fellow officers he might not be trusted again.

Nevertheless, I knew my visit back to The Block was a very good move. I hoped that revealing myself in a friendly way as a cop to the many people working on The Block would one day produce relationships with informants and sources who could provide me with information about crimes being committed. That turned out to be true; I would report several crimes from Block informants for the next 40 years, including a major bribery scheme involving the theft of $3.5 million in city school funds.

The temperature must have been in the high 90s when I went inside the old Maryland Penitentiary downtown. I got there at 11 in the morning, which was a bad move; inmates still needed to be fed lunch before a correctional officer could escort them to see visitors. I had called the warden in advance, since I was not on a list of visitors for the inmate I wanted to see. I explained to the warden my highly unusual reason for visiting the man. The warden was nevertheless accommodating. I did not tell him I was a police officer. I didn't want to use my position to gain advantage.

As I waited, I thought, "How many inmates will turn 21 knowing that their sentence is life without parole?" The waiting area was packed and very loud; it made me sad when I saw how many young mothers were there with toddlers. In an effort to quiet the young ones, the adults were happy to give the children coins for the vending machine. I thought, "This is not their first rodeo."

It was nearly 3 p.m. when the public announcement system called my name and directed me to a particular window. The man on the other side of the thick window was unkempt, with long hair and a pronounced scowl. He was in his early 30s.

I picked up the phone to speak to him through the glass. Here I was, finally face to face with Elmer Scaggs, the man who sired the children I now considered my own.

"Mr. Scaggs," I said. "My name is Jim Cabezas. The reason I'm here is that Dee and I are now married and I would like to adopt Diana and Joey." I knew that Dee had never visited him in prison and that he had not seen his children since they were babies. "I have a government job and I make a good salary." Scaggs did not utter a single word. His eyes were as cold as ice. He seemed proud of his jailhouse tattoos on his fingers and his neck. They were inked with words, like "born to lose" with one word on each finger. Some words were misspelled.

"If you agree," I said, "I will send the warden a legal document which requires your signature and a public notary's signature."

He continued his silence. It really unnerved me.

Then he stood and motioned the officer to take him back to the general population.

When I got outside, Dee was anxiously waiting in the car. I told her what happened and that I had no idea whether Scaggs would agree to the adoption. This is something I really wanted, to give the children my last name and commit myself to them as their father.

Three weeks later, I received his permission to adopt the kids. They both agreed to change their last names to Cabezas. Diana made no changes to her first and middle names, but Joey decided he wanted to drop his middle name, Elmer, after his biological father . He replaced it with James, after me. I was thrilled.

30
WORKING WITH PROFESSIONALS

Just a few weeks after I resurfaced and began working as a detective in ISD, I was detailed to the Maryland Office of the Attorney General, assigned to help in some criminal investigations that would teach me a whole new set of investigative skills I could never have learned on The Block.

The attorney general's office gets its authority from our state's constitution. Its primary purpose is to provide legal representation to the governor, members of the General Assembly, the judiciary and all of the state's agencies, such as the departments of education, corrections and health. The AG's office is not usually known for conducting criminal investigations. It is a little-known fact that an approval letter from the governor is required before any criminal investigation can be initiated by the office. That puts the investigation at a disadvantage because the highest officials in the governor's office will know about it. One could only assume they are all honest people, but in Maryland in those days that was not always true.

Usually the job of prosecuting criminal cases is left up to Maryland's 24 state's attorney's offices, located in each county, including Baltimore City, which is an independent entity not located in any county.

When I got to the AG's office, I reported to Assistant Attorney General Deborah Jennings, who was leading a criminal investigation into the state's recently legalized Maryland Lottery.

She was trying to determine if merchants hoping to obtain lucrative lottery machines were asked to pay thousands of dollars in bribes to get an inside advantage to have machines installed in their businesses. Acting Governor Blair Lee authorized the investigation after three shopkeepers said they were approached by people claiming to have influence with the Lottery Commission.

When the state opened its Maryland Lottery in May 1973, it was the state's first legal lottery in 122 years. After more than a century of tax-free, illegal lotteries run by gambling syndicates on the streets, in bars and in factories, it was about time that the state government got in on the action. With the creation of the Maryland Lottery Commission and the installation of hundreds of machines connected to a central computer, ticket sales on the opening day were so brisk that businesses sold out of their first week's worth of tickets in just a few hours. There was a frenzy leading up to that first day, with politically well-connected people getting jobs at the Lottery Commission and contracts to print the tickets. So it was no surprise in late 1977 that someone might have sought bribes from businesses who wanted the machines installed in their stores.

Debbie Jennings was unlike any supervisor I'd ever worked for. Aside from being a woman, she was quite young—perhaps not yet 30—and exceptionally bright. She treated me with the utmost respect and provided guidance and direction that I never got from Sgt. Crab. The attorney general's office was a whole different world for me. The lawyers scrupulously followed the law. I knew I would never see a briefcase with a hidden, illegal recording device. The atmosphere was so different from the strip clubs on The Block.

"Everybody's hair is done nicely," I thought. "They keep their clothes on. They wear tailored suits, perfume and aftershave. And unlike the scent of The Block, no one smells like urine."

Jennings was one of five prosecutors in the Criminal Investigation Division, which was headed by Robert Ozer. I was assigned as lead investigator to the lottery inquiry, along with a Maryland state trooper, named Donaldson. I don't recall his first name, but we called him "Doc" Donaldson. When we first got there Jennings explained to us that the accusation of bribes solicited to get lottery machines was just an allegation. It was up to us to find evidence to either "exculpate or inculpate" the case. Having not gone to law school, I had to raise my hand to ask what those words meant. I was embarrassed. I didn't know what the lady was talking about. Exculpate, I learned, means to exonerate someone of fault or blame, while inculpate means you have enough evidence to charge someone with a crime.

Despite my deficient legal knowledge, I was excited to have the opportunity to work a sophisticated investigation. These were very serious allegations. I did have some advantages because of my street knowledge. When one of the lawyers asked, "There are 15 bars here, does anyone know anything about them?" I could tell them that a certain bar was known for narcotics distribution or another bar was known for its video poker machines where bartenders made illegal payouts to winners of the so-called "amusement" machines. Another bar, I told them, was known for its brisk sports bookmaking business. These were all places that had applied for lottery machines. I also had an above-average skill for writing reports, which the team found helpful.

We began with a map of all the places that had gotten approval for the lottery machines. We had received a tip that someone at a vending machine company called Midfield Vending was soliciting bribes in return for a guarantee that a machine would be placed in a particular business. We didn't know whether Midfield actually had a contact inside the Lottery Commission, or was running a scam. I wrote a search warrant executed at the vending machine business on DeSoto Road. When we got there we searched the office for any names of Lottery Commission field agents on documents or rolodexes, but didn't find any.

The prosecutors were tough and aggressive. We met as a group every two days. I'll never forget one meeting that CID chief Ozer attended. He told us, "If we have to subpoena every swinging dick out there we're going to do it. We're going to bring these people in before the grand jury."

This would be my first grand jury investigation. I learned the grand jury has three purposes: to secure tangible evidence (such as business or bank records) by issuing subpoenas, to subpoena a person to testify and to decide whether to indict someone. I also learned that in bribery cases the person who testifies before a grand jury is automatically given immunity from prosecution. If the person doesn't commit perjury, he or she won't be charged with a crime. So, you've got to be very careful who you offer that immunity. You don't want to give immunity to a person you suspect of murder, for example.

Donaldson and I were assigned to interview a state lottery field agent suspected of soliciting bribes in exchange for placing machines in city businesses. The agent, Carlton Dotson, reviewed applications that came into the Lottery Commission before the machines could be placed in businesses. The geographic area Dotson covered was the same as the area where tipsters said bribes were being solicited.

Donaldson and I made a cold call one Saturday to Dotson's home in Northwest Baltimore. He answered the door and we introduced ourselves as Detective Cabezas and Trooper Donaldson.

"We have some questions we want to ask you," I said.

He did not ask why we were there or what we wanted to ask him about.

That was strange. If a police detective and a state trooper came to your door, wouldn't you ask them what they wanted to talk to you about?

Instead, he just said, "Come on in."

He directed us to the kitchen, where we sat at a round table covered with junk mail and newspapers.

"For the purpose of thoroughness," I told him, "I'd like to record this interview, but I can't record it unless you specifically express you are in agreement."

"I don't care," he said. His manner was very relaxed, even nonchalant.

I turned on the tape recorder and spoke into it. I recited the day's date and the time. I stated where we were and indicated that everyone in the room agreed to the use of the recording device. I had each of us say, "I consent" into the recorder to make it clear everyone agreed. In Maryland, recordings can only be made legally if all parties agree—unless, of course, a law enforcement officer has permission from a judge for a secret wiretap.

Donaldson and I told Dotson upfront that the attorney general's office had received information that bribes might have been paid to guarantee businesses lottery terminals. I began with open-ended questions that were not at all accusatory:

"Are you employed?"

"Where do you work?"

"What are your job duties?"

"Describe a typical day at work."

This was a very different type of interview from the ones I conducted as a police officer in the Eastern District. This was an investigation involving white collar crime—a huge difference from the interrogations of drug dealers and other street people.

When I interviewed a drug dealer like Jarbo I would have to know how to speak his street language. I would say, "You're fucking lying to me, you lying piece of shit."

But I would never say that to a person like Dotson, who had a professional job.

After several more non-confrontational questions we were ready to begin a careful interrogation.

I turned to Dotson and said, "The fact is, we are here because we have information that accuses you of demanding bribes."

With that, his head hit the table and he passed out.

Donaldson immediately went to his aid to revive him, while I spoke into the tape recorder:

"For purposes of this recording Mr. Dotson has fainted." I then announced the time and said the interview had concluded.

Once he regained consciousness, we asked Dotson if he needed to call a doctor or go to the hospital, but he said he was fine. He stood up and walked us to the door.

Dotson was later indicted for seeking bribes from two West Baltimore businessmen. He was only tried on one of the charges, but a jury acquitted him. Apparently the jury did not believe the testimony of the business owners who accused Dotson of demanding bribes. The owner of Midfield Vending Company pleaded guilty to obstruction of justice, forgery and making false representations to businessmen he solicited for bribes. He received a two-year suspended sentence and was fined $4,000.

In those days the attorney general's office was at 1 South Calvert Street in the heart of the downtown business district. I often went with lawyers from the office for happy hour after work on Thursdays or Fridays, just up the block at Peter's Pub inside a historic early 20th-century brick building with arched windows.

One afternoon I walked in and saw Howard Glashoff. He was one of the police officers fired after the strike. I had met him years before at the Tic Toc Club when I began my deep covert assignment. Back then, of course, I only posed as a former cop who had to leave the department because I had gotten into some sort of trouble. I never let Howard know I was working as a deep covert. Now I was hanging out with lawyers from the attorney general's office. What must Howard think? I was in a bit of an awkward position. I thought to myself, "Jesus, I just left all these land mines behind. Now they are coming back to haunt me."

If Howard wondered what I'd really been doing for the last several years, he didn't let on.

He didn't ask the question and I didn't bring it up. When he saw me he may have assumed I was a civilian investigator. I wasn't going to touch it. He just said hello and we hit it off. Howard stood 5 feet 10 inches, had blonde hair and brilliant blue eyes. He wasn't Hollywood handsome, but he was an attractive man who always dressed impeccably. He bought his clothes at Hamburger's Department Store just a few blocks from Peter's Pub. He had a quick mind and was hilarious. He was also a raving liberal. I never had a friend as liberal as Howard.

He was working as an investigator for the Baltimore City state's attorney's office, just up Calvert Street in the Circuit Courthouse. It was at Peter's Pub that he introduced me to his boss, Mary Ann Willin, who had recently become the first woman deputy state's attorney for the city. Her boss was state's attorney William Swisher, a man who wasn't the most dedicated public servant. Mary Ann, like Howard, was very smart and laser-focused on her job. When I got to know her better she told me it was Swisher's job to get elected so she could run the office.

At the time I met her, Swisher was under federal investigation for mail fraud and extortion involving his relationship with Jack Pollack, Baltimore's last big political boss. Federal prosecutors would charge Swisher with accepting bribes to hire people with political connections to Pollack. They would also accuse Swisher of accepting a $25,000 bribe to stop a city corruption investigation. (A federal jury acquitted him of the charges in December 1979.)

Mary Ann was working on the investigation of a high-ranking police commander, Lt. Col. James H. Watkins. I told Mary Ann about some unusual conversations I'd had with Paul Balton, who owned the Harem

Club on Howard Street. Balton seemed to know Watkins better than any strip club owner should know a high ranking police commander. Balton even referred to Watkins by his street name as "The Bear." I asked myself, "Why would a strip club owner know the Bear?" Watkins didn't conduct vice investigations. He was in charge of a squad that investigated narcotics distribution in the public housing high rises. (Years later I learned that there may well have been a drug connection between Balton and Watkins. I heard that someone broke into Balton's Harem Club and stole a kilo of cocaine or heroin from his safe on two different occasions. Of course, he could not report the theft to police.)

Mary Ann thought what I told her was interesting enough for me to testify before a grand jury. It was my first time testifying as a law enforcement officer. I was a bit nervous going in, but she explained the grand jury process is absolutely secret. Everyone must take an oath of confidentiality. If they break that oath they can be fined and jailed. It was especially memorable because my testimony was the first time I told anyone outside the police department about my covert life.

I testified to what I knew about narcotics trafficking in the city and told the grand jury that Balton knew Watkins. (I later remembered that dinner I'd had with Balton and his wife at the Inner Harbor when I realized he must have known all along that I was a deep covert officer. I have always wondered if Watkins was the one who told him. If true, it is a chilling thought that a high-ranking police officer would ever put another officer in such danger.)

Watkins was eventually indicted and tried, but, much to the disappointment of prosecutors, he was acquitted of corruption charges in June 1979.

During my time at the AG's office I also assisted in a most unusual investigation of an unscrupulous Catholic priest named Father Guido Carcich, who directed a multimillion dollar charity operated by the Pallottine Fathers. According to articles in the *Washington Post* and the Baltimore *Sun*, Carcich gave only a tiny fraction of the funds raised to help the poor. Instead, he used the money to invest in real estate and make loans to politically connected businessmen. He even loaned $54,000 to Governor Mandel to help finance his divorce.

On a Friday afternoon I volunteered to serve a subpoena at the Pallottine office on North Paca Street downtown. I had the subpoena in an envelope folded like a letter. In those days we served the original document with a grand jury foreperson's signature. I took the subpoena out of the envelope and knocked on the door. It was a warm afternoon, with clouds gathering fast. No one answered. I waited 30 seconds, and knocked again.

Suddenly the skies opened and it started pouring. Here I was, raised as a devout Catholic, about to serve a subpoena to a priest, and the skies open on me. I looked up into the rain. "Hey God," I said, laughing, "I'm only the messenger." By the time the door opened, blue ink was running down the page. I apologized to the person who answered the door. The man said not to worry. He would give the document to their lawyer.

While my professional life was going very well, I was even more pleased with my home life.

Not long after I adopted Diana and Joey, I bought our family of four a home in a nice, quiet neighborhood in Northeast Baltimore. We would expand to five on March 23, 1978, when our son, James Vaughn Cabezas, was born. During Dee's pregnancy we were all quite nervous because of her previous ectopic pregnancy. Even Diana, who rarely showed compassion, displayed genuine care toward her mother during those months. James was born at Franklin Square Hospital after a long, hard labor in which Dee insisted on a natural childbirth with no drugs to numb her pain. Despite our worries during Dee's pregnancy and her difficult delivery, James's birth was an occasion of true joy for me.

31
A LAWMAN WITHOUT A GUN

Back in 1973 I was fascinated by the federal investigation of Vice President Spiro T. Agnew for taking kickbacks from engineers who got no-bid contracts when he served as Baltimore County executive. He kept taking payoffs after he became governor and vice president. In the years that followed I grew increasingly curious about the investigative steps used to probe political corruption.

For the next four years, other high-profile political corruption cases were in the news constantly. Four months after Agnew's guilty plea and resignation as vice president, Baltimore County's top prosecutor, state's attorney Sam Green, was convicted of conspiring to take money from a man who wanted his arrest record expunged. The most salacious news from Green's trial—in the very courthouse where he reined as top prosecutor—was evidence of his sexual exploits with nine women working in his office. Green, a married man, met his secretaries for sex in motel rooms, in an aide's apartment and even at his desk while opening mail. The next month, Baltimore County executive Dale Anderson, Agnew's successor, was convicted of conspiracy for extorting almost $40,000 from contractors doing work for the county. Nine months later came the guilty plea of Anne Arundel County executive Joe Alton for extorting kickbacks from consultants. When Anderson arrived at a federal prison in Pennsylvania the following year, Alton was there to welcome him.

Two years later state delegate George Santoni was convicted in federal court of attempting to extort almost $15,000 from a contractor in exchange for his help getting custodial and demolition contracts from Baltimore City. The contractor turned out to be a phony company set up by the FBI. Three months later, Maryland's most powerful politician, Governor Marvin Mandel, was convicted in federal court of pushing legislation to benefit his friends, who gave him hundreds of thousands of dollars in bribes and gifts.

These cases, along with the Watergate investigation that led to President Richard M. Nixon's resignation in August 1974, taught me that there is no particular political party or geographical jurisdiction that has a monopoly on immoral behavior and disdain for the integrity of public office. The corrupt mind has no boundaries: suburban or urban, Democrat or Republican, it doesn't matter.

After I resurfaced and began working at the attorney general's office I wondered if I could begin a new phase of my career investigating white-collar crime and political corruption. It certainly would be a far cry from my days on The Block or on the beat in the Eastern District. I could tell from Maryland's rich history that there would likely be plenty of greedy politicians to ferret out. The problem would never go away by itself.

I also knew that my eyesight would not stay stable forever. In the back of my mind I thought, "At some point I will need to find a job where I don't need to carry a gun." If my eyes eventually failed me, I reasoned, maybe I could transform that misfortune into an opportunity.

In 1978 that opportunity arrived.

I was told by an ISD supervisor that I was being assigned as an investigator to the new Office of the State Prosecutor (OSP), dedicated to investigating political corruption. Maryland had never established such an office before, but now, after so many high-profile convictions of politicians, there was a clamor from the Maryland General Assembly and the public to create a state office exclusively dedicated to flushing out political fraud, bribery and influence peddling, as well as maintaining integrity in government and the election process.

To me, the assignment was the perfect chance to learn new skills for investigating crimes of corrupt elected officials and candidates for office. I could not believe my good fortune. I would still be employed by the police department and technically assigned to ISD as a detective, but I would be detailed for most of my time at the Office of the State Prosecutor. For now, I would continue carrying a gun, but I hoped it would soon lead to a career where I would not have to wear a firearm.

It was a dream come true. I hoped my new assignment meant that Commissioner Pomerleau had confidence in me. I also wondered if the commissioner had assigned me to act as his eyes and ears. If so, he was wrong. I wasn't going there to be his spy.

The new office was created by state legislation and signed into law by Acting Governor Blair Lee III (formerly the Lieutenant Governor), who was filling in while Governor Mandel was in federal prison. After a long search, a specially designated State Prosecutor Selection and Disabilities Commission chose Gerald D. Glass as the first state prosecutor. Jerry was a former Baltimore City assistant state's attorney, in charge of the economic crimes unit, where he won convictions of city sheriff Frank Pelz for bribery and city councilman John Schaefer for violating conflict of interest laws.

Lee approved the appointment, saying the new office would "keep a sharp eye on white-collar crime" and "clean up whatever problems exist in this state and do it ourselves without the federal prosecutors."

Although Lee appointed the new prosecutor, Jerry would be completely independent of the governor, the legislature or any other state law enforcement agency. After spending my career under the thumb of supervisors who took their marching orders from an authoritarian police commissioner, I would now be working for a new boss who answered to no one.

On my first day, I walked the short distance from the Baltimore police headquarters to the new OSP office, happily singing the song from the new hit film, *Saturday Night Fever*.

The song, "Staying Alive" by the Bee Gees, had a catchy, addictive tune.

Whether you're a brother or whether you're a mother
You're stayin' alive, stayin' alive
Feel the city breakin' and everybody shakin'
And we're stayin' alive, stayin' alive...

Then I heard that little voice in my head I hadn't heard for a while. In my youth I called it "Chilo" but I knew now that it was really my father's voice.

"How are you? It's been a long time," I said to the voice.

"It has been. And you have been doing fine without me," I imagined Pop saying.

"Thank you Pop. I miss and love you very much."

"You and I will always will be as one," said Pop. "Listen very carefully. You are fortunate to have been assigned to this new office. You have never investigated politically powerful people before and you have no idea what will come your way. You cannot make a single mistake. Keep your mouth shut, except to ask questions. And remember, no question is stupid."

I found Jerry Glass to be a gregarious man with a good sense of humor who was very knowledgeable about Maryland's criminal law and rules of evidence. He treated me with respect and never looked down on me because I wasn't a lawyer. Our office was in the same downtown building as the attorney general's office, just a few floors up. We had a small staff with a deputy state prosecutor, Gerald Ruter, and one other staff attorney, Neal Janey. A financial auditor was assigned to our office, Marcelino Ferrer, who would become invaluable to us. We also had three administrative staff employees.

Many in the legal and political communities were dubious that we could succeed. They considered our office underfunded; they doubted we would be able to fulfill our mission to ferret out corruption and election law violations and successfully prosecute those indicted.

We set out to prove them wrong.

For the next 38 years I would work with my colleagues to investigate dozens of corrupt elected officials, law enforcement officers, government lawyers, political operatives, public educators, bureaucrats and private contractors who robbed public bank accounts and campaign treasuries, violated tax and election laws, took bribes, paid kickbacks and conspired to enrich themselves at the cost and detriment to the citizens of Maryland.

My associates and I would catch them using all the tools available to us. We won court approval to wiretap their phones. With subpoenas we scrutinized their bank, business, payroll and campaign finance records. With warrants we searched their homes for thousands of dollars in hidden cash, ill-gotten fur coats and stolen gift cards. We watched them from our cars and ran surveillance as we walked past their homes (once nonchalantly pushing a baby buggy with a doll). I combed through trash for bank envelopes from bribers and dove into dumpsters for copies of doctored campaign finance records. I honed the skill of extracting confessions with the kindest care, once even getting an admission of guilt from a legislator right in his Annapolis statehouse office.

With our state mandate to investigate bribery, misconduct in office, election law violations, perjury, obstruction of justice, extortion and violations of government ethics, no dishonest public official was exempt from the OSP's scrutiny.

I investigated state delegates and senators who used their elected positions—and campaign funds—for personal gain. There was the suburban Prince George's County council member who raided his campaign funds and skipped town before his sentencing. There was a Baltimore City comptroller who commandeered tax dollars through a fictitious employee. There was a sex-crazed county executive from affluent suburban Anne Arundel County who used his police detail for campaign work and to cover up his sexual escapades. I arrested a state trooper for taking bribes so vehicles with faulty brakes could pass inspection.

There were three city school principals who stole precious public school dollars from their own student funds. My staff tracked phony bills from the owner of a tutoring business who forged parents' signatures to earn $150,000 for nonexistent lessons for special education students. We also caught a wealthy businessman conspiring with a school employee to steal more than $3.5 million for phony school boiler repairs.

We caught two savvy political operatives for tape-recording a phony Election Day call to keep thousands of voters away from the polls. We investigated the perennially corrupt city liquor board, zeroing in on a politically well-connected bar owner and the city's chief liquor inspector for bribery and conspiracy. My office made a dent in a long-standing illegal video gambling syndicate, winning convictions of 11 companies and 25 people for illegal gambling and for filing false taxes. Our efforts helped the state collect almost $4 million in fines and taxes.

We even investigated the infamous illegal tape recording of a young woman named Monica Lewinsky confiding to a friend named Linda Tripp that she was having an affair with President Bill Clinton.

During my tenure there seemed to be an epidemic of corrupt local sheriffs prone to pilfering from their government bank accounts and campaign funds. We arrested four of them, including a Baltimore City sheriff who tried to wheedle out of his charge by offering me a $2,000 bribe—caught on videotape.

And yes, we investigated a Baltimore mayor for taking thousands in gift cards from developers doing business with her office. We even confiscated fur coats—a Persian lamb and a mink—that she bought with a gift certificate from one developer, whom she also happened to be dating.

Back in 1978, though, I was a green investigator in a new office with no track record.

Our first big case began in October with a newspaper article from the Baltimore *Evening Sun*. The article, by Kevin Abell, reported a conflict-of-interest scheme involving Donald H. Noren, the state's top environmental health official. Noren had acquired interest in a tract of land in Anne Arundel County just as his agency changed rules to allow development of the very same property. Before he changed the rules, the property was useless, banned from development because of a limit on sewer hookups for new homes. One of the other investors in the land deal was Maurice "Mo" Wyatt, who had worked as Governor Mandel's patronage chief, a powerful position that allowed him to dole out coveted jobs in state government.

The day the article was published Lee asked the OSP to begin an investigation of the case.

"I seriously want to get to the bottom of this," said Lee. "This sort of thing simply has to stop in the state, and the chips will fall wherever they may."

Shortly after our investigation began, we started to look beyond Anne Arundel County to Baltimore County, where another sewer moratorium, called the Gwynns Falls Sewer Moratorium, barred newly constructed buildings from being connected to the sewer. This created great hardship for builders who were unable to complete their houses and apartment complexes and pay their construction debts.

Our investigation focused on the years 1974 to 1976 when the state established the moratorium to stop 5 million gallons of raw sewage from overflowing into the Gwynns Falls stream system every day. The state's Department of the Environment understood the hardships facing builders, so the agency allowed them to appeal their sewer applications to the Board of Review, in the hopes that they could get a waiver to the moratorium and complete their projects.

While we moved our investigation to the Gwynns Falls area, we continued to focus our attention on Wyatt and Noren, who at the time was assistant attorney general assigned to the state's Environmental Health Administration. He represented the agency when developers appealed their cases to the Board of Review. It made sense to look for any connection between Noren and the developers because he had sway over the board to award the highly coveted exceptions to the moratorium.

This case would take us more than a year to investigate and it would eventually involve interviews with potential witnesses, grand jury testimony and a thorough review of state health records, bank accounts and several trash cans. I would learn to write my first application for a telephone wiretap—and listen to my first wiretapped phone conversations. Our investigation would lead us to a third person, a lawyer well known in Maryland politics who had served on the Baltimore City Council and was now a judge on the District Court. Before we were ready to indict anyone, we knew the stakes were very high. We all knew that if we did not succeed in convicting anyone in this case, the future of our fledgling office was in jeopardy. But if we won, we all hoped we would be in business for many years.

As for my job as investigator I asked myself, "What do you know about building apartment buildings or how to finance them? What do you know about hooking them up to sewer systems? What do you know about state regulations involving the dumping of raw sewage? What do you know about the Baltimore County developers building hundreds of apartments, despite a moratorium?" The answer was "nothing."

I remembered Pop's voice telling me that no question is too stupid.

I went to the health agency and asked the receptionist if she could introduce me to someone who could explain the rules of the sewer moratorium. Before long a gentleman with white hair came around and invited me to his cubicle.

"What are your questions?" he asked.

"What is needed to issue an occupancy permit?" I asked.

"You have to be able to flush a toilet," he answered.

And so, my career investigating political corruption began.

32
POLITICS IN THE SEWER

We knew we needed to cast a wide net before we could even think about narrowing our investigation into a possible bribery scheme that circumvented the Gwynns Falls Sewer Moratorium. As we started our work we hoped that, if bribes were paid by developers, we might begin to see something suspiciously in common among the projects that got special approval to hook up to the sewer system.

This would take some time.

We knew all the ways citizens could bribe someone in public office. They could pay cash, of course. They could bribe in the form of plane tickets or exotic vacations. They could offer a luxury car, or even a boat, to a public official who otherwise would not be able to afford such a luxury. They could actually offer anything of value, including sex, known as carnal bribery. We supposed a bribe could be paid by personal or business check, though I assumed no one would be so stupid as to leave such an easy trail.

We knew to look at Donald Noren because he was the state official who advised the Board of Review to approve exemptions for developers. We already knew that he had engaged in unethical behavior when he bought into a tract of land in Anne Arundel County just as his state agency freed it up for development. That was a violation of the public trust. We had no idea whether any of the three other men (including Wyatt) involved in the Anne Arundel deal had done anything unethical or illegal. We also wondered if any of them were involved in the Gwynns Falls cases in Baltimore County.

We subpoenaed records for the Anne Arundel County deal. Then we subpoenaed state records that would give us names of every lucky developer who got an exemption so we could search for a common thread. It turned out that exemptions had been granted to six owners of apartment projects totaling 1,400 apartments, as well as one developer of 22 homes for sale.

The cast of characters was growing. We would need to interview as many of them as we could before we issued grand jury subpoenas requiring them to testify.

Early on I went to interview one of the partners in the Anne Arundel land deal, Guido Iozzi Jr., a former ironworker who became head of the Baltimore Building Trades Council before he spent five years in federal prison for racketeering and threatening contractors to make payoffs. His cellmate was none other than Jimmy Hoffa, the infamous Teamster leader who disappeared in 1975. Jerry Glass and Gerry Ruter thought I should go with one or two other staff members to interview him. That was a bad idea, I told them.

"Iozzi is known for his quick temper," I said. "He's also an excellent street fighter."

"If two or three of us show up, he will be on the defensive."

So I went alone.

I arrived at his East Baltimore rowhome, finding it not far from City Hospitals, where I convalesced from Stevens-Johnson Syndrome as a boy. I knocked on his door and he opened it, wearing a sleeveless white undershirt with suspenders, just like any respectable mob guy about to sit down to dinner. I showed him my Baltimore police ID and told him I needed to ask him some questions. "I also have a subpoena," I said.

"Come on in," he said, in a very gregarious manner.

"We just sat down to dinner. Have some spaghetti. Take your coat off. Loosen your tie and relax," he said as he poured me a glass of wine. I sat down at the table with Iozzi and his wife.

I told him, "I'm assigned to the Office of the State Prosecutor. We're investigating allegations of bribes in return for development approvals."

"Hey look," he said. "I know when I've committed a crime and I haven't committed any crimes that you are investigating. Go ahead and ask your questions. I don't have anything to tell you."

As he served me spaghetti and salad, I asked a series of questions concerning the hardship exemptions.

"I don't know any of those properties," he said. "I don't know any of those people."

I also asked him about Noren, but he wouldn't come forward with any information, so I finished eating. It was very good homemade spaghetti.

When I got up to leave I took the subpoena out of my breast pocket and handed it to him.

"Just leave it on the table," he said, as if getting a subpoena was an everyday occurrence. "I'll give it to my lawyer."

We had so much work to do that Jerry Glass called ISD and asked for another detective to help out. They sent us my good friend Charlie Walas, whose keen intellect and great sense of humor was a great boost to our investigation.

Charlie and I tried to come up with ways to shake the trees to see what evidence fell. One day we tried to interview Louie Comi, a convicted gambler who we knew ran the largest fencing operation in the area. Certainly, we thought, Comi and Iozzi knew each other. As we rapped on the door, I said to Charlie, "Do you have your gun?

"Why the fuck are you asking me that question?" he said.

"I accidently left mine at home," I said.

"Aren't you supposed to have my back?" he asked.

"I do have your back," I said, "But today it's without my gun."

At that point the door opened. Comi told us nothing, other than the usual "call my lawyer" before he slammed the door.

One day Charlie went to an open house at Noren's home in Towson, after learning that the house, which came with a swimming pool, was for sale. He took a woman along so he wouldn't look suspicious. He cased the house for any obvious mail or notes that would offer some evidence. He had no luck. When he turned to leave, the real estate agent asked if he was interested in buying the house. No, he said. "We're not pool people."

We worked with a third investigator from the state police, John Nagengast. One day John and I decided to drive to Wyatt's home in Baltimore County. We wanted to see if there was a new car in the driveway that might have been a bribe. John brought his dog on a leash. I brought a baby carriage with a doll I'd purchased, so we could fit into the neighborhood. We cased the house, but we didn't find anything suspicious.

After obtaining the records naming all the Gwynns Falls developers, we continued our interviews. One man's name sounded familiar to me, but I couldn't place him. Samuel Gorn was the developer of an apartment project called Kingswood Commons on Rolling Road in the Catonsville area of Baltimore County. The sewer moratorium had stopped his project for 270 apartments dead in its tracks. He had already spent $3 million, poured 145 concrete slabs and had 70 apartments under construction. We figured the guy must have been desperate to get an exception to the moratorium and finish the project.

I went to interview him at the Horizon House apartment building that he owned on North Calvert Street. As soon as I saw him, I knew where I'd met him before.

"Do you remember me from the Harem Club?" I asked. "Are you still taking photos?" He was the businessman with the hobby of photographing strippers with his big old press camera.

"Now I'm in a different role," I told him, showing him my police ID. When I identified myself as an investigator for the Maryland prosecutor's office, he almost died. He refused to answer my questions, but said he would call his lawyer.

"Make sure your lawyer calls our office within 48 hours," I told him before I left.

Our investigation could not be complete without what we called "trash rips," or simply rifling through someone's trash late at night, searching for evidence. I had done plenty of trash rips during drug investigations in some of the city's toughest neighborhoods. But now, I had a higher class of trash to sort through. I was looking for any paperwork that might identify a bank account or other financial records we were not aware of. I came up with nothing suspicious.

As we closely reviewed the state records on the developments, a pattern finally emerged. We began to see a familiar name pop up. Allen B. Spector, a well-known lawyer in Baltimore, had represented some of the developers. That raised eyebrows. We all knew Spector was very active in Democratic politics and had been a member of the Maryland House of Delegates and the Baltimore City Council. He had resigned recently to take a judgeship, handing over his council seat to his wife, Rochelle "Rikki" Spector.

We also knew that Spector was politically connected to Governor Mandel, who appointed Spector to the District Court for Baltimore City in 1977, just before going off to federal prison. Of course, we knew that Mandel's appointments secretary (more aptly known as his patronage chief) was none other than Mo Wyatt, who was partners with Noren and Iozzi in the Anne Arundel County land deal. Our office sent out numerous grand jury subpoenas while Marcelino Ferrer, our auditor, began to pour over bank records that we'd subpoenaed.

It was Ferrer who found the smoking gun. He traced money going from three developers (including Gorn) to Spector's bank account, from Spector's bank account to Wyatt's bank account, and from Wyatt's bank account to Noren's bank account, just in time for the Board of Review to grant the very same developers exceptions to the sewer moratorium. I had thought that such sophisticated and politically astute men would never be so careless as to pass on bribes in the form of checks, but damned if they hadn't made it easy for us to trace, like Hansel and Gretel leaving a trail of bread crumbs through the forest. We were astonished that their hubris led them to believe they would never get caught.

When totaled, we found that the developers paid Spector $20,000 for doing virtually no legal work. He gave $11,300 of that to Wyatt (who had been in law practice with Noren). Wyatt, in turn, gave $5,650 to Noren. All of these transactions were followed with the swift go-ahead from the state's Board of Review for the developers to finish their projects.

I was brought into the grand jury to provide the status of the investigation.

In other cases I'd seen grand jury members literally fall asleep during testimony, but not on this case. They hung on every word, every bit of evidence. One asked me, "These are all wealthy, professional people. Why would they take such a chance for such a small amount of money?"

"It's not the necessarily the first million which gets someone caught," I said, "but the million plus a dollar," meaning that they could have been doing this for a long time before we found out about it.

As the investigation continued, we knew that we could not request court-ordered wiretaps of phones until we exhausted every other investigative method.

We first obtained a court approved Penn Register, also known as a dialed number recorder. It printed out the phone numbers of calls made to or from the suspects' homes, as well as the date, time and length of the calls. This information was necessary to demonstrate to the judge that communication was taking place among the three suspects.

Finally, I was assigned to write the request to the Circuit Court for a wiretap. I had never been assigned such an important task and I was determined to get it right.

Luckily, Judge Robert C. Murphy, chief judge of the Court of Appeals, had published a law review article with the steps required for requesting a wiretap. For me, it was manna from heaven.

Once the wiretap was approved we had the phones tapped for Spector, Noren and Wyatt.

This became arduous work for me and the other investigators. We had to listen to conversations from 6 a.m. to midnight for 30 days. We had to be careful to turn off the listening device when they called their lawyers, because these were legally restricted conversations we were not allowed to hear. Although we each worked 12 hour shifts listening to their conversations, we never heard them talk about the bribery scheme.

We did, however, have one very frightening moment while listening to the wire one evening. I was monitoring a conversation between Spector and an unidentified friend. Spector said he was in the bathtub and I could hear the water splashing as he talked. He was telling his friend how people committed suicide during the Roman Empire by slashing their wrists in a tub of hot water. He sounded depressed, and very possibly drunk. I began to panic.

Spector knew he was under investigation. His law partners and secretary had already appeared before the grand jury and the files from his old law firm had been subpoenaed. I envisioned him as a desperate man who thought there was no way he could resolve his problems and continue his life.

I was legitimately concerned for his safety, though of course I could never let him know I was listening in on his phone line. Another investigator and I decided to call the police anonymously. We told them there was a disorderly man at Spector's address.

Soon, we heard Spector hang up the phone. We assumed he got out of the tub to answer the door for the police. We did not know for sure that day whether he attempted suicide. Later, to our relief, we discovered that he had not.

At this point in the brief existence of the Office of the State Prosecutor, we had only prosecuted a few public officials for very minor crimes. We had done nothing to prove the necessity of the office. For all of us as professionals in law enforcement, the success of this case was essential. If we failed, there would be no future for the office.

I spoke about it with a friend, FBI agent John O'Neill, who worked the public corruption squad.

"The book on your office is that you won't survive," he said. "Nobody in the General Assembly really wants your office to succeed. Their hope is that you guys will do a head dive," meaning we would fail.

On December 7, 1979, after 14 months of investigation, a grand jury indicted Spector and Wyatt for paying bribes to a public official during the years 1974, 1975 and 1977. Noren was indicted for accepting the bribes. If convicted, each man could go to prison for as long as 12 years and be fined $5,000 for each charge. The developers who made the payoffs to Spector were not indicted. Instead, they all agreed to cooperate and testify for the prosecution.

The indictment was big news in Baltimore, with headlines on the front pages of all the newspapers and on television and radio.

A retired judge from Howard County, James Macgill, heard the case so no city judge would have to oversee the criminal trial of a colleague. That would be too close for comfort. All three defendants were tried together. They chose to have the case heard by the judge, instead of a jury. That meant the defendants were hoping to convince the judge that we didn't have the evidence to prove a bribery scheme, according to a strict interpretation of Maryland's laws. A jury might not care about the subtleties of the law and just base their verdict on evidence and their gut feelings.

We did not demand that the three men be arrested and jailed (or granted bail) before trial. This was not a crime of violence. There was no worry that they would skip town, so we felt the best way to proceed was a criminal summons that required them to appear in three weeks to be arraigned.

Going into the trial, the defendants and their lawyers expressed complete confidence that they would be cleared of all charges. The three defendants had hired knowledgeable lawyers who had reputations for convincing courts that their clients were innocent.

"I expect to be totally vindicated either by pre-trial motions or by the trial itself," said Judge Spector.

Wyatt added, "I am confident I have done nothing illegal or improper. I am convinced that I will be totally vindicated in the matter."

33
REVEALING THE TRUTH

The trial began in the Baltimore City Circuit Courthouse on North Calvert Street. I was sequestered from sitting in on the trial, in case I had to testify, but the case was easy to follow later in the newspapers. Gerry Ruter, as the lead prosecutor, began his opening statement laying out the case to the judge and saying that Spector used his "political muscle" to get developers exemptions from the moratorium.

"As soon as Judge Spector was paid his fee he immediately gave about half the amount to Mr. Wyatt, who then immediately gave half of that to Mr. Noren," Gerry told the judge.

He also laid out the amounts of money that our office found through bank records.

Noren, Gerry said, was paid "to keep his eye on things so that each of Judge Spector's clients got what they wanted." He described Spector as a "man who could get things done."

Spector's lawyer, Paul Mark Sandler, a skilled local defense attorney, disparaged the state's case in his opening statement, calling it "a man in the moon case" where the prosecutor took a simple conflict of interest—that was perfectly legal—and stretched it into a full blown bribery scandal. The charges, he believed, would never stick. He claimed Spector had no knowledge that the "legal fees" were funneled to Noren.

Veteran defense attorney Russell Smouse, representing Wyatt, claimed that his client received a fee for offering his legal expertise on residential developments to Spector. Since Wyatt was much younger than Spector (he was only 31 years old at the time) that was a stretch, I thought. Smouse, too, belittled the state's case to the judge: "The evidence will not amount to criminality. It is, at most, a case of inferences."

As testimony began, one of the three developers, Bernard Rome, testified that he paid Spector $2,500 if he could get on the Board of Review's agenda for a hearing, plus another $2,500 if he won approval to hook up 22 homes he was building.

"It was common sense that I didn't want to spend $5,000 unless there was some sort of success story," he said.

Gorn testified that he paid Spector because "he knew his way around. I would have used any legal means and paid any reasonable fee to achieve release from the sewer moratorium," he said.

The case continued with bank employees testifying about the checks paid from the developers to the three men. The auditor from our office, Ferrer, testified about the transfer of bank funds, calling it "a question of washing money," which prompted fierce objections from the defense.

Gerry emphasized that Spector appeared to do no actual legal work for his fees. His office files on Gorn contained only four pieces of paper; one was a bill for $10,000. There was also evidence of a cover up. Some of the checks paid from Spector to Wyatt contained a note that they were "for Butterfield," a reference to an unrelated personal injury case handled by Spector's law firm.

When the state finished, the defense surprised everybody and declined to present a case. No evidence. No testimony from the three men. They apparently reasoned that our case was so weak they didn't need to mount a defense. They were betting they could just convince the judge that the prosecution did not follow the state's bribery laws.

I was finally allowed into the courtroom to hear the closing arguments.

The defense attorneys really laid down their contempt for the government's case.

Sandler called it a "disgrace," claiming the state "did not prove the defendants agreed to conduct illegal actions, nor did they prove any specific public acts influenced" Noren.

Russell White, Noren's lawyer, told the judge, "The best that the state can infer is that Mr. Noren got money from developers as a gift. A gratuity is not a bribe and the mere acceptance of money does not infer bribery."

Smouse piled on: "The state's case is not even tissue thin. It is totally deficient."

When it was Gerry's turn to rebut them, he said, "The state does not have a tissue-thin, circumstantial case. I would gladly walk the Grand Canyon on that tissue." He noted that the developers paid Spector on a contingency basis so he would only get paid if they won approval to complete their developments.

The verdict came a day later.

My palms were sweating as we waited for Judge Macgill to deliver his decision. I sat with the other investigators on a hard bench usually set aside for witnesses. The courtroom was packed with anxious relatives of the defendants, as well as curious lawyers—both prosecutors and defense attorneys—who had been following the case closely. In a city with a rich history of political corruption trials, this one stood out because it involved three lawyers—one who was a judge.

There is an advantage to hearing a verdict from a judge, who will hopefully explain the reason for his decision. If a jury heard the case, all we would hear is a verdict of guilty or not.

In this case, Judge Macgill was ready with a long, thorough explanation of his decision.

He first appeared to agree with the defense that the state's case was based on circumstantial evidence, even though we believed we had enough direct evidence with bank records and testimony from the developers.

Nevertheless, while the defense argued that circumstantial evidence was not enough to prove a bribery scheme, the judge disagreed.

"Circumstantial evidence is not weaker, or of a lesser quality than other kinds of evidence," he said.

"The facts of the case," (meaning the testimony and bank records) "do not make (Mr. Noren) guilty of bribery, nor do they make Judge Spector or Mr. Wyatt guilty of bribery," he continued. "To find one or more of these defendants guilty of bribery, it must be established beyond a reasonable doubt that the moneys were paid and received pursuant to a corrupt agreement."

The judge went on to note a contradiction in Gorn's testimony. He hired Spector "on a contingent fee basis, contingent on his securing relief from the moratorium." However, Spector labeled his fee from Gorn as "an annual retainer."

The judge also noted testimony from another developer, Richard Davison, who went to see Spector because he believed that as a city councilman, Spector knew his way around the bureaucracy and could expedite the moratorium appeal so he could complete 204 apartments. Rome, the third developer, retained Spector with the same kind of contingency fee arrangement, paying the lawyer $2,500 after he received a hearing before the Board of Review and paying the remaining $2,500 only if the Board granted him relief.

"Rather promptly," noted the judge, "after his clients met with success and after he was paid the agreed fees, Judge Spector paid a portion of them to Mr. Wyatt and Mr. Wyatt in turn, and just as promptly, paid a portion of his portion over to Mr. Noren. It is of some significance, I think, that the amounts paid to Mr. Wyatt went into his personal account and from that account he paid Mr. Noren who deposited his portions in his personal account. I think that it is also of some significance that Judge Spector's files . . . contain no lawyer's work product done by him, nor any evidence of any work done for him by Mr. Wyatt.

"I think that I, like a jury, may use my common sense and experience in life in evaluating evidence and on that basis it is difficult for me to believe that persons dealing in commercial transactions, much less partners and friends, transfer substantial sums of money to each other without either explanation or inquiry. . . . It has been said as to circumstantial evidence that before a verdict of guilty is justified, the circumstances taken together must be inconsistent with . . . every reasonable hypothesis or theory of innocence."

Finally, the judge got to the point.

"I find here no reasonable hypothesis or theory of innocence when I consider the circumstances I have mentioned as well as others in evidence which I have considered, but may not have mentioned. In the light of all of the circumstances, taken together, I find in each case, beyond a reasonable doubt, that the moneys which passed from Judge Spector through Mr. Wyatt to Mr. Noren were made pursuant to a corrupt agreement or agreements and constituted bribes offered and accepted."

When he was finished city councilwoman Rikki Spector leaned forward and put her hand on her husband's shoulder. A detective with the state's attorney's office slid across the bench next to me and whispered in my ear.

"Jim, is there any way you can avoid arresting them," he said. Apparently, someone in authority—I had no idea who—had sent him to make sure they weren't taken in a paddy wagon to be fingerprinted, booked and put in a holding cell. It would particularly look bad to see a sitting judge led away in handcuffs.

"We're not here to embarrass anyone," I told him. "We're going to issue criminal summonses to their attorneys, so they can appear later for sentencing." The men promptly left the courthouse with their lawyers and families. As Councilwoman Spector walked past me, she turned and pretended to spit on me.

After the verdict I gathered with the rest of the staff and we happily walked the two blocks back to the office. When we arrived, we found crepe-paper streamers hanging from the door. The secretaries pulled out two bottles of champagne. We all went to the conference room to celebrate. Jerry Glass thanked everyone for all our long hours of work.

"Cherish this moment," he told us. We all knew what he meant. We had no idea what cases would come next—or whether we would be so successful in the future.

The defendants appealed their convictions to the state's highest court, the Court of Appeals, which upheld their convictions. I felt very strongly that all three men should go to prison. In reality, though, they had no prior criminal records and were not violent offenders. There was also no expectation that they would repeat their crimes.

They were each given a two-year suspended sentence, two years' probation and fined $15,000.

The far worse punishment they faced was the loss of their livelihoods. Spector, the first judge in anyone's memory to be convicted of a crime while on the bench, resigned before the governor could fire him. He, Noren and Wyatt were disbarred from practicing law in the state of Maryland.

34
A MEANS TO AN END: THE TOOLS OF INVESTIGATING POLITICAL CORRUPTION

Years ago, during a long stationary surveillance of drug dealers inside a vacant storefront, I observed a spider weaving a web. As I watched for more than an hour, with a street light shining on it, I learned that it was not possible for the spider to jump onto one thread without disrupting the rest of the web. It is the same with criminal investigations. Each step must be carefully planned and executed, to make sure not to disrupt evidence to be gathered. I would not want to interview an elected official I suspected of robbing his campaign coffers, for example, without first tracing suspicious transfers from his campaign bank account or obtaining cell phone records to figure out who he was talking to.

The mission of the OSP, as we call the Maryland Office of the State Prosecutor, is to investigate four crimes: bribery, misconduct in office, election law violations and ethics in government violations. The state prosecutor can also charge people with perjury, obstruction of justice, or extortion if those crimes are discovered during the course of an investigation. At the request of a state's attorney we can also investigate multijurisdictional street crimes, such as an auto theft ring.

In regard to public officials, there are three types of criminal misconduct:

1. Nonfeasance: The accused is a public official and not just a public employee. A public official is someone who has taken an oath of office, serves in a position with term limits, or who exercises sovereignty, or power, of the state.

To prove nonfeasance, you must show that the public official failed to carry out his duty under the color of office because of a corrupt motive, which can range from personal benefits to a wish to harm someone. Say you have a liquor board commissioner with a secret financial interest in a bar that is selling alcohol to minors. When the case comes before the liquor board, the commissioner fails to disclose his ownership and minimizes the violation to protect his interests.

2. Malfeasance: The accused is charged with a common crime while on duty as a public official. For instance, a police officer responds to an alarm at a jewelry store. While investigating the break-in, he steals diamonds. He can be charged with criminal misconduct as well as theft.

3. Misfeasance: A public official wrongfully performs his duty due to a corrupt motive. For instance, a police officer gives a speeding ticket to a driver who was not speeding; the driver turns out to be dating the police

officer's girlfriend, proving a corrupt motive.

Complaints about alleged crimes come to the OSP from many sources. Over the years I took hundreds of calls from strangers alleging crimes that included bribery, theft, obstruction of justice and perjury. I also got tips through news reporters, law enforcement colleagues, businesspeople, elected officials and from a large pool of informants I gathered over decades in law enforcement.

Some were extremely polite and helpful. Others were rude, hostile, or even paranoid. No matter how the caller behaved, I had to remain unbiased and fair.

Every now and then a caller would be so abusive, I would politely hang up. One time an angry complainant called back and told me to "Eat a bag of dick."

"Thank you very little," I said before I hung up again.

Once our office receives a credible tip or complaint, we have many investigative tools at our disposal. Here are a few examples of how we used a few of these tools:

Getting an informant to wear a wire

Bribery case against state police officer Leo J. Konopacki Jr. Early in my career I got a call from a former prosecutor I knew, who was then in private practice. He was representing Charlie Taber, who owned an auto repair business in West Baltimore that inspected vehicles for the state. Taber told him that state police officer Leo J. Konopacki Jr. had demanded bribes after learning Taber's log books showed phony inspections. If Taber didn't pay the officer, he would report the auto repair owner for his wrongful conduct and shut him down. We got Taber to wear a wire and heard the officer demanding the bribes. Konopacki, a 17-year police veteran, pleaded guilty and spent 90 days in federal prison.

Scrutinizing campaign finance reports for violations

Violations of campaign finance laws can range from theft of funds to receiving donations that exceed the legal limit to making illegal loans from one campaign to another. Here are a few examples:

State delegate Nathaniel Oaks. In November 1987 The Evening Sun reported that state delegate Nathaniel Oaks billed his campaign for out-of-state traveling expenses, then turned around and charged the state government for the identical expenses. The article cited 11 examples of the double-dipping scheme totaling more than $5,500. The reporter, Dan

Fesperman, scrutinized Oaks's campaign reports, then reviewed state reimbursement records for members of the General Assembly. The next day, my boss, state prosecutor Steve Montanarelli, began an investigation, finding that Oaks stole more than $10,000 from his campaign funds.

In November 1988 Oaks was convicted of stealing the campaign funds, perjury and misconduct in office. He was given a five-year suspended sentence, three years' probation and ordered to perform 500 hours of community service. He also had to pay a $1,000 fine and resign from office. However, he won back his seat in the House of Delegates in 1994. In 2017 he replaced a state senator who resigned. After a long FBI investigation he was indicted again on charges of bribery and wire fraud involving payoffs he took from a businessperson cooperating with the FBI. He was also charged with obstruction of justice for reneging on an agreement to become an FBI informant. After pleading guilty and resigning from the state legislature—yet again—Oaks was sentenced to 3 ½ years in federal prison in 2018, fined $30,000 and given three years' probation. At his sentencing, a federal prosecutor called him "profoundly corrupt."

Mayoral campaign of Catherine Pugh, elected Baltimore mayor in 2016: During a hotly contested Baltimore mayoral primary I got a call from a source who asked, "Have you looked at Pugh's campaign reports?" He was referring to the mayoral campaign of state senator Catherine Pugh. I said, "No, should I?" He told me it appeared that the reports showed more money than the campaign actually had. I ordered the reports and assigned two investigators to analyze them.

They discovered two problems. One involved suspicious donations of $18,000 involving a young aide to Pugh, who had worked in her state senate office and later in City Hall, after her election. The aide, Gary Brown Jr., had illegally funneled the funds (well above the $6,000 legal limit per contribution) through the bank accounts of his mother, stepfather and brother. After a thorough review of the campaign account my investigators interviewed his mother and stepfather, who admitted that the money donated under their names was not their own. They also said their son must have received the funds from someone else because he did not earn enough money to donate $18,000 to a political campaign. Brown was convicted of election law violations and received probation before judgment and one year of supervised probation. He continued his job working for the mayor.

We also discovered an illegal loan of $100,000 to the Pugh campaign from the political slate of James T. Smith, a politician from the separate jurisdiction of Baltimore County. Smith was a former Baltimore County executive and Circuit Court judge. Smith's campaign slate was fined $3,000 for the illegal loan, while Smith got a job as one of the new mayor's top aides.

Using a witness for live testimony

Bribery and conspiracy case against Baltimore's chief liquor inspector and a local bar owner: In the late 1990s Mike McDonough, a long time deputy state prosecutor with our office, contacted a potential witness in a case we were developing against the corrupt Baltimore City Liquor Board. The witness, Charlie Wilhelm, was already an FBI informant in several unrelated cases involving a crime ring he had operated out of the Hampden neighborhood and The Block. The ring sold drugs, ran an illegal lottery, and had a lucrative loan sharking business. Wilhelm was living in hiding in Alabama after testifying at a murder trial against his former partner, William Isaacs.

With the FBI's help, McDonough contacted Wilhelm to ask if he paid bribes to liquor inspectors. Wilhelm had managed a bar on the city's east side, where he bribed liquor inspectors to look the other way when he kept the bar open after mandated closing time. More important, Wilhelm told McDonough, he bribed the liquor inspectors to give him advance warning when the police were about to raid his bar to crack down on illegal video gambling machines. These machines were a big draw in bars all over Baltimore, where bartenders made illegal payouts to game winners. Unlike legal gambling, where the government gets its cut, the video gambling machines raked in tens of thousands of dollars each week in untaxed income for the bar and machine owners.

Wilhelm described the routine bribes he and another bar owner paid to inspectors, including the chief liquor inspector, Anthony Cianferano. Wilhelm also told McDonough about a close associate of Cianferano's, former state delegate Billy Madonna, whose political connections allowed him to recommend the appointment of liquor inspectors. I eventually met Wilhelm on one of his trips to Baltimore under FBI watch. He recognized me from The Block and we talked about all the people we knew in common.

Wilhelm was physically intimidating and had a reputation for threatening people with physical harm. But he also could be very personable. When it came time for the trial of Cianferano and Madonna in 1999, Wilhelm was one of several people who testified about the bribery scheme. He said he paid bribes to Cianferano and other inspectors. Unfortunately, the judge threw out the bribery charges, perhaps because she didn't believe the testimony of other witnesses. I felt Charlie's testimony was very credible.

197

The two men nevertheless pleaded guilty to conspiring to thwart the city's liquor laws. Both got probation, $1,000 fines, and were ordered to perform 300 hours of community service. The chief liquor inspector lost his job.

Interviewing a suspect to gain a confession

State delegate Sylvania Woods: In 1990 we got a tip that Sylvania Woods, a state delegate who headed the Prince George's County delegation, had misused his political office to sell phony cell phone contracts that allowed him to collect nearly $50,000 in fees and commission. He also raided his campaign funds for personal use. The General Assembly was in session when I went to Annapolis to visit him. As always, I prepared my questions beforehand, arranging them carefully to solicit the most truthful response. I went with a retired city police officer working with us, so he could take notes while I asked the questions. I knocked on Woods's door. We identified ourselves and I politely said, "We don't want to disrupt any legislative duties, but we have some questions."

When I conducted interviews of suspects I was always careful to wear a "white hat" so I never appeared to be confrontational. That would play poorly before a jury, which might think I was intimidating or threatening the suspect.

"There is an allegation you are misusing your office and doing it for personal benefit," I told him. I was careful not to use the word "corruption." It would scare the hell out of him.

"I haven't done anything wrong," he said.

"I'll tell you what we have," I responded.

I then laid out the evidence against him: he had used his state office letterhead to obtain fraudulent cell phone contracts in the names of numerous people, including several General Assembly colleagues, who never requested—or received—the phones. The scam earned him $46,000 in fees and commissions.

When I was finished he asked, "Is that a crime?"

I told him it was indeed a crime and asked for his explanation, which led to his confession.

Our investigation prompted Woods to resign from office before he was indicted. Several months later he pleaded guilty to felony theft and misconduct in office. Because he had already resigned from the legislature, a judge gave him five years' probation.

Using an undercover detective, stationary surveillance, recorded phone calls and search and seizure warrants

Bribery case of Prince George's County officials Robert L. Isom and Robert L. Thomas: In 2004, my boss, state prosecutor Robert Rohrbaugh, received a call from the chief legal advisor to Governor Robert Ehrlich, who said he had been contacted by a New Jersey businessman with a disturbing story about a contract to install security systems in Prince George's County government buildings. A Prince George's County official told the businessman he could guarantee an exclusive, $1 million contract in exchange for $250,000 in bribes.

We got the businessman to meet with the caller and his partner, and pay the first installment of that "bribe" (money we actually borrowed from the state police) at a meeting we set up under heavy police surveillance. We had business cards printed that showed John Poliks, a veteran police officer working in our office, was a partner of the New Jersey businessman. They met with the county officials at several restaurants, including Rip's Country Inn, a popular restaurant in Bowie. The businessman carried a leather portfolio with a wireless microphone that picked up the conversation about the bribery scheme. Subsequently we wrote several search and seizure warrants for the suspects' homes and offices and confiscated computers and government records.

Isom, deputy director of the county's Department of Environmental Resources, pleaded guilty to conspiracy to commit bribery in exchange for his testimony (and a reduced sentence) against Thomas, the county's deputy director for the Office of Central Services. Thomas was convicted of conspiring to commit bribery and sentenced to two-and-a-half years in state prison, five years of supervised probation, 500 hours of community service and $10,000 in restitution.

Use of media tip and search and seizure warrant

Illegal use of an anonymous robocalls designed to suppress the vote: On Election Day in 2010 I got a call from Jayne Miller, the veteran investigative reporter for WBAL-TV. She said, "Hey Jim, what are you guys doing about this robocall?" I said, "I don't know what robocall you're talking about." She then told me about a very peculiar and suspicious late afternoon prerecorded campaign call concerning the race for governor: incumbent Democrat Martin O'Malley was running against Republican Robert Ehrlich, who was attempting to regain his seat after losing it the previous election.

The call, to more than 100,000 voters in Democratic households in Baltimore City and Prince George's County—both with large African

American populations—told voters, "Governor O'Malley and President Obama [who was not on the ballot] have been successful. Our goals have been met. . . . Relax. Everything is fine. The only thing left to do is to watch it on TV tonight. Congratulations and thank you." The call went out two hours before the polls closed. Even more suspect was the fact that the call was anonymous. It omitted the required authorization line identifying the candidate that produced the call. The robocall was clearly a dirty political trick to get Democrats to stay away from the polls, so Ehrlich could gain ground from voters in more Republican areas of the state.

We soon learned that the call was produced by a company in Virginia hired by Julius Henson, a political campaign consultant working for the Ehrlich campaign. We obtained a search and seizure warrant for his home in East Baltimore. We sent out John Poliks, who took on many of my duties after I lost my sight. John searched the house and came up with a key piece of evidence: a campaign document called the "Schurick Doctrine" proposing to "promote confusion, emotionalism and frustration" among black voters, who were likely to vote for O'Malley. This was our first evidence of the involvement of Paul Schurick, Ehrlich's campaign manager.

Henson, a high-priced campaign consultant, was known for his aggressive and sometimes hostile demeanor. During Schurick's trial, my boss, Maryland prosecutor Emmet Davitt said, "It's not just a political dirty trick. In the state of Maryland it's against the law."

Schurick was convicted of conspiracy and election law violations. He was sentenced to 30 days on home detention, four years' probation and ordered to perform 500 hours of community service. Henson was convicted of conspiracy and was sentenced to one year in prison with all but 60 days suspended. He also got three years' probation and was ordered to perform 300 hours of community service. He was banned from working on a political campaign during his probation.

35
THE STATE OF GAMBLING: OPERATION QUARTERMATCH

Maryland is a gambling state. Our inhabitants have an alarming appetite for illegal wagering that is almost as insatiable as their hunger for steamed blue crabs from the Chesapeake Bay. From sports betting and street lotteries to poker card rooms and cock or dog fighting, Marylanders love to play the odds.

By 1984—long before casinos were legalized—one of the most popular and lucrative illegal gambling operations in the Baltimore region was called video poker. These games of chance were played on bulky machines found in hundreds of bars, liquor stores, laundromats and even bowling alleys. They were essentially slot machines without the slots to deliver winnings. Instead, a bartender or store clerk discreetly paid out a winner, hoping no vice cop was watching. The owners of the pokers, as they were nicknamed by local criminals, pretended they were as legal as candy or cigarette machines. The big difference was that the poker machines brought in tens of thousands of dollars each week, nearly all of it untaxed.

Not surprisingly, the people who owned the machines were very rich, even after splitting the proceeds with the bar owners. The illicit operations were worth the occasional bust (and a legal slap on the wrist) from local vice detectives; the bar owners knew they might very likely go out of business if not for the income from the machines. After all, there was a limit to the amount of beer a person could drink; there seemed to be no limit to the number of quarters a Maryland gambler could plunk into a poker.

In the summer of 1984, I got a call from an investigator at the Maryland State Police, who told me his agency had picked up intelligence claiming that a New Jersey mob family might be supplying video poker machines to Maryland's well-known vending companies. Whether or not the intelligence was true, I already knew from my police work that the video gambling business was so widespread that the vendors were stiffing the IRS out of income tax and the Maryland treasury out of millions in amusement taxes each year. I met with Gerry Ruter and our new boss, Steve Montanarelli, who had replaced Jerry Glass as the state prosecutor. Steve, a former Baltimore County deputy state's attorney, was (like Jerry Glass) a first rate prosecutor and I was honored to work for him. Steve was a tall, imposing lawyer whom I had met years before when he was prosecuting a Baltimore County man accused of stealing a lawn mower. The defendant was one of my best drug informants, providing high quality information that led to important drug arrests. I asked Steve to stet, or set aside, the case if my informant made restitution for the stolen lawn mower. Steve agreed.

I recommended that our office undertake a multi-jurisdiction investigation of tax fraud by numerous suspected video gambling machine companies which had hundreds of machines placed in bars and other businesses throughout the region. Our investigation would involve the Maryland State Police, as well as police departments for Baltimore City, Baltimore County and Anne Arundel County. Luckily, there was already a joint law enforcement association called CLEIG (Combined Law Enforcement Intelligence Group) made up of intelligence units from those agencies.

I had high hopes for the investigation. I believed that if we successfully prosecuted enough businesses, and if they received stiff fines, they would think twice about continuing their illegal enterprise. It could be the death knell of the video poker industry, although the Baltimore County vice detectives doubted the enterprise could ever be stopped by pure enforcement. This would also be the most complex investigation to date for me and for the state prosecutor's office.

Among all the capable detectives and supervisors who would work on the case there was one particularly tenacious Baltimore County vice detective named Doug Dunlap, who had an uncanny resemblance to the actor Robert Duvall. Dunlap had been investigating illegal gambling for years. When we met with Gerry Ruter, we explained how the video poker business worked, including the intricate relationship between the machine owners and bar owners. He was quite surprised that machine owners actually pay a few thousand dollars to the bar owners to place the machines in their establishments. Each machine had an electric counter that tracked the number of quarters placed into the machine. It also had a knock-off switch to reset the machine.

We all agreed to target the big vendors who owned and distributed the poker machines, rather than the small businesses that housed them. Gerry Ruter pointed out that a jury might be sympathetic to a small bar owner, but not so forgiving to a wealthy vending machine company owner who doesn't believe in paying taxes.

Our investigation was shaping up to be the largest state investigation of illegal gambling in anyone's memory; we would need more than a dozen undercover police detectives and a robust surveillance effort, not to mention voluminous search warrants. We dubbed our investigation "Operation Quartermatch," because quarters were used by the gamblers and winners got their illegal payouts only after they accumulated enough points for a cash payout.

I found it interesting that the police chiefs expressed logistical concerns about our plan to seize more than 200 machines. Since each weighed hundreds of pounds, the commissioners wanted to know how we would transport and store them. The Baltimore County vice unit found an aging, vacant house to store the machines they expected to seize from their jurisdiction. A county engineer inspected the structure to make sure it could hold the weight. Thankfully, the building passed inspection. Similar arrangements were made for storage in other jurisdictions.

Our next step was establishing legal proof that the dozen companies we were investigating were indeed the ones that supplied hundreds of the machines to local businesses. For this undercover job I called on my mentor, Eddie Crowder, from my early days on the police force. Along with his partner Lorenzo Gray (who was later murdered in the line of duty) Crowder had taught me how to conduct drug investigations and to "always protect your next step," a lesson I never forgot.

I instructed him to wear a suit and tie to take on the persona of a computer salesman.

Eddie was a gregarious man, so pretending to be an outgoing salesman would come easily to him. I also reasoned that since Eddie was African American and the people working at the vending companies were white, they would feel uncomfortable brushing him off before first hearing his sales pitch because that might make them appear racist. I figured no one could turn away Eddie and his contagious smile. We gave him fake business cards identifying him as a sales representative for a company that sold IBM computers and sent him to visit a half dozen vending companies. At each location Eddie asked to speak to someone in the company who could talk about the computers they used. I was right; no one turned Eddie away.

Once he got into a conversation he was able to learn what type of business they ran and enough detail about their computerized financial records to prove that they did indeed supply the illegal poker machines.

We then decided to conduct surveillance of the vending companies' "route" men. These men were crucial to the operation because they traveled specific routes and emptied or "dumped" thousands of quarters out of the machines each week. They paid out the bar owners' share and took the rest back to the vending companies. A route man read the counter on every machine, checking that the number of quarters matched the counter to make sure the bar owner hadn't broken into the machine and stolen some of the profits.

First, we used mobile surveillance teams to follow the route men from the suspected vending companies to determine which bars they visited. We then stationed several plainclothes investigators at each bar, pretending to be regular patrons nursing a beer. We could not assign one investigator to show up at more than one bar because that might make the route man suspicious, so I assigned six different detectives to six different bars. This strategic tactic—one man, one bar—would also hopefully prevent any of our investigators from getting drunk, a slip up that a defense attorney would love to exploit. They were instructed to watch the route man at work and listen in on his conversations with bartenders or managers.

The surveillance went like clockwork (even though we found no evidence that the New Jersey mob was involved in the Maryland operation) and we gathered enough evidence to move forward with a request for search and seizure warrants.

Our next big hurdle involved making sure our investigation was completely safe from any leaks in the police departments to the targets of our inquiry. History had shown us that dirty cops are all too willing to accept bribes from gambling operators in advance of vice raids or arrests. I had sadly learned that lesson in the 1970s when several Western District officers and commanders (including one of my police cadet teachers) were convicted of taking weekly bribes from illegal lottery operators.

Out of an abundance of caution, I discussed with the other investigators which judge we could trust to handle the documents requesting search and seizure warrants. Since the District Court is a statewide system, we could pick just one District Court Judge in any of our jurisdictions to consider all our requests. Detective Dunlap recommended Baltimore County District Court Judge Patricia Graham because she was the newest judge to the bench, so new that she might be the least likely judge to be influenced in any way that might compromise her judgment.

After Judge Graham agreed to Detective Dunlap's request to review what he described as a very sensitive and confidential warrant, she visited the county's vice unit in a safe house in Towson. At Detective Dunlap's request, she was given a crash course on video gambling by FBI supervisory special agent Bill Holmes, the leading authority on the topic. By the time Holmes finished his lecture, which we dubbed "video gambling 101," (including a demonstration on a previously confiscated machine) the judge had a good working knowledge of the business.

Detective Dunlap then arranged for the investigators to visit with the judge at her home, rather than her court chambers, to review the lengthy application for search and seizure warrants. When Judge Graham was satisfied that there was sufficient probable cause to authorize the warrants, we began to mobilize.

We planned March 7, 1985, as our "raid day." I was excited about the success so far of our investigation and I hoped nothing would go wrong with the machines we confiscated.

Detective Dunlap and his partner James McConville got approval to use a large copy machine, fondly known as "Big Bertha," in Baltimore County's police headquarters. The investigators brought in five boxes of copy paper for the photocopying extravaganza; they needed to make enough copies to hand to every person at a raid site. We had 84 search warrants, each about 150 pages long, and we needed to make three copies of each document. The team had a long night ahead of them with Big Bertha, which overheated several times. The warrants were so thick that detectives had to drill holes and add screws to hold them together. Judge Graham later arrived at the safe house to sign them.

When the day of the raid arrived, I could not have been more thrilled. In my career, raid day has always been one of my favorite moments of an investigation. I was in the OSP office (which had moved from Baltimore to an office building in Towson) monitoring the events. I was surprised by a visit from my police supervisor from downtown, Maj. Bert Shirey, the director of intelligence. I assumed he would stay downtown in police headquarters to monitor the raids, but he apparently wanted a closer look. I think he may have worried that the evidence—those very heavy machines—might be damaged in transit, marring our investigation.

That day, we quietly rented several Ryder trucks to haul the machines away. Since we needed to employ about 100 uniformed officers to issue the warrants, we told them to come to a staging area to prepare for a visit by President Ronald Reagan, who was actually nowhere near the Baltimore area. Once the uniformed officers had gathered, their names and badge numbers were recorded; they were told they could not leave or use any telephones. Then they were told the real reason for their assignment.

Within an hour, all the raid teams arrived in 84 locations without a hitch. The officers seized 300 machines and thousands of documents confirming the generated revenue.

I was so pleased the raids were going well. But several hours into the operation, I got a phone call. It was Dee, crying so hysterically I could not understand what she was trying to say. Whatever she was telling me, I knew it had to be bad. "Please calm down so I can understand what you're saying," I told her.

She told me that James had passed out while sitting at his desk at Hazelwood Elementary School. He was taken by ambulance to Franklin

Square Hospital. I went into a panic. I told Maj. Shirey, "My son's in the emergency room. I have to go." The major said, "Family first. Please call when you know more." As I drove to the hospital, I screamed, "God, you owe me one. Please help James. I love him so very much." When I arrived I was greatly relieved to find James awake.

"Little mouse, how are you feeling?" I asked.

"Pop, I'm not sure," he said.

I came to the side of his bed and gave his hand a squeeze.

"The doctors will find out what happened and make you well again."

I stayed a while, kissed him on the forehead and promised I would be back soon.

"OK Pop," he said with a smile. After he fell asleep Dee asked, "When will you be back?"

"As soon as I can," I said.

It turned out that James had passed out into a diabetic coma and was diagnosed with juvenile diabetes.

By the time I returned to the office, Operation Quartermatch was just about complete.

Auditors from the state comptroller's office were recruited to review the financial documents seized and to calculate the money found in the machines. They determined that each machine generated between $500 to $1,000 per week, or $26,000 to $52,000 a year. The amusement taxes collected from those machines were based on only a tiny fraction of the true income, so the state was losing out on millions of dollars each year. Gerry Ruter filed gambling fraud charges against 12 companies and their owners. All were found guilty and fined $3.7 million.

I honestly thought the convictions would become a major deterrent and diminish the number of pokers, but I underestimated the thirst of Baltimore gamblers and the businesses that fed off them.

A year after our raid, I got a call from John Gavrilis, a lieutenant in the Southeastern Police District. He asked me to speak with a young police officer named Timothy Godwin who reported that the owner of a bar in East Baltimore had offered him a bribe. I spoke to the officer, an honest young man, who told me this story:

Officer Godwin answered a call from Robert Bricker, the owner of the Ponca Bird Inn, a clean, nicely decorated restaurant-bar in a working class neighborhood. When he arrived, the officer saw ten video poker machines. Bricker asked for the officer's help with a bar employee he suspected of stealing quarters from the machines. I had to wrap my head around this bit of information for a minute: the bar owner was asking the police to stop an employee from stealing money from an illegal operation. Bricker also complained to the officer that his establishment had recently been raided by vice cops and hinted that he could use the officer's help in preventing more raids. He then offered a bribe, which the officer refused.

Undeterred, Bricker dropped the crumpled bills into the back seat of the police cruiser as Officer Godwin was about to drive away. I was quite familiar with Bricker and the Ponca Bird Inn; I had passed along information that led to the vice raids, which netted $24,000 in cash from the machines. After my conversation with Officer Godwin, Charlie Walas and I followed up on the attempted bribe by going undercover to the bar, where we ordered burgers (which were excellent) and watched the bartender making payouts to the gamblers. I then arranged for a sting operation with another officer wearing a hidden recorder. Bricker was recorded admitting he tried to bribe the officer. The bar was subsequently raided and another $52,000 was seized. Bricker was convicted and sentenced to 18 months, with all but 60 days suspended. I received a Meritorious Conduct Award from the police department for my work on the case.

Despite our best efforts with Operation Quartermatch and raids at businesses like the Ponca Bird Inn, the illegal video gambling industry lived on for years in Baltimore City and Baltimore County (though it was banned in other suburban counties). In fact, it grew exponentially after Quartermatch despite a Maryland Court of Appeals ruling that the machines were illegal gambling devices. To make matters worse, there seemed to be no political will by the state legislature to acknowledge the machines were illegal and to ban them statewide. For all our hard work, the proliferation of pokers was like a metastatic tumor that spread despite every known medical intervention.

The machines even continued attracting gamblers after casino slots were legalized in Maryland in 2008. Today, I suspect many gamblers don't want to leave their provincial comfort zones to pay for parking at a glitzy casino. They would rather continue their old habits at neighborhood bars, where the pokers now take $20 bills, instead of quarters.

36
A TIME OF SETBACKS

Over the next couple years, I oversaw several investigations of public corruption while splitting my time as a detective for the police department, where I investigated drug dealers selling heroin and crystal meth, as well as adult book stores selling pornography. My career was thriving. My early job evaluations from Jerry Glass at OSP to my police supervisors could not have been more complimentary: "I believe that the greatest achievements of this office have been a direct result of Detective Sergeant Cabezas's assignment here. . . . The organizational and leadership ability possessed by Detective Sergeant Cabezas enables this office to be very effective in the detection, investigation and subsequent prosecution of complicated and sophisticated criminal schemes. The high respect in which Detective Sergeant Cabezas is held by other state and federal law enforcement agencies causes this office to benefit."

But he could not help noticing the toll my hard work took on my family:

"I continue to believe that Detective Sergeant Cabezas goes above and beyond the limits expected of him, many times to great personal hardship to himself and his family, to initiate and complete investigations..."

How right he was. Dee, understandably, felt she was not getting enough of my time. Unfortunately, she responded by drinking and smoking heavily. She would sometimes come home drunk, wake me up and begin to argue. Once I realized that Diana, Joe and James had taken notice, I suggested we seek marriage counseling. We attended counseling twice a week for three months, but she kept drinking. More than once she asked me to cut back my work hours, but I refused: "I wish I could, but in order for me to do my job properly I can't spend less time working." It was like I had two jobs, one at the state prosecutor's office and one at the police department where I supervised six detectives.

In response to our family turmoil, Joe—who was seventeen at the time—surprised us by deciding to join the Navy.

"Are you sure?" I asked. "You're a starter on Poly's football team and you have good grades. So what's up with wanting to join the Navy?"

He said he wanted to go to sea and learn how to work on nuclear weapons. He also could get his GED while in the Navy. Since he was not eighteen he needed an approval letter from Dee and me. Though I suspected he really wanted to get away from our unstable home life, I did not voice my suspicions. We indeed were a dysfunctional family. In the end, Dee and I met with the recruiter and signed the authorization letter. Diana had more serious problems. One day she came home from school to tell her mother that she was pregnant.

"Oh my God who is the father?" asked Dee.

"Mom I don't know if the baby will be white or black." She dropped this bomb without showing any emotion, then left the house.

As it turned out, she was not pregnant, but made up the story to hurt her mother.

On three occasions, Dee and I returned from dinner to find that Diana had rearranged all of the living and dining room furniture.

One spring evening, I was sitting on the porch when I noticed a new yellow Corvette circling the block. On the third go around, the driver stopped, got out and began walking up the steps.

"How are you sir?" he politely asked me.

"Let me ask you one question before I tell you how I'm doing," I answered. "Why are you here?"

"I have a date with Diana," he answered.

"How did you two meet?" I asked.

"At the Red Rooster Inn," he replied, naming a bar where Diana should have been barred for being too young to drink.

"Oh, and who do you think I am to Diana?" I asked.

"Well, I have no idea," he answered.

"I am her father and she is only 17 years old. And by the way, I'm also a cop," I said.

He immediately walked down the steps, got into his Vette and drove away. Just then, Diana yelled from her bedroom, "Dad is my ride here?"

"He just left," I told her. "And I want your fake ID you use to get served."

In a confidential discussion with Joe, I learned that Diana was frequently skipping school to drink beer and had a reputation for being promiscuous. I sought legal advice and prepared a petition seeking the court's help in getting Diana placed in an institution for troubled adolescents. During her six-month stay, she met with counselors and participated in group sessions. The counselors told us that Diana believed her mother had abandoned her when she married me, even though I adopted her and her brother. Instead of gaining a father, she believed she had lost her mother. Four months later, Diana was with child; she moved to New York State where her fiancé was stationed in the military.

At the same time my family was falling apart, my eyesight was quickly deteriorating.

I had glaucoma in both eyes that made my sight cloudy and blurred. While a person without glaucoma has eye pressure measured between 10 and 18, mine was 32, a dangerous level. At nighttime when it rained, every street light bounced around my field of vision surrounded by halos. When I saw an oncoming car, its lights would blind me for three seconds. No matter what prescription eyeglasses I wore, they did not help on a rainy night. Often I pulled over and waited for the rain to stop.

In 1984 I was still seeing Dr. Scholz. He had been my doctor since I was a trusting boy with two loving parents and a bright future. I was now 34 years old, an orphan in a troubled marriage with three children. And I was going blind.

As I've written, Dr. Scholz tried every technique he could think of to keep my sight intact and to lubricate my painfully dry eyes. In addition to my impaired vision, I had no working tear ducts, since they were burned by the Stevens-Johnson Syndrome. Dr. Scholz had prescribed several types of eye drops and even experimented with contact lenses to keep my eyes lubricated for nearly three decades. I had so much faith in him that when he suggested I participate in a clinical test with a new eye ointment that might improve my dry eye syndrome, I agreed without hesitation. The test was conducted by an ophthalmologist named Scheffer C.G. Tseng, who was doing post-graduate research at the Wilmer Eye Institute at Johns Hopkins Hospital.

On the day of my first appointment I walked into Hopkins Hospital's Wolfe Street entrance and headed to the basement where Dr. Tseng had a work area. He had no receptionist, or even a waiting room. I found the hallway outside his office lined with about 15 folding chairs set out for patients, though I was the only one there. I knocked on his door and announced myself. He said, "I'll be right with you." An hour went by, maybe 90 minutes. Finally he opened his door and invited me inside. He conducted a very thorough examination of both eyes. He was quiet and professional and told me he was very close to discovering an eye ointment that could be a miracle cure for dry eye. It could change my life. The ointment was made with a Vitamin A concentrate. I thought if he was right it could indeed change my future. He gave me the ointment in a little silver tube with a black top and told me to apply the ointment to my eyes twice a day.

I visited his office every week for about four months, juggling it with my duties overseeing Operation Quartermatch, as well as my police work. While I waited to see Dr. Tseng, I never saw another patient, either on the folding chairs in the hall or in his office, but he still kept me waiting for about 90 minutes on each visit. I was using up all my medical leave from the police department and paying to park outside the hospital.

Worse, the treatment did nothing to alleviate my symptoms or reverse the damage of dry eye. The tests Dr. Tseng performed to gauge improvement in my eyes actually made them temporarily worse. He conducted what was called the Schirmer's test by placing a small strip of orange-colored paper the size of a matchstick deep between my eye ball and eye lids to see if the gland produced sufficient tears to maintain proper eye fluid. I could see that the paper was still dry when he removed it. The test irritated my eyes and made them very bloodshot; it was hard to see. I told Dr. Tseng I was worried I could not see well enough to drive, but he assured me my sight would get better. This went on for four months, until he moved to Harvard University, where he continued treating 300 patients as part of his study

After Dr. Tseng left for Harvard, my vision worsened.

The police department's chief physician reported the vision in my left eye was 20/200. That meant that from 20 feet away I could only see what someone with normal vision could see from 200 feet away. In my right eye I had 20/70 vision.

I was about to take the exam to become a lieutenant and I knew my deteriorated eyesight would become an issue. The department's chief physician wrote, "I do not feel this gentleman is qualified for promotion with his current vision."

Maj. Bert Shirey ordered me not to drive a police car until my eye problems could be corrected with new glasses or some other remedy. Aside from the problems with my eyesight, he wrote in a memo to the personnel department that, "Sergeant Cabezas is one of the most productive and efficient employees."

I am embarrassed now to admit that I prepared for the eye exam required of lieutenant candidates by cheating. I memorized about a dozen lines of the eye chart until I could recite them forwards and backwards. It took hours of practice, but I passed. I knew it was morally wrong but I was eager to be promoted up the chain of command in the department where I had spent my whole career, not just for the increase in salary, but for the chance to oversee major criminal investigations. My cheating on the vision exam created a huge conflict with my conscience. On bended knee I prayed that God would send some sign of direction and guidance. None came. Luckily, I knew that if my eyesight was too poor to drive, I had the authority to order subordinates to drive me wherever I needed to go.

At some later date I would need to update my skills at the firing range. There certainly was no way to cheat on that test, but I decided that was a hurdle for another day.

37
THE DIRTY BASTARDS

For years, as part of my police work, I stayed in touch with people I knew from my covert years on The Block. After I resurfaced, the revelation that I was a cop—not a cab driver—spread like wildfire. I used the news to my advantage as a detective and developed a few of the bartenders, sex workers and doormen as informants to keep me posted on loan sharking and gambling scams. They also acted as my eyes and ears on the Pagans, the outlaw motorcycle gang that supplied the majority of dancers and strippers to the bars. I found it interesting that the Pagans parked their motorcycles in a neat row facing the street, so they could make a quick getaway, though not before a police officer could jot down the numbers on their license plates, all lined up at the curb.

One of my informants was Dave Dykes, a bartender at the Block Show Bar. He was the lovable loser who always bet on the slowest horses at the track and had a corny sense of humor. His real name was Dave Shiner. He once gave me information that led to the arrest of two child molesters. Another informant was a bartender at the Great White Way named John Riley, a big man with sandy-colored hair, who also told bad jokes and liked to sing the song, "Just a Gigolo." They would page me with the numbers 411 when they had information for me. Their motives for helping me were hardly altruistic. I knew they both wanted to have an "ace in the hole" in case they were ever arrested. Being an informant might get them off the hook.

In April 1984 I was listening to the radio when the announcer reported a terrible fire had been deliberately set on The Block. A witness had seen a man stuff a plastic bag filled with a liquid through a broken window in the door of the 408 Club that led to four apartments upstairs. A blaze immediately broke out, engulfing the entire building. Five people were dead. One was Dave Dykes. Another was the beautiful dancer who went by the name Duchess. (Her brother was the Pagan who put a knife to my throat many years ago.) Duchess's real name was Gail Lyn Kamzura. She was 26. The only person to survive was John Riley, but he was badly burned and clinging to life at the burn unit at City Hospitals. He died 11 days later.

I know this sounds callous, but when I heard about Dave and John, my first thought was, "I just lost two informants."

A city man, Gordon Wiggs, was arrested for setting the fire. Prosecutors and police sought the death penalty. They said Wiggs lit a match to flammable liquid in the door leading to the apartments as revenge against Duchess, whom he considered his girlfriend. He was apparently jealous of her relationships with other men.

I followed the trial closely. I had been gone from The Block for eight years, but I still felt sympathetic to the people there, even if we were not kindred spirits.

Wiggs's trial included testimony from a peep show clerk who saw the defendant carrying a plastic bag and walking toward the 408 Club 15 minutes before the fire broke out just before 5:30 a.m. Another witness testified to hearing Wiggs exclaim that Duchess would soon learn what it felt like to be "Joan of Arc," referring to the martyr who was burned to death.

Wiggs's lawyers did their best to sow doubt among the jurors about his guilt and even insinuated, by describing the immoral behavior of people working on The Block, that the victims deserved what they got for their degenerate lifestyles. Apparently the jury agreed. Much to the shock of the prosecutor, Mark Cohen, Wiggs was acquitted. Mark later told me that some of the jurors thought the victims were second-class citizens. I was frankly stunned by the verdict and sad that justice did not prevail. I was disgusted that the jury did not convict a man I believed to be a murderer, based on proof beyond a reasonable doubt.

At home, our family problems worsened. Not long after Diana moved away, I learned that Dee had been spending thousands of dollars on clothes, shoes, jewelry and bar bills that we could not afford. We were in debt to the tune of $17,000. I took a second job as a night security guard at the downtown Holiday Inn to pay her credit card bills. Not surprisingly we argued about her compulsive spending and I wondered how much longer I could stay married to her.

I heard Pop's voice asking me, "What about James?" He was only eight years old.

Pop's voice was not as reassuring as it was in the past. "You know what to do," said the voice. Well, I didn't.

It took a while for me to figure it out, on the night before I was scheduled to take the exam to become a lieutenant. I had studied for months from an administrative manual that was three inches thick, along with a big stack of training books.

I was asleep when Dee came home drunk. She woke me up and slapped me on the head. Without saying a word, I dressed and drove to the Holiday Inn where I knew I could get a free room because I worked there. I was finally able to get some sleep before the exam. Pop had been dead now for many years, but as always, he was right. I did know what to do.

Two days later, I had a long conversation with James. I explained that his mother and I would be separating. Frankly, I don't think the little boy understood. I promised that we would see each other every week, and we did. I moved in with my good friend Howard Glashoff. Joe was in the Navy, stationed in Philadelphia, but I felt bad about leaving James. It would take a year for the divorce to be final.

Despite the stress at home, I managed to score so high on the lieutenant's exam that I ranked number two on a list for promotion. At the same time I had the first in what would become many years of catastrophic eye problems. I was at home alone painting the porch and steps when suddenly I noticed a dark curtain moving from the inside of my left eye toward the outside, cutting off my vision. I knew that I had a true medical emergency that required immediate surgery. I was certain that the curtain that moved across my eye was a detached retina. I would go blind if it wasn't repaired. I called the office of Dr. Bert Glaser, whom I knew from Dr. Scholz to be one of the best retina specialists in Baltimore.

Dr. Glaser operated twice at Johns Hopkins Hospital, but the eye did not repair. After the second try, one of Dr. Glaser's associates came in to say, "The surgery has not been successful. We would like to try again." "No," I told him. "I can barely see out of the eye anyway, even before the retina detached, because of the cataracts."

I still had light coming into the eye, but I could not see images. Now I was down to one eye.

Meanwhile, the colonel of the Criminal Investigation Division offered me a position as one of three commanders of the homicide unit. The very same day, state prosecutor Steve Montanarelli offered me a permanent job as chief investigator. That meant I would no longer have to juggle my police duties with my political corruption investigations. I recognized my great luck in getting the full time job in the OSP office and quickly accepted Montanarelli's offer. I already understood the need to root out political corruption. And, finally, I would never again have to carry a gun.

I resigned from the BPD in August 1986 with genuine mixed emotions. Maj. Shirey kindly told me that I did not need to report for duty on my last day, but I needed quiet time sitting at my desk in the office of ISD one last time.

I arrived at the office at 5 a.m., knowing that I would be alone. I had turned in my keys the day before, but I had a spare set. When I opened the door, I decided to leave the lights off. I sat at my desk, reflecting on my 15 years on the police force. Despite my negative experiences with corrupt and racist cops, my unpleasant assignment spying on the striking officers, the painful isolation of my years as a deep covert, not to mention the department's failure to solve my father's murder, I also had a long list of good reasons why the department had treated me so very fairly.

For one, despite all my eye problems, which led to many days of medical leave, my supervisors were always supportive. They allowed me to have a second job at the Holiday Inn. They let me take home an unmarked police vehicle. I'd won many commendations for solving crimes and making arrests in dangerous situations. I remembered the officer who administered my very first vision test to become a police officer. Realizing my eyesight was far from perfect, he had asked how much I wanted to be a cop. When I answered "more than anything in the world," he hesitated for a moment, then told me I had passed. There was the very proud moment of giving the valedictorian speech at the police trainee graduation and that first midnight shift walking the foot post at North and Greenmount avenues in the bitter cold.

Pop had been so delighted that I was part of a community of law enforcement officers and making new friends in the department, especially those who were African American. Coming from another country, he understood the importance of knowing people from different races and circumstances. Despite my many sacrifices over the years, it certainly had been the right career for me.

When I joined the department, I assumed I would retire as a member of the force. But somewhere along the trail of life, I heard someone say, "When man plans, God laughs." Now that I was leaving, I believed I had worked each case to the fullest extent possible and that I never shirked a task. I knew all my police training had prepared me to become the Chief Investigator for the Office of the State Prosecutor. I left my old desk in police headquarters before anyone showed up for work. When I arrived at the OSP office, I tossed the spare keys in the trash.

A few years after my unfortunate experience at the Wilmer Eye Institute with Dr. Tseng, I was reading my morning paper, *The Sun*, as usual at my kitchen table.

I wore heavy coke bottle glasses so I could see out of my right eye. I also held a large magnifying glass over the newspaper.

Out of habit I always scanned the paper for any medical news involving the treatment of eye problems. On page seven I stopped and placed my magnifying glass over the headline: "Hopkins probing research; Questions raised over eye salve work."

The article, by the *Sun*'s medical reporter, Patricia Meisol, began:

"The Johns Hopkins University is conducting an inquiry into whether university rules on scientific research were violated by a former researcher who allegedly made a personal fortune on an eye ointment that has proved largely ineffective."

Before I read any further I knew who the writer was talking about. My heart raced as I read on. "The University said it would look into the propriety of clinical tests on an experimental drug for 'dry eye' conducted at its Wilmer Eye Institute by former postgraduate researcher Scheffer C.G. Tseng, who subsequently formed a business to sell the product."

I banged the table with my fist when I read his name. I instantly felt abused. I thought, "Now I get what people mean when they say 'there ought to be a law.'"

This was the very first news I'd heard about Dr. Tseng's private company formed with his boss, Dr. A. Edward Maumenee, director emeritus of the Wilmer Eye Institute and one of the world's leading ophthalmologists. A Harvard ophthalmologist would also join the business, called Spectra Pharmaceuticals. Based on the promise of the eye ointment, the doctors stood to make good money. In those days, medical ethics standards weren't as strict as they are now, so the doctors went ahead and sold millions of dollars in stock and paid themselves hundreds of thousands of dollars based on their claims that the eye ointment did wonders for patients' eyes.

I could only imagine what Dr. Scholz must have thought, having sent me to Dr. Tseng, assuming I would be in good hands.

In reading subsequent articles in *The Sun*, I learned that I was one of 22 original patients in Dr. Tseng's study at Hopkins back in 1984. I was frankly surprised to hear there were as many as 22 patients, since I never saw any of the others when I went for my weekly visits over four months.

What really got me angry was news I heard later that the "success" of the eye ointment was reported in the scientific journal *Ophthalmology* in 1985. It made this false statement: "After treatment, all patients demonstrated clinical improvements in symptoms [and] visual acuity," based on various eye tests including the Schirmer's test that I found so painful. The study concluded, "Most importantly, this topical vitamin A treatment caused the reversal of squamous metaplasia as evidenced by impression cytology," meaning that it reversed the painful dry eye syndrome. "Therefore, this treatment may represent the first nonsurgical attempt to treat these disorders." Well, that was a lie. I knew that since I was one of the original 22 patients. The article's statement that all patients saw improvement could not possibly be true.

I later learned that the medical ethics scandal involving the for-profit company selling stock based on faulty medical data was reported in newspapers throughout the country. They noted that Dr. Tseng and his family made $1 million based on the phony promise of the eye ointment. Harvard, as well as Hopkins, conducted their own ethics investigations, but Tseng never lost his medical license.

Another *Sun* article noted that investigators at Hopkins were asking,

"Where are the 22 patients?" Apparently they never were able to find all of Dr. Tseng's research records. I am honestly skeptical that there were another 21 patients.

In fact, in all the articles written over the years about this medical ethics scandal I never found one that interviewed a single patient. Certainly no one ever contacted me about my experience. For all I know, my account here is the first to record a patient's experience with the failed experiment of the vitamin A ointment.

While preparing to write this memoir, I requested my medical records from the Wilmer Eye Institute from those months of treatment. I was told they had no such records. When I got that news, my anger from more than 30 years ago resurfaced. I thought, "That dirty bastard."

38
SMALLTIMORE

Smalltimore is a nickname we use for Baltimore because people we meet seem to know somebody else we know, whether we're connected through the neighborhoods we grew up in, the schools we attended or the places where we work and worship. It's a big city that feels like a small town. For a criminal investigator gathering informants and sources, I couldn't be in a better place than Smalltimore. Over the decades I made a point of keeping in close contact with hundreds of people who might someday help me solve crimes, including a detective in another police department, a curious auditor in City Hall, and a bartender from The Block. They all knew somebody who knew somebody else who committed a serious crime.

If it wasn't for those Smalltimore connections, I might never have caught a city comptroller stealing thousands through a fictitious employee, a businessman stealing millions from city taxpayers through phony boiler repairs, or a suburban county executive committing misconduct in office for sending his police detail on political errands and guarding his county car while he had backseat sex.

As they say in *Law and Order*, "These are their stories":

Erwin Burtnick was not your typical bureaucrat. A long time city auditor, he had a strong sense of duty and more energy than most government workers I've known. A slim man, he was intense, inquisitive and talkative. And he was relentless in protecting the taxpayers' money from waste or fraud.

Erwin was never content just to sit at his City Hall desk. He would walk two blocks to police headquarters and appear on the sixth floor, telling property crimes investigators about the theft of tires or other items from the city shop that repaired government vehicles. When he finished with them, he would come upstairs to ISD on the eighth floor. We all knew Erwin. He would stand with his arms behind his back and look down at whatever reports I had on my desk. It took me a while to realize he could read upside down.

By 1992, Erwin had risen to the position of assistant comptroller. That year he got a new boss when former city council member Jacqueline McLean was elected comptroller, the third highest elected office in the city. Shortly after McLean took office, Erwin later told me, she shocked the staff by telling them that she had ordered the city curator to remove all portraits of previous comptrollers who were white men. Of course, that was all of them. McLean was the first woman and the first African American to be elected to the position. She then made an even more bizarre announcement:

she would not consider any applicant for a job in her office who did not have a vagina. About six months after she took office, McLean abolished Erwin's position and he lost his job after 26 years with the city.

Erwin sued the city and began to scrutinize McLean's hiring practices, looking for a pattern of sex and race discrimination against white men. He read the Board of Estimates' weekly agendas and noted that McLean had hired two contract employees, both women. He asked around about them. One was known to many people in City Hall. But the second woman was a mystery. Her name was Michele D. McCloud. No one he spoke with had seen her—or any of the news releases she was hired to write. When the board approved a pay increase for McCloud, Erwin became particularly suspicious. A contact in the finance department confirmed the phantom employee was in fact being paid.

At about the time Erwin was making inquiries about McLean's mystery employee, I got a tip about a questionable city lease of office space in a private building. The tipster was a real estate agent working in the city's real estate office, which came under the supervision of McLean. When I met the agent, he was playing the music from *Phantom of the Opera*, which my wife and I had just seen at the Morris Mechanic Theatre. We chatted about the musical before he told me that the city had recently approved a $1 million lease of space in a building in the classy Federal Hill neighborhood. McLean had rushed the lease through the Board of Estimates without telling its members—including the mayor—that she and her husband owned the building. The income from the lease was apparently intended to bail out her debt-ridden travel agency.

As part of our investigation of the lease deal, we invited Erwin to give us some background about McLean. We were surprised when he told us there was another matter we should investigate: a potentially fictitious employee McLean had on the city payroll.

We learned through subpoenas that City Hall paid McCloud with checks sent to a Northwest Baltimore beauty shop, Salon Me'Chelle, run by the comptroller's sister, Wyonna Fountain. Det. Sgt. Rick Barger and I visited the salon. I showed my identification and said, "Excuse me. We're here to chat with Jackie McLean's sister."

"Get the fuck out of my shop. You're trespassing," the sister told us. She was lucky she was not indicted for conspiracy for receiving the checks on behalf of the comptroller. We made every attempt to establish that McCloud was not actually a person. Barger spent 40 hours reviewing security video from Harbor Bank, hoping to find footage of McLean opening the account in the fictitious name, but he found nothing.

We subpoenaed records from the same bank, making sure to include a nondisclosure order that barred bank officials from revealing our investigation to McLean. I also called McLean in an attempt to interview her, but she refused to answer my questions.

Finally, we sought a search and seizure warrant for her office in City Hall. The judge who reviewed our affidavit was Gary Bass, a former prosecutor I worked with on drug cases when he worked for the Baltimore City state's attorney's office. Quite the speed reader, he raced through our affidavit and said, "This reads like a novel," then signed the warrant. I wanted to proceed as discreetly as possible. We certainly didn't want to bust down the comptroller's door in City Hall. I called George Balog, the city's longtime director of the Department of Public Works. I had known him for years. "We have a sensitive, confidential investigation going on," I told him. "We need a key to Jackie McClean's office."

He was glad to help, but didn't ask what we were doing. I don't think he wanted to know.

"You have my word," he said. "I won't tell a soul." Barger and I arrived at City Hall at 9 p.m. during the Christmas holiday, 1993. As we'd expected, it was a ghost town, except for the police officer guarding the front door, who was half asleep when we showed him our identification. He was stunned to see us and not sure if he should let us in, until Barger told him he was from ISD. We made our way to McLean's office on the second floor. I put the key in the lock and was relieved when the door opened.

We went through the outer office where thousands of Board of Estimates agendas and city contracts were stored, then headed inside the comptroller's rather grand private office, with its refurbished 19th-century windows and high ceiling. I looked out her window. Off to the right I could see the edge of the all-too-familiar red-light district at the corner of Holliday and Baltimore streets, the neon lights bouncing off the wet blacktop left from the day's snowfall. I took a split second to reflect. "I have come a long way," I thought.

We were looking for any paperwork that mentioned the name McCloud. We noticed right away that the place had been cleaned out. There were few files and no diplomas or pictures on the walls. Not even a coffee mug. We took an appointment book and five telephone message books that were inside a red attaché case marked "The Honorable Jacqueline McLean, City Comptroller."

We also found a pad of paper with one sentence written dozens of times in McLean's handwriting: "Teach my hands to walk against my adversaries." I found it very disturbing. Barger copied it down and later quoted it in a memo to Steve Montanarelli and the OSP staff. Before we were done, we made sure the office was in the same order that we found it. We locked the door behind us and were finished before midnight.

We should not have been surprised that McLean had cleaned out her office. The writing was on the wall for weeks leading up to our search. The Baltimore *Sun* was filled with articles by reporters JoAnna Daemmrich and Kim Clark about the comptroller's alleged misdeeds, including the building lease and the fictitious employee. It turned out that they too were speaking to the persistent Erwin Burtnick.

McLean was indicted on February 25, 1994.

The reporters wrote, "City Comptroller Jacqueline F. McLean, the financial guardian of Baltimore government, was indicted yesterday on charges of stealing thousands of dollars in public funds and steering a lucrative city lease to a family-owned building. A grand jury accused Mrs. McLean of felony theft and misconduct in office for allegedly authorizing $25,189 in payments to a fictitious consultant called Michele McCloud."

McLean lost her job as comptroller. Her trial was postponed as she fell into depression, attempted suicide and was hospitalized in a mental institution. When she finally came to court she appeared emotionally unstable and pleaded guilty. Steve Montanarelli asked the judge to send her to prison for six months, but she got probation instead. McLean repaid the money she stole. "I'm extremely ashamed of my actions," she said in court. "I cannot drive through the city of Baltimore without crying."

McLean died six years later at the age of 57.

After I resurfaced from my covert assignment on The Block, I made a point of going back to people I knew—bartenders, doormen, dancers—to reveal my true identity. I assured them that I had no police files on them, so they had no reason to believe I was after them for criminal activity. I gave out business cards and told them to write my work phone number down somewhere safe and destroy the card. I cultivated them as informants or sources who might report crimes that no one else in the police department or the OSP office knew about. I made a point of listening to their stories and treating them with respect. Then I waited patiently. I think this is one of the reasons for my success: I know how to make informants.

Two of the people I kept in touch with were a gregarious bartender and a quiet dancer whom I met on The Block in the 1980s when they were in their 20s. Most Block couples hop from one bed to the next, but this particular couple stayed together. They kept in touch with me, I believe, because they liked being treated with a kindness quite foreign in a red-light district. By 2004 they were living in a suburb south of the city and had a grown son. The bartender contacted me one day with a story about the possible theft of government funds.

"My son works for a boiler repair company," he said. "There is some sort of payoff scheme going on with Baltimore City government." Over the phone he didn't tell me which city agency might be involved, but when we met at a bar in Glen Burnie near his home he named the boiler company: All State Boiler, owned by Gilbert Sapperstein. The city employee involved in the scheme, he said, was Cecil Thrower, who worked in the Department of Public Works. The boiler company, his son told him, was billing Thrower's agency for repairs that were never made. If true, I knew that the boiler company would be paying kickbacks to Thrower to keep the scheme going.

"I don't have to talk to your son," I told him, "but I would appreciate it if you would talk to him and get as much information as possible." I didn't know if the son would feel comfortable talking to me. He could be a clam. I went back to the OSP office and began researching basic questions: Does someone named Cecil Thrower work at DPW? Yes. Is there a man named Gilbert Sapperstein who owns All State Boiler Services? Yes.

As our investigation continued, we discovered that the theft had been going on for six years. Thrower was a longtime city worker, responsible for overseeing repairs to two large steam boilers at the Back River Wastewater Treatment Plant. He was authorized to hire All State Boiler for "as-needed" repairs. A cynic would say that "as needed" referred to Sapperstein's company needing money for doing no work, while Thrower signed off on dubious invoices in exchange for "as-needed" kickbacks, or bribes.

We arrived at Sapperstein's business with a subpoena for his invoices and contracts, looking for evidence of bills going to DPW and payments coming back to the company. There were so many invoices and payments for repairs and parts, I could tell it was a scam. "How many pieces of equipment could they possibly need?" I wondered. The payments also came in chunks of $5,000, the maximum amount the city could pay out without getting approval from the Board of Estimates. It was very suspicious.

When it came time to subpoena the city for its records, we wanted to be as low key as possible. Instead of going directly to DPW, where employees might be hostile, we went to the city solicitor's office so the lawyers could quietly get the records for us.

By the time Thrower lost his job and pleaded guilty to bribery, he had paid Sapperstein's company almost $140,000 of taxpayers' money through inflated invoices and received between $1,500 and $2,000 in kickbacks.

As for Sapperstein, we discovered the $140,000 he stole from DPW was just the tip of the iceberg. Exposure of the first scam sparked several other investigations into similar thefts of millions from Baltimore City schools. School auditors found suspicious transactions between Sapperstein's company and a school employee named Rajiv Dixit, who oversaw repairs to school heating and plumbing. From there the case mushroomed with the aid of a U.S. postal inspector, the U.S. Attorney's Office, the city's audit department and numerous staff from our office working thousands of hours.

In the end the state won guilty pleas from seven people, including Dixit. His kickback schemes had hummed along for 12 years before we caught him. He so enriched himself that he was able to buy two gas stations. Dixit lost his job and pleaded guilty to bribery, theft, embezzlement, extortion and conspiracy. The government seized his gas stations. He repaid the school system a half million dollars he stole. He was sentenced to five years in prison. Sapperstein plead guilty to bribery and theft. Before he left the courtroom he wrote checks to the financially strapped school system for $3.5 million and $140,000 to DPW. He also gave $250,000 to the CollegeBound Foundation and paid the government $120,000 in fines.

We discovered that Dixit had kickback scams with nine other businesses, including one run by a father and son who pleaded guilty to conspiring to defraud the school system. When I heard the son's name, I shook my head in recognition: James Duklewski was one of my high school fraternity brothers in Sigma Kappa Phi. Again, Smalltimore.

How incredible that all these schemes to steal millions from the city were cooking under our noses for 12 years. All it took to uncover them was one conversation with a bartender from The Block who liked me because I treated him with respect.

39
DEPRAVITY IN OFFICE

By 2012 I had lost all my sight, but was still working as the OSP's chief investigator. One Sunday I got a call at home on my cellphone from a Maj. Ed Bergin in the Anne Arundel County Police Department. I didn't know Ed, but he got my name from a mutual friend and colleague, Hank Snow, a retired Anne Arundel County police detective. Yet another Smalltimore connection. I had worked with Hank at CLEIG (Combined Law Enforcement Intelligence Group) and knew him as an honest, straightforward, down to earth cop. I assumed Ed Bergin came from the same honorable police stock.

Bergin supervised the police officers forming the security detail protecting the Anne Arundel County executive, John Leopold. He said he had a very sensitive and serious matter he needed to discuss. "I feel absolutely duty bound to tell someone what I think are crimes being committed by Leopold," he told me.

Bergin went on to say that he had already approached his boss, the Anne Arundel County police chief, James Teare Sr., and told him of the alleged crimes. But the chief just brushed him off and made it clear he would do nothing because Leopold was his boss.

Bergin gave me a few details over the phone: his security staff had complained to him that Leopold was ordering them to conduct campaign activities, picking up contribution checks, posting Leopold campaign signs and driving the county executive to look for his opponent's signs, so Leopold could personally yank them out of the ground.

Although Bergin said he felt morally obligated to report what he believed were crimes, he also was very worried about keeping his job. I knew he was in a tough spot.

"I don't want my name thrown out there. I could get fired," he said. I tried to make him feel comfortable. "We at the state prosecutor's office are very familiar with these types of investigations and we know if we don't maintain the confidentiality of complainants, we might as well shut the doors."

The next morning I went into work and told my boss, Emmet Davitt, about the call and noted that I thought the accusation against Leopold would need our immediate attention. Davitt called in his deputy prosecutor, Mike McDonough, and they agreed Bergin should come into our office as soon as possible. The major arrived at 6:30 that evening.

He spent almost two hours giving us details of Leopold's misconduct. That was just barely enough time to scratch the surface. In addition to crossing the line between government and politics to use county police for campaign work, he told us that the county executive also ordered police officers to compile dossiers on his political enemies by illegally accessing a criminal database.

Then he told us that his police officers were being used to protect Leopold during his prolific sexual activities on county time. He ordered officers to guard his county car while he had dalliances in busy parking lots. Apparently his backseat assignations had been going on for some time: someone called 911 three years before to report naked people inside a Chevrolet parked outside Nordstrom. The license plate was a dead giveaway: "County Executive 1."

For the head of a county government with more than a half million people, Leopold seemed to have plenty time for sexual liaisons during work hours. And he was not a young man. He was in his late 60s. We also learned that he used his security detail to run interference between his live-in girlfriend and his mistress while he was in the hospital after surgery. Later, he ordered an officer and a female employee to unzip his pants in his executive office to empty his urinary catheter bag during the work day.

I thought, "Here is yet another example of a political leader abusing his authority for his personal benefit and that's a crime."

I also realized that Chief Teare was likely guilty of criminal misconduct for aiding Leopold in his crimes by refusing to intervene when his officers were ordered to do the executive's dirty work.

As always, we proceeded cautiously, so as not to disturb that precarious spider's web of investigation. We considered the very delicate issue of asking police officers to speak with us about criminal conduct involving their police chief and county executive. Bergin was nervous enough. I could only imagine how rank and file officers might feel.

Bergin suggested that one particular officer might speak with us in confidence to begin our investigation.

I discussed with Davitt and McDonough the investigative steps we should take to get the best evidence to get to the truth. We decided to subpoena several officers to testify before a grand jury. They would have to tell their supervisors that they had no choice but to answer our questions under oath. They could even make it appear as if they were testifying against their will. As always, we were protecting our next step.

A year after our investigation began, Leopold was indicted by the Anne Arundel County grand jury on four counts of misconduct in office and one count of misappropriation of county funds. Davitt told the media, "Public officials criminally abuse their public trust when they treat public resources as their personal property and public personnel as their personal servants. These abuses will not be tolerated."

Leopold's lawyer insinuated that his client was charged for political motives.

I told *The Sun* that nearly all the cases our office investigates are "complaint-driven."

"There has never been a prosecution from this office that was politically driven."

I did not attend the trial, since I was working on other investigations, but the salacious testimony was reminiscent of the 1974 trial of Baltimore County state's attorney Sam Green, which meticulously laid out his sexual encounters with nine female employees.

One *Sun* article about the Leopold trial described how police corporal Howard Brown drove Leopold every week to the parking lot at an Annapolis bowling alley to meet a county employee for a sexual encounter.

"Brown said he would drive Leopold to the meetings after lunch on Tuesdays," the *Sun* article said. "Brown said he would look inside the other cars parked in the lot to make sure that they were not occupied, and then position himself so that he could see anyone entering the lot.

He said Leopold would enter the employee's car for the meeting. After at least one such meeting, he said, Leopold described receiving "the best oral sex he'd ever had."

Brown also testified that Leopold "told him to watch a cash box at a political fundraiser, to plant campaign signs for him, and to compile a dossier on his 2010 challenger."

Then there was the embarrassing testimony about Leopold's catheter bag:

"Crying as she testified, a former scheduler for Anne Arundel County Executive John R. Leopold told a judge Friday that she emptied her boss's urinary catheter bag several times during the workday and went along with planting signs for his 2010 reelection campaign because she feared for her job. 'It was my experience that you don't tell him no because then he considered you unloyal,' said Patricia Medlin, a 15-year county employee. 'People lost their jobs. I've seen it.'"

The trial was a huge embarrassment for Leopold, but also a disgrace for Chief Teare.

Davitt told him he had to resign or face charges. We wanted to abate the situation as quickly as possible in the interest of justice. If we charged Teare, a very good police department would linger for months waiting for the outcome of a trial; that could damage recruitment efforts of new officers as well as everyday operations. Getting him to resign in disgrace was a more efficient way to exact justice.

Teare had already been denounced by the County Council with a vote of no confidence while local unions had asked him to resign. Davitt, my boss, made the announcement of the chief's retirement to make it clear he was leaving the job under pressure to avoid charges.

In January 2013 Leopold was found guilty of two counts of misconduct and suspended from office. He was sentenced to 30 days in jail, ordered to serve five years' probation and perform 400 hours of community service. He was fined $100,000.

In 2018, five years after serving his sentence, Leopold decided to get back into politics. He filed to run for the Maryland House of Delegates. "I have paid my dues," he said. "I have learned my lesson and moved on. I feel I have a responsibility to be ethically impeccable." He lost the Republican primary, placing last.

40
THE ART OF STEALING TRASH

Whether you're investigating a former state legislator for drug trafficking with the mob or a suburban county councilman for looting his campaign funds, sifting through their trash for evidence can be a very satisfying mission for an investigator. For me, it was especially exciting because it gave me the opportunity to find the one piece of evidence that would prove a case beyond a reasonable doubt.

Before the digital era, when so much evidence was on paper, a trash rip (also known as a trash run) was one of my favorite investigative tools, second only to a raid with a search and seizure warrant. I used to say, "Trash is my life." I was only half joking. When I lost my eyesight I was sad knowing I would never conduct another trash rip.

There truly is an art to stealing trash. You can't just take it. And you don't necessarily want to send a rookie. It takes a real pro. Evidence I found—an envelope from a briber's bank, or credit card receipts from a pornography business—led to coveted search warrants of suspects' homes and offices, which led to more evidence of a crime. Finding tangible evidence in trash also came in handy for bribery cases, since Maryland law requires independent evidence to corroborate testimony of someone involved in the conspiracy.

I always began by casing the neighborhood where the suspect lived so I could learn when neighbors put out their trash. Once the trash is placed on the public sidewalk, it is fair game for criminal investigators; the Supreme Court ruled in 1988 that trash is considered abandoned property. I began my trash rip dressed in dark clothing, in the dead of night, at 2 or 3 a.m., parking my car blocks away. I switched off the overhead light so no one would see me when I quietly opened the door. I walked to the trash can outside a suspect's house and took the bag to a street light so I could see the color. (I never used a flashlight, since it could draw attention.) Then I put it back in the can. I walked three or four blocks to find a trash bag of the same color and removed it from the neighbor's can. I returned to the suspect's can and switched the bags, walking back to my car as quietly as possible. I drove out of the neighborhood without turning on my headlights for 30 to 40 yards. Because of my diminished vision in my right eye (I was already blind in my left eye), I could only do this when the streets were dry. Rainy nights, with light bouncing off the wet pavement, wreaked havoc on my eyesight.

I never worried too much about my safety, since most of the white collar criminals I investigated lived in low-crime suburban communities like

Hunt Valley, Fallston and Annapolis.

But even though I was far from the dangerous neighborhoods that I policed as a young officer, I still had a lesson to learn about never being too cautious. Back in the mid-1980s I was stealing trash belonging to the disreputable George Santoni, a former member of the Maryland House of Delegates previously convicted of extorting kickbacks on city contracts. Now I was investigating him, along with the FBI, for racketeering and drug dealing with the New Jersey mob. I had been sifting through his trash twice a week for six months. The evidence was remarkable. I found credit card receipts showing he had a lucrative pornography business connected to the mafia. I also found paperwork for limited liability companies he owned that would be otherwise hard to trace. I knew the FBI was tapping his phone, but I did not know the FBI had occupied the house across the street from his Hunt Valley home so they could watch his comings and goings. One day I was talking to my good friend, FBI agent John O'Neill, who was overseeing the investigation. "You know, I just saved your ass," he said with a grin on his face.

"What do you mean?" I asked. FBI agents, he told me, had heard Santoni talking angrily on his wiretapped phone. "Some motherfucker's been stealing my trash," he said. The former member of the Maryland legislature then said he would fill a shotgun with rock salt and shoot the culprit in the ass. O'Neill and the other agents thought it was hilarious. Of course, I didn't find it very funny. John and I decided I would take Santoni's trash for just another two weeks so he would not become suspicious that the FBI might have heard his threat on a phone tap.

In 1987, after a two-year investigation, Santoni pleaded guilty to drug and racketeering charges and was sentenced to eight years in federal prison.

In 1989, Mike McDonough, the deputy state prosecutor, received a tip from a Maryland state trooper alleging that the International Harvester company had an inside track to sell trash trucks to the city. Our office began an investigation of a possible bribery scheme involving Floyd Dearborn, who supervised the city office that purchased trucks and other vehicles. We found evidence that Dearborn was tailoring specifications for new trucks that perfectly matched equipment sold only by subcontractors of International Harvester, as well as K & L Truck Equipment Company. In return, principals of the companies were paying Dearborn tens of thousands of dollars in cash bribes, paid vacations, clothing, and a car phone.

My initial trash rips outside Dearborn's suburban Harford County home turned up the name of his bank. We then subpoenaed the bank for his records, which showed he was depositing hundreds of dollars of cash into his account, in addition to his city paycheck.

We had already interviewed Keith Graham, president of the K&L Truck Company, who admitted to bribing Dearborn. I knew we'd also need to find independent evidence to help prove our case for bribery, so I continued sifting through his trash for about three months.

One night I found an empty bank envelope from Maryland National Bank. I knew this was not Dearborn's bank. It was Graham's bank. I immediately understood this was an important piece of evidence. We soon discovered that Graham's bank records showed he had withdrawn thousands of dollars the day before I found the envelope.

That empty bank envelope in Dearborn's trash finally connected the two of them. More importantly, it gave me probable cause to write a search and seizure warrant for his home.

After a judge signed the search warrant, Charlie Walas and a state trooper went with me to Dearborn's house. It was a very nice suburban home and Charlie noticed a beautiful, decorative vase covered with a gold lid. Charlie opened it and stuck his hand inside.

"Look what I found," he announced, as he pulled out $8,000 in cash.

It turned out that Dearborn's wife was a shopaholic, so the house was filled with items of clothing that she had never worn. We found a box with 400 decks of cards, all unopened. They had more expensive habits: two quarter horses stabled nearby.

We confiscated the cash and took all his financial and tax records.

In 1992 Dearborn and all the businesspeople who paid him off pleaded guilty to bribery charges. We collected more than $250,000 in restitution. Dearborn, after agreeing to testify against his co-conspirators, was sentenced to four months in prison, fined $10,000 and ordered to pay another $25,000 in restitution.

In November of 1989 the state prosecutor's office had more cases than it could handle. I was assigned to two of them. They involved coming in contact with dirty evidence (literally, not figuratively) that made me so physically ill I nearly died.

One case involved an allegation of police and prosecutorial misconduct in a murder investigation in Calvert County in Southern Maryland. The other involved allegations that a Prince George's County councilman was stealing funds from his campaign.

Mike McDonough drove me down to Calvert County so we could reexamine the evidence in the murder case. A woman had killed a man with a .357 magnum revolver. A grand jury declined to indict her because of evidence that she was defending her husband as the victim attacked him. The fight was so violent that the husband lost an eye. The father of the dead man argued that the shooter should have been indicted for murder and that the county sheriff and the state's attorney mishandled the investigation. We eventually determined that the case was handled properly. Of all the evidence I examined, I will never forget what happened when I opened the sealed plastic bag containing the victim's bloody shirt and blue jeans. The stench of death and dried blood was so strong that it knocked me back and I stumbled slightly. I believe I might have inhaled some toxins that day that got into my system.

I did not feel sick immediately, so I went on a trash rip the following day to Prince George's County to investigate a county councilman named Anthony Cicoria. On this particular mission, a 4 a.m. dumpster dive, I brought Eddie Crowder with me. As always, I prepared in advance so I would know what to look for. I had contacted someone familiar with Cicoria's office building and learned where his staff's trash was dumped, as well as the color of their trash bags.

Eddie and I arrived at the dumpster without any special gloves or protective masks. In those days there was no protocol requiring us to wear anything to shield us from disease. Eddie cupped his hands and I stepped on them, as he boosted me over into the dumpster. I did not realize that a medical clinic next door threw its waste in the same dumpster, so it was even more unsanitary than an ordinary dumpster. I did find the right bag, which was full of identifying documents (like phone bills) belonging to Cicoria's office. I also found an invaluable piece of evidence: the carbon paper occasionally still used in those days to make copies. I later held the carbon paper to the light and read an expense report that proved the councilman was stealing campaign funds.

Cicoria was indicted and his criminal case was quite a drama. He was convicted of misappropriating campaign funds. While on probation he fled to Florida with a false driver's license and illegally used a county government credit card. He was subsequently sentenced to nine years in prison, but Governor Schaefer commuted his sentence a year later, so he could slip out of prison just before Christmas.

That day after our dumpster dive, Eddie and I were hungry so we went to a 7-11, where I ate a Bahama Mama hot dog, without first washing my hands. A few days later I would learn that my unsanitary searches had consequences.

41
A CONVERSATION WITH DEATH

For a long time after Pop's unsolved murder, I gave up religion. I hadn't set foot in a Catholic church in 15 years, except for an occasional baptism or wedding.

In 1986 I had a change of heart. I felt something was missing in my life and I decided it was my relationship with God. I had an urge to return to prayer. It had brought me comfort as a child and as a young man. Now I needed it back in my life.

I visited Pastor Frank Callahan at St. Margaret Church in Bel Air and told him I had been angry with God for so long because of Pop's death, but now I regretted my decision to leave the church. I wept profusely as I spoke with the priest. He was understanding and heard my confession. That day I left the parish office, singing the George Jones country-and-western lyric, "When I slammed the door to heaven I should have known hell stays open all night long."

I started to go to daily Mass before work at 8:30 a.m. as well as Sunday.

I was living in Bel Air, where I purchased a home with two master bedrooms so my best friend, Howard Glashoff, could live there with me. My youngest son, James, spent each weekend at my home. We had a wonderful relationship and went to Mass together on Sundays. He studied the catechism and made his Confirmation at age 13. Joe was in North Carolina, working after leaving the Navy. Diana was still living out of state. Except for my deteriorating eyesight, I was enjoying good health. I was in great shape from daily long distance jogging. I had money in my pocket. I was very pleased with my job and happily single once again.

On November 4, 1989, just a few days after breathing in the fumes from the bloody clothes in the Southern Maryland murder case and diving into the dumpster filled with medical waste in the Prince George's County theft case, I was home alone feeling extremely sick. I had a spiking fever and aches throughout my body. I was dehydrated with horrible stomach cramps. I thought I had the flu.

I managed to drag myself to a doctor. He said my symptoms sounded like the flu and he gave me the heavy-duty antibiotic Cipro that is given to people exposed to anthrax.

"If you don't improve in two days get to an emergency room immediately," he told me.

The next day there was no improvement. I was vomiting and had diarrhea. The following day I managed to get to the family room to lie down. When I tried to get up, I could not move. When Howard got home, he took one look at me.

"Enough of your macho bullshit," he said. "I'm taking you to the hospital."

As my dear friend picked me up, I could feel a raging fever. He got me in the car and raced to the emergency room at the Greater Baltimore Medical Center, about 45 minutes away. A nurse hooked up a drip and told me that I was seriously dehydrated. Soon after she drew a blood sample, I passed out.

When I woke up I found myself in the Intensive Care Unit. I was exhausted and thought I was dying; I felt comfort in the blue skies and white puffy clouds I saw in my mind. Just then, I felt a pounding at the foot of the bed. I opened my eyes. There was my good friend, FBI agent John O'Neill, slamming his fist and yelling.

"You are not dying on me." He continued hitting the foot of the bed with his fist. I weakly smiled. "I love you," he said.

I was diagnosed with a staph infection of the aorta in the heart, a very serious condition. After asking me many questions about where I had been and what I was exposed to, I told them about the bloody evidence and the dumpster dive. Though I'll never know for sure how I got the infection, I believe that it was from the toxins I breathed in from the dead victim's bloody clothes.

Within two days I was transferred to nearby St. Joseph's Hospital, where cardiac doctors were ready to operate.

They began treating me with medications to get the infection under control. They did not have my medical records from my primary physician, Dr. Harvey Mishner, and I was not coherent enough to alert them against giving me the one antibiotic that might kill me: penicillin. This was the medication that produced Stevens-Johnson Syndrome when I was eight years old.

Very soon after receiving an IV of penicillin, my skin began to blister. I had an itchy, blotchy rash everywhere. I had horrible memories of the 40 days I spent in the hospital as a child. Once the medical team learned about my medical history, they began giving me heavy doses of Benadryl into an IV to counteract the allergic reaction. They were very concerned.

The cardiologist at St. Joseph's Hospital, Dr. Joseph D'Antonio, explained that I needed emergency surgery, or I would die. The operation was performed by a talented surgeon named Garth MacDonald. He removed my aortic heart valve, which was overwhelmed with staph infection, and replaced it with a synthetic one. Howard stayed with me the entire time. He told me he had taken care of everything back at the house: he cleaned my bathroom, washed my laundry and changed my sheets.

No one could ask for a better friend.

After the surgery I was in and out of consciousness, but I heard a nurse enter the room. Howard was sitting at the foot of my bed and she loudly admonished him to get off.

"What do you charge to haunt a house?" Howard asked her.

There would be no truce between the two for the next 40 days.

One day after the heart surgery, I heard Dr. D'Antonio say, "Stand back. I need an all clear." My heart had stopped. He used electric shock paddles to restart it. Several hours later, I was vomiting blood after developing a huge hemorrhage in my stomach. It was like a scene from *The Exorcist*. My sons were in the room and I could hear crying. I have no recollection of the next two days, but learned the hemorrhage was sealed when I awoke.

During my long stay in the hospital I had many visitors, including former city councilman Tony Ambridge and my boss, Steve Montanarelli, and his deputy, Mike McDonough. Mike told me that Steve was despondent over my brush with death. I was like a son to him and he was like a father to me. I often worked Saturday mornings, as did Steve. We enjoyed talking about our families and our mutual love of classical music, especially opera.

The many get well cards reminded me of my 40 day stay at City Hospitals in 1958. Howard's loyalty was remarkable. He visited every single day. He was God's gift to me. There was only one uncomfortable occasion when two ladies I was dating visited at the same time. Ouch! Somehow, it all worked out. Thank you Sweet Jesus.

I was indebted to many wonderful nurses and technicians. Sue Williams was my primary nurse and Erin Blind was my primary technician. These ladies had a very good sense of humor which made the time pass. Before leaving the hospital, I penned the following: "While Jesus pensively walked along the water's edge, his face was frowned. He worried, as he knew full well, that his gift of free will was both good and bad. As the sun faded into the horizon, he smiled. He found a remedy for his concern. He would create a special set of angels. In time society would call them nurses."

On December 23, Howard drove me home. How wonderful to be home for Christmas and to be able to sleep in my own bed. He had stocked all sorts of goodies, including spiked eggnog. Thankfully I had accumulated enough medical leave that I didn't lose any salary.

When I was admitted to St. Joseph's Hospital, I weighed 176 pounds. When I got home I weighed 136, though my love handles were still there. Go figure. I have always been a big eater and I very much enjoyed getting back up to 170 pounds. For the next two weeks a nurse visited to administer an antibiotic drip.

I was a long way from distance running. I felt weak, so I built up my strength by walking thousands of steps inside the house every day. While I was convalescing, I wrote this poem:

Conversation with Death

Death, you have so often come that I know you well
But I have no fear. There are times when you are cruel without compassion
It is shameful that you prefer to act savagely without warning
You strike at any hour, day or night choosing to be precise or capricious
Yet there are times when you tenderly visit in mercy and you are welcomed
Age, gender, race or ethnicity matters not to you
But I do not hate you; you are the Omega, part of the cycle of life
I have heard, tasted, felt, smelled and seen you
You have changed the life of so many without any regard but to satisfy yourself
Now you ask why I have no fear.
The answer is simple
I have never been without the love of God, family and friends.
Their wisdom, affection and tenderness shines in me.
Cocooned in a protective love
Death, these many years, you came but a heartbeat away more than once
Frustrated were you
One day you will have me and I will rest in perfect peace

42
A SONG IN MY HEART

The hospital staff had treated me so very kindly that I decided to thank them by hosting a happy hour party at the popular Mt. Washington Tavern, the restaurant-bar that Howard and I frequented on Fridays. I called Sue Williams and told her to invite the staff, as well as boyfriends, husbands, girlfriends and anyone else they wanted to bring. It was my treat. That Friday in February of 1990 was the beginning of a new world for me. Sue and Erin brought a very attractive friend, a high energy lady who had a beautiful and engaging smile. Her name was Laura Pelesh. I had actually noticed her before at the bar. She was always impeccably dressed and in good spirits. She loved to sing and had a beautiful voice. In fact, she knew every word of every song, from Broadway musicals to top 40 hits.

I had never introduced myself to Laura because I was dating other ladies. Once we met that afternoon at the happy hour, I learned that she taught third grade in the Baltimore County public schools. It was a profession I very much admired. Howard, as always, was a very generous man; he kept ordering Laura (and the other guests) peppermint schnapps. For several months after the party, I saw Laura on Fridays, but did not immediately ask her out. I did learn more about her, though. She had studied classical piano for eight years. Like me, she had experienced loss at an early age. Her father suddenly died of a brain aneurysm and heart problems when she was still in college.

On June 19, 1991, Laura and I went on our first date to catch an Orioles game. John O'Neill was also there and I was proud to introduce Laura to him. The Twins won 8 to 4, but we didn't care, since we enjoyed each other's company. She thought my driving was odd, though. While searching for a parking space, I reversed the car abruptly and jerked my head in either direction, as if I was going down an alley looking for a suspect. We continued dating for a year and discovered that we wanted to commit to each other for life.

No one marries with the thought of one day getting divorced. But it happened to me twice. During both of those marriages I did experience love, but the love I had for Laura was so much more powerful. Laura was a very funny lady and our commonalities were striking. We were both devout Catholics. We preferred live theater to movies. We loved music, especially Jimmy Buffet, socializing with friends, and watching college basketball. Our life together was truly grand. We were made for each other. It's a cliché, but it was the truth.

On June 7, 1992, we were in the kitchen of my Bel Air home on a sweltering day.

"Are you going to turn on the air?" she asked.

"Yes I am," I answered. "After I ask you to marry me."

When she said yes, I saw tears of joy in her eyes.

Laura and her mother began an invitation list, searched for a venue for our reception and, of course, shopped for the all-important wedding dress. I had received an annulment from the Catholic Church after my divorce from Kathy, so I was free to marry again in a Catholic church.

On June 19, 1993, we were married at the Church of the Immaculate Conception in Towson. Howard was my best man. John O'Neill was there, too, as well as Pete and Mary Ann Saar. By then she was head of Maryland's Department of Juvenile Services. Pete was an assistant state's attorney.

Laura wore a wedding gown of silk, with puffed sleeves and a long train. She carried white roses and orchids and, as she came down the aisle, she was truly radiant.

We had a traditional Catholic wedding and live music that included a violinist, flutist, and a trumpet player. A lovely mezzo-soprano, Laura's cousin Barbara Tobler, sang "All I Ask of You" from *The Phantom of the Opera*.

Laura and I had a huge group of friends that included many of her fellow teachers.

We chose an excellent band to play Top 40 music.

Our wedding reception was on the top floor of the historic Belvedere Hotel in Baltimore, an ornate building nearly 100 years old. The ballroom where we celebrated has an arched ceiling 36 feet high with crystal chandeliers. While finalizing reception plans a few days before the wedding, Laura noted that the forecast called for 103-degree heat. She pointedly asked if the management could guarantee the hotel's air conditioning would be working. Yes, she was assured.

On our wedding day, the temperature reached into the 90s as our limo from the church turned onto Chase Street and pulled up to the Belvedere. We immediately saw fire trucks as we were greeted by my old friend from my early days on the police force, Wayne Carneal, and his wife, Fran. They anxiously gave us the bad news: the air conditioning unit had caught fire.

For the next four hours our 150 guests sweated the night away. Laura will never forget how the butter on the dinner tables began to melt. The top tier of our four-tier wedding cake, encased in butter cream icing, began to sag like the Leaning Tower of Pisa until it was whisked into a refrigerator. Our wedding pictures and video would forever show the glistening faces of our happily sweaty guests.

The heat did not deter our friends from dancing the night away to tunes like "Sweet Caroline" by Neil Diamond. At some point I saw a trash can filled with women's pantyhose, discarded in the heat. Our wedding album would include photos of the firefighters outside the hotel. The management was so apologetic that they gave us another reception several weeks later— for free. We honeymooned in St. Thomas.

Shortly before the wedding, we wrote letters to each other committing to our marriage.

Mine was in the form of a poem:

> *There is the marvel of Fall's*
> *Golden colors and there is your beauty,*
> *Your charm;*
> *There is the excitement of Winter's*
> *first snowfall and there is your song,*
> *your laugh;*
> *There is the freshness of Spring's*
> *air and there is your enthusiasm,*
> *your smile;*
> *There is the welcomed warmth of Summer's*
> *sun and there is your care,*
> *your love;*
> *There are all of these pleasures*
> *because through you, God has touched me.*

Laura wrote me a letter that ended with this:

I want to promise you a few things on this day. I will always love you with all my heart. My love for you grows deeper and stronger every day. I will always be honest with you and communicate with you my thoughts, feelings, and needs. I will always trust in you that the decisions we make will be what is best for each other and our relationship. Finally, I will always give you the support and encouragement you need throughout the ups and downs of our lives. I love you bunches, Jim Cabezas, forever and ever and ever!

Like any newlywed couple, Laura and I learned many personal details about each other. My biggest concern was always the health of my eyes and how long I would maintain a quality of vision. But of course, we would find out soon enough.

43
I SHOT THE SHERIFF, BUT NOT THE DEPUTY

I waited in a McDonald's parking lot just west of the city until the unmarked car arrived. The Baltimore City sheriff, Shelton J. Stewart Jr., was in the passenger seat. His deputy, George Cunningham, was driving. As I climbed into the back seat I noticed that Sheriff Stewart was in full uniform. "How stupid is that?" I thought.

"Hey guys, how's everything going?" I asked, as casually as I could.

I expected the sheriff to respond with some sort of chit chat, but he got right to the point.

"This is for you," he said. He turned and handed me an envelope.

I tried not to miss a beat.

"Sheriff, with all due respect, business is business. I'm going to have to count this," I said.

"Ok," he responded.

I opened the envelope. It was full of $100 bills. I counted aloud, as clearly as I could.

"One hundred, two hundred, three hundred," until I got to $1,000. When I was finished I told him, "Hey, I'll do what I can for you."

I went back to my car and waited for them to leave.

An investigator from the Baltimore County state's attorney's office approached me. I quickly handed him the envelope.

"Did you get the sound?" I anxiously asked him.

"Yes," he said.

I was greatly relieved. I had just taken a "bribe" from the sheriff, in exchange for using my influence at the OSP office to drop charges that he violated state election laws by pocketing campaign contributions.

Our exchange was caught on an audio wire I wore inside my coat; hence my reason for counting the $100 bills aloud. The county police also had videotape of the sheriff's car driving into the McDonald's lot.

Stewart had been elected to office less than two years before, in 1986. The job of Baltimore's sheriff, to serve warrants, guard courtrooms, and oversee evictions, is quite limited, compared to the city's police department. Still, it is a coveted elected position. In those days the sheriff oversaw a $3.9 million budget with 150 employees. Stewart beat 11 other candidates, even though he had no law enforcement experience. Instead, he had spent 20 years working in public relations for the state's transit administration.

His legal troubles began shortly after the election when I got a call from one of his opponents, who claimed to have knowledge that Stewart wasn't reporting all his campaign contributions. Our investigation found that the tip was correct and he was indicted for perjury, conspiracy and violating campaign laws.

He was awaiting trial when I got a call from deputy sheriff George Cunningham. I knew Cunningham socially through a friend. (Yes, this is yet another Smalltimore story about how I helped solve a crime because of who I knew.)

Cunningham told me, "I think our sheriff is stupid." He told me that Stewart wanted to run for mayor and felt the election law indictment would be a cloud over his head. He wanted to find a way to remove it. Shelton apparently knew that Cunningham was acquainted with me and asked his deputy if he could talk to me so this cloud could be removed.

Cunningham called a few days later,

"I think he wants to pay you a bribe," he told me.

I spoke with my boss, Steve Montanarelli, who knew that any arrangement for me to accept a bribe under surveillance would have to take place outside the city, since the Baltimore City state's attorney's office (located in the same courthouse as the sheriff's office) and the city police had a conflict of interest.

We contacted Baltimore County assistant state's attorney Frank Meyer, who was chief of the office's investigations division, to make the arrangements in the county, a jurisdiction separate from the city. That's how we got to the McDonald's parking lot in Woodlawn outside the city line.

Stewart was indicted for bribing a public officer and obstruction of justice after a grand jury listened to the audio tape, watched the video and heard my testimony. At his trial, his defense attorney did not refute what was on the audio and video tapes. Instead, he claimed that Cunningham had entrapped his boss. The lawyer called Cunningham's involvement in the case "skullduggery" and referred to the deputy as a double agent, simultaneously working for the sheriff's department and the state prosecutor.

In the end, the defense attorney used a "stupidity defense." He claimed that Sheriff Stewart was induced to take the bribe because "he isn't the smartest man in the United States . . . this case was one of gullibility."

Stupidity, indeed.

On the witness stand the sheriff tried to get the jury to believe that he never gave me the money. His deputy, he said, must have dropped it to me in the back seat of the car. He also insisted that the prosecution had doctored the audiotapes. He wanted the jury to believe that everyone was lying—his deputy, me and the prosecutor—and that he was the only one telling the truth.

The jury convicted him of obstruction of justice, but they were deadlocked on the count of bribery. Obviously, some of them bought the argument of entrapment.

Sheriff Stewart was stripped of his office after his conviction, but he was not a man who could take a hint. He called the Maryland attorney general's office and asked if this was in fact a crime that required him to leave office. He was told unequivocally, "yes."

Later, I received a call from someone in the sheriff's office, concerned that his boss had locked himself inside his office and refused to leave. Stewart, the caller worried, was having a meltdown and had his service revolver with him.

I told him that getting Stewart to leave his office was out of our jurisdiction.

Later I heard that someone contacted George Russell Jr., a prominent local lawyer, former judge and city solicitor, who finally convinced Stewart to leave.

Shelton Stewart wasn't the only Maryland sheriff who pledged an oath to enforce the law but did not believe it applied to him.

In my years in the state prosecutor's office, we investigated at least five other sheriffs around the state. Sheriff James Taylor from Dorchester County on the Eastern Shore pleaded guilty to misconduct for stealing money confiscated by the county's drug task force where he worked. Then he violated his probation and got 60 days in jail. In Prince George's County a deputy sheriff named Wendy Tyler stole hundreds of dollars from a deputy sheriffs' association she headed. She even used the group's money to buy herself a French poodle. She pleaded guilty and got probation.

In Carroll County Nicholas Plazio, a former major in the sheriff's department, pleaded guilty to providing false testimony in a murder trial. My office forced a sheriff in Calvert County to resign for harassing a woman after she filed a complaint against a deputy sheriff—her former boyfriend—for falsely imprisoning her by following her in his squad car, handcuffing her and issuing a trumped-up traffic ticket.

Another Eastern Shore sheriff, John Ellerbush, went to jail for stealing $40,000 in county funds from a DARE (Drug Abuse Resistance Education) program.

I proved the theft after spending two weeks interviewing shop owners where the sheriff made purchases with the stolen funds.

After I gathered all the evidence I was ready to make a cold call. I drove to his home three times until I finally found his marked sheriff's car outside.

As I knocked on his front door, I could feel my adrenaline racing. How I spoke to him was just as important as what I said.

When he came to the door I introduced myself.

"The purpose of my visit is to ask you questions regarding matters of your office," I said in a very nonthreatening and professional manner.

He invited me inside and we sat down at a dining room table.

He noticed that I was carrying a thick three-ring binder.

"I'm hopeful for your complete cooperation," I told him.

He nodded in agreement.

"What I have in this binder is a series of invoices of purchases made by you with money you illegally took from the office."

As I methodically produced copies of checks from the DARE fund, along with the corresponding purchases he made, his face started to lose color. After producing the fourth set of documents, I said, "Sir, what do you have to say about your conduct?"

He then nervously spilled out a full confession, shaking his head in shame.

I've long wondered if the epidemic of lawless Maryland sheriffs has something to do with the fact that each is elected, and answers to no other state official.

Perhaps their complete independence from oversight makes them reckless.

As the saying goes, "Absolute power corrupts absolutely."

44
PRINCIPALS WITHOUT PRINCIPLES

Back in 2005, after our office put an end to a 12-year, multimillion dollar kickback scheme involving business owners bribing a Baltimore City school official, I truly believed the convictions we won would act as a deterrent to others thinking of stealing from the school system. As an extra warning, we staged a media event on the courthouse steps with one of our investigators handing a giant check to the city school's chief for $3.5 million, recovered as restitution in the kickback scheme. In law enforcement, we believe if we can stop a crime before it happens, we're way ahead of the game.

How wrong we were. The corruption in city schools seemed to be without end.

In the ensuing years, our office won convictions of three city school principals for stealing thousands of dollars from their students' activity funds. Another employee, in charge of renting school buildings to outside groups, confessed to me that he stole more than $200,000.

And the owner of a private company providing tutoring services for special education students was convicted of overcharging the school system to the tune of $150,000.

I was especially unnerved by the thieving school principals, who should be role models for students and teachers. It is their duty to set a school's moral and ethical standards. Laura spent her three-decade career teaching third grade in public schools, so I took the crimes personally. How was it that they lost their moral compass, stealing from the very children they were supposed to be educating? Why they took a wrong turn from that high road, ducking into an alley like a common criminal, I do not know. I have always wondered about their motives. Was it greed, need or an addiction?

Lewis Williams had a job renting school space to outside groups, like the drum and bugle corps, Girl Scouts, Boy Scouts, religious and community groups.

As he received rental checks, he deposited them in a Mercantile Bank account he set up under the phony name L.E. Williams Enterprises and kept the money for himself. Since his bank fraud was a federal violation, the case was handled by the U.S. Attorney's Office as well as our office. Williams, who had a history of tax liens and bankruptcy, used the money to buy two cars, a Cadillac and an Infiniti, two $6,000 watches and to pay off credit card debts.

By the time I brought him into the OSP's conference room, we had already traced much of the $220,000 he stole from the school system.

Before I turned on a tape recorder with his consent, I thought in advance how this recording would sound to a judge or jury if the case went to trial. As always, I was very careful how I asked questions and, especially, how I waited patiently for an answer. I knew that if there were any long pauses after my questions, those guilty silences would provide jury appeal. The longer it takes for a suspect to answer a question, the easier it is for a prosecutor to convince a jury or judge of guilt beyond a reasonable doubt.

I began by showing Williams the first check from a pile, made out by him to the Mercantile account.

"What were the circumstances under which you issued this check?" I asked calmly.

Williams did not respond immediately. I stayed silent and patiently counted the seconds to myself. When I got to 24, I knew I had him. I still had my eyesight intact and saw his head bowed. He appeared remorseful, but gave me no explanation.

It turned out that we didn't need to bring our case to a judge or jury. In 2004 he pleaded guilty to felony theft in Baltimore circuit court and guilty of bank fraud in federal court. He was sentenced to 18 months in federal prison.

In 2009 I got a call from a friend, a former *Sun* reporter, who told me the school system had paid a private contractor for non-existent tutoring sessions for her son. The contractor, Tracy Queen, was able to defraud the school system by forging the mother's signature on dozens of phony time sheets. After discovering the fraud and complaining to school officials, the mother (who is now the co-author of this book) was concerned that school officials failed to report the crime to any law enforcement agency, though they did break off their contract with Queen's company. Our office began an investigation which revealed that Queen, who operated Queens Mobile Education, had forged the signatures of 250 parents of special education students and stolen $150,000 of city school funds. She pleaded guilty, was sentenced to ten years in prison (with all but 18 months suspended) and ordered to repay the money she stole.

William Howard was the principal of Coppin Academy High School when he pilfered more than $10,000 from the school's student activity fund. By the time we caught on to his crime he had moved on to another job at St. Mary's College in Southern Maryland as assistant vice president for academic services. I called his office to arrange a meeting on the pretense that I wanted to know how the college was accommodating students with disabilities. I told his receptionist, "I'm blind and would very much like to talk to him because I obviously come from that community." When I arrived with another investigator, Latisha Beal, I immediately told Howard that I had misrepresented the reason I needed to talk to him, so as not to embarrass him. Of course, I also liked the element of surprise.

"Our office received a complaint that you misspent funds from Coppin Academy. I'm not here to establish whether or not you stole the money. I'm here to ask you why you did it."

Though I was legally blind, I could still see a little bit and noticed how he shook his head and hung it in shame. He then gave us a full confession.

"I wanted to buy my fiancée a very nice diamond wedding ring and my intention was to pay it back," he said. I knew a year had gone by and he had never reimbursed the account and had already left the school. He was given probation before judgment, four years' probation, ordered to repay the money he stole and to perform 150 hours of community service.

Western High School is one of Baltimore's premier public high schools. It sets a high standard for its all-girl student body. Alisha Trusty was its principal; she unfortunately set a pretty low standard for herself. Our office was contacted by the school system's Office of Legal Counsel, which found irregularities on Western High's student activities account. Our investigation found that Trusty stole $54,000 to pay credit card bills, legal fees and her gas and electric bill. She stole almost $3,000 from the fund for a 19-day stay in a New Jersey hotel while she was on paid medical leave from her school principal job. And she double dipped by stealing $10,000 from the fund for a work-related trip when she had already been reimbursed by the school system.

Trusty pleaded guilty to the theft and was given five years' probation and ordered to repay the money she stole. Trusty told a judge she was "very ashamed" and noted that the theft cost her a 17-year career in education.

Leslie Lewis was principal of the Baltimore Community High School, a public charter school that later closed.

She stole about $15,000 from a student activity fund from school uniform sales and other fundraisers to feed her gambling habit at the Maryland Live Casino, where she made 49 ATM withdrawals. Lewis also was accused of falsifying school purchase orders to buy $40,700 worth of merchandise, including Bose speakers, Apple computers and iPads, projectors, printers and cameras. She was also charged with stealing four flat-screen TVs from the high school. She was sentenced to 90 days in prison, five years' probation and ordered to pay $59,000 in restitution.

A wunderkind's fall from grace

By 2016 I had spent more than a decade investigating theft from public schools. I thought nothing could shock me, until a complaint came into our office. The complainant was a parent with children in Baltimore County schools, who was known for her public criticism of the school board. The parent suggested our office investigate Dallas Dance, the suburban county's dynamic young superintendent, who was hired at the age of 30 to run the state's third largest school system with more than 100,000 students.

The same year Dance was hired, in 2012, the school system also hired a private education company, SUPES Academy, on a no-bid contract for $875,000 to train 25 principals a year for three years. The following year Dance took a side job consulting for SUPES for $147,000 to train principals in Chicago. He failed to get permission from the school board before he began working the side job for SUPES and did not report it on his financial disclosure forms. But in 2013, the *Sun*'s education reporter, Liz Bowie, found out about Dance's consulting work and reported it. Two years later, she reported that the head of the Chicago public school system, Barbara Byrd-Bennett, pleaded guilty to federal charges for her involvement in a kickback scheme in which SUPES promised her hundreds of thousands of dollars in exchange for no-bid contracts worth $20 million.

By the time the Baltimore County parent called me, she had obviously read all this news, though I had not followed the story as closely. Now she suggested Dance's relationship with SUPES, like Byrd-Bennett's in Chicago, might be illegal.

The parent said, "Isn't it odd to you that it was a sole source contract and there was no bidding?"

I was very careful when I answered her.

I knew she was a gadfly and might repeat to the media whatever I said. I simply told her I would prepare a report to Emmitt Davitt, the state prosecutor, and we would take her report under advisement.

But I was thinking, "This is a great tip. It's not frivolous in any way." I had not been aware of the Chicago case and immediately went online to find the newspaper articles.

I wrote the report and met with Davitt and Mike McDonough. We assigned the case to one of our investigators, Tim Frye. We issued a subpoena to the school board for Dance's personnel file, as well as his financial disclosure statements (which he signed under penalty of perjury) that did not show his contract agreement with SUPES. Of course, we also subpoenaed Dance's bank records that showed the deposits from SUPES.

I retired before the case was complete, but knowing how hard teachers work, I found Dance's conduct despicable. Dance was Laura's ultimate boss in the school system and I knew she and her colleagues would be very disappointed to hear the news.

After I retired Dance pleaded guilty to four counts of perjury for failing to report the outside income on his financial disclosure forms. He was sentenced in 2018 to six months in prison and ordered to perform 700 hours of community service. Davitt noted that Dance showed a pattern of "blatant deceit" by not reporting the consulting work.

The Sun reported Dance's statement from the courtroom the day he was sent to prison:

"I'm embarrassed. I'm ashamed of myself...That's remorse I'll have to live with for the rest of my life."

As for Bennett, the Chicago Public Schools CEO, she was sentenced to four-and-a-half years in prison for her kickback scheme with SUPES. At her sentencing, Byrd-Bennett tried to blame the stresses of a job running one of the largest, and poorest, school systems in the country.

But in the end, she told the judge, "I wish I had magic words or a better explanation."

The prosecutor in the case, though, gave a clearer reason:

"Naked Greed."

45
THE PRESIDENTIAL SUITE

In early 1998, the nation was consumed with the shocking news that President Bill Clinton had had a sexual relationship with a former White House intern named Monica Lewinsky. The details appeared in an explosive article by *Newsweek* investigative reporter Michael Isikoff. He reported that Lewinsky and Clinton lied under oath in a sexual harassment lawsuit brought by another woman named Paula Jones, by denying they had sex in the White House. Their perjured statements caught the attention of independent counsel Kenneth Starr, who was investigating Clinton for other alleged crimes.

In public, Clinton vehemently denied that he had lied. Pointing his finger at the media, he said, "I did not have sexual relations with that woman, Miss Lewinsky. I never told anybody to lie, not a single time— never. These allegations are false."

As the scandal hurtled toward a vote of impeachment in the House of Representatives, our staff at the OSP office zeroed in on one possible crime that directly concerned us: Lewinsky's telephone conversations describing her affair with the president were surreptitiously tape recorded in Maryland by her friend and confidante, Linda Tripp. If, in fact, Lewinsky did not consent to the tape recordings, Tripp's act was clearly a violation of Maryland's Wiretapping and Electronic Surveillance Act, which states that it is unlawful to tape record a conversation without the permission of all the parties. A violation of the wiretapping law is a felony punishable by imprisonment up to five years and a fine up to $10,000.

As news of the sex scandal continued, political pressure mounted in Maryland for someone to investigate Tripp for violating the wiretapping law. In the Maryland House of Delegates, 49 Democrats signed a letter urging an investigation. One delegate called the case "a slam-dunk felony violation."

The initial investigation was announced by the Howard County state's attorney, but she quickly passed it on to our office, since she had no investigators to handle the case.

In the spring of 1998, my boss Steve Montanarelli called a meeting with Mike McDonough and two investigators, John Poliks and myself. Mike, a great legal researcher, zeroed in on a case called Kastigar v. the United States, in which a witness granted immunity to testify about a crime cannot be prosecuted elsewhere for the same crime with the same evidence. If Congress granted Tripp immunity to testify against Clinton, our office would have to find new evidence against her and build a Chinese wall between the case in Congress and a case in a Maryland court. It would be a herculean task.

With the Kastigar case weighing heavily on our minds, we proceeded cautiously with the most logical plan: interviewing Monica Lewinsky to determine if she had granted permission for Tripp to tape record her conversations.

We decided not to send Lewinsky to testify before a grand jury because a transcript of her testimony would be made available to Tripp's attorneys, who might use it to their advantage.

Instead, John Poliks and I would interview her, so I could subsequently tell a grand jury what she told us.

"My name is Jim Cabezas," I told her when she answered the phone. "I am the chief investigator for the Office of the State Prosecutor, and my boss believes it is the duty of our office to investigate whether the Maryland wiretap statute was violated during your telephone conversations with Linda Tripp," I told her.

"You are not a suspect in any way. You are a witness," I said.

Lewinsky came to our office in Towson with two lawyers. I remember her as a poised, well-educated, polite young woman caught up in a scandal that we all realized threatened to bring down the president.

As I often do, I put myself in the position of someone victimized as a result of a crime. I believed Lewinsky was clearly a victim, betrayed by Tripp, who was willing to break the law in her zeal to harm President Clinton's reputation. Our interview with Lewinsky was straightforward. We only needed to know the circumstances of her phone calls with Tripp and whether she gave Tripp permission to tape record them. We did not need to ask her any details of the phone conversations; doing so might appear unethical, with two male investigators unnecessarily asking her specific questions about having sex with the president. I decided that we would just ask general questions.

Therefore, the session began benignly enough:

"How did you meet Linda Tripp?"

After every answer, we simply followed up with: "Then what happened?"

Lewinsky was very forthcoming. She explained how she met Tripp at the public affairs office of the Pentagon.

Then we got to the big question. "Did you ever give consent to the tape recordings?"

"No," she said, "I felt betrayed."

The interview ended after three hours. As we continued our investigation, John and I visited Tripp's suburban cul-de-sac in Columbia and spoke with neighbors and others who knew her. One woman we met told us that Tripp confided how she hid the tapes in the valance of her living room curtains. While certainly intriguing, the statement did not provide sufficient probable cause for us to execute a search warrant of Tripp's home. What a pity! We did, however, bring the woman to testify before a grand jury.

At some point during our investigation, Steve Montanarelli got a visit from Tripp's high-powered defense attorneys, Joseph Murtha and Anthony J. Zaccagnini, who pressured him not to seek charges against her.

I came to view Tripp as a bully after learning of the pressure she put on Lewinsky to embarrass the president. I was not surprised when in July she accused our office of conducting a politically motivated investigation.

Through her lawyers, she issued a statement claiming that the announcement of the investigation by our office "is the latest in a series of attempts to intimidate me."

Meanwhile, our investigation continued to nail down every detail of Tripp's actions, including where she purchased the tape recorder—at a Radio Shack in the Columbia Mall. We even got grand jury testimony from members of her bridge club who said Tripp told them she was secretly recording Lewinsky's conversations. To protect the bridge club ladies from being seen by the media going into the grand jury room in the courthouse, we took the very unusual step of using a county school building for the grand jury to hear the ladies' testimony.

The investigation lasted for more than a year. We even interviewed Paula Jones's lawyers. In July 1999 a Howard County grand jury indicted Tripp for illegally taping the conversations.

Shortly after the indictment was announced, *Sun* columnist Michael Olesker interviewed me.

"The grand jury action screams out that Ms. Tripp did not accidentally cross over the line but that she eagerly jumped and did so willingly and repeatedly," I told him.

"What the grand jury reminds us," Olesker wrote, "in this postscript to the degrading White House sexual scandal, is that Tripp lied in all the scuzziest ways. She lied when she shamelessly called herself Monica Lewinsky's mother confessor, and she lied when she tried to skirt the edges of the law, and she lied again when she tried to declare her back-stabbing-for-profit an act of national patriotism."

As we long suspected, a legal challenge was immediately launched by Tripp's lawyers, using the Kastigar case to argue that Tripp had already received immunity from Congress, so she could not be charged in Maryland.

A pretrial court hearing on the matter was scheduled with Lewinsky as the star witness in December 1999.

It was my job, along with John Poliks, to get her safely to and from the courthouse. That was easier said than done, with scores of reporters and television cameras expected to search for any glimpse of her. Mike McDonough and I picked up Lewinsky at Penn Station in Baltimore without anyone recognizing her. We took her to the Sheraton Hotel in Towson to spend the night before the following day's testimony. To prevent anyone from identifying her through hotel records, we reserved the room in the name of an assistant attorney general. We slipped into an elevator with her and headed up to the hotel's top floor. As we approached her room, we all began to laugh. A sign on the door read, "Presidential Suite." Even Lewinsky thought it was funny.

The next morning, as John and I arrived to pick her up for the 30-minute trip to the Howard County Courthouse, we found her in her nightgown, getting her breakfast from room service.

"I'll be with you shortly," she said.

Once we arrived at the Ellicott City courthouse, John parked his van outside the sally port where they take in prisoners, hoping to avoid the long line of local, national, and even international reporters and photographers lined up on the walkway from the parking lot to the front entrance of the courthouse. There were only a few press people outside the sally port when we took her in, but as soon as somebody yelled, "there's Monica," a mob moved in and waited for us to leave.

Since I had to testify about our investigation, I was sequestered outside the courtroom, so I did not hear Lewinsky's testimony.

When it was my turn, I noticed the packed courtroom, as one of Tripp's defense attorneys tried to throw me off my guard by asking me a personal question.

Though I was blind in my left eye, I still had decent vision in my right eye and wore very thick glasses.

"Can you see what I'm holding in my hand?" he asked.

"No sir," I answered.

"What a cheap, offensive shot," I thought.

Leaving the courthouse was not as difficult as we thought it would be. I did check for any television helicopter that might follow us, but I was grateful there was none.

We had asked Lewinsky to wear a large hat and sunglasses to avoid being recognized in the train station, so she wore a large beret. John bought her a coffee, a snack, and a newspaper to bury her face in once she got on the train. While we waited with her on the wooden benches, not one person seemed to recognize her. We escorted her down to the track and John got on the train with her to make sure she was seated safely.

He and I stood on the platform as the train pulled away, watching Lewinsky wave goodbye.

That was the last time we saw her. She never returned to Maryland to testify at a full trial. The case against Tripp was in fact dismissed because of the immunity deal she received from Congress. Lewinsky, shamed for her involvement with Clinton, stayed out of public view for many years. Almost two decades later she became a public activist against bullying.

46
NEVER SAY DIE

While confronting my failing eyesight, I followed Pop's philosophy: "Never say die." I aggressively sought every possible medical procedure that might improve my vision and alleviate the pain of eyelashes that grew inward and scratched my tender eyes.

I never feared these eye operations, no matter how grueling. Even if a procedure failed, I hoped the doctors might learn something useful for another patient. I never had the feeling of shoveling sand against the tide. I refused to allow blindness to lower my high expectations for my quality of work, family life, and friendships.

In the decade between 1990 and 2000, I put my eyes in the deft hands of seven of the country's most skilled ophthalmologists, from Baltimore to Boston. After eight surgeries, though, I only had fleeting improvement in my sight. My aggressive battle with blindness also had an unintended consequence. It left me without any sick leave remaining as a state employee. When I requested more time off from the state's leave bank, I was sent first to be examined by a state doctor.

I had no idea when Laura drove me to that appointment in January 2001 that a heartless doctor, who was not even an ophthalmologist, would turn my life upside down after examining me for just 60 seconds.

My journey leading up to that day, despite my upbeat outlook, was often painful, leading me, at times, to desperation. In addition to several excruciating procedures to pluck my eye lashes that grew inward, I had a much-dreaded detached retina in my right eye. Since I was already blind in my left eye, this was the most worrisome problem and I had great hope that the retina could be repaired.

On Memorial Day weekend 1997 Laura and I were having drinks with friends at a restaurant in Timonium. We were sitting outside on a deck that looked out over a well-lit billboard. One minute I could see the billboard. The next minute it was gone. It was as if a black curtain had come across my right eye. As I went into a quiet panic, my senses blocked out all the conversations around me. This is how I had gone blind in my left eye, so I was well aware of the long and precarious road ahead with another detached retina. When I told Laura, she was very supportive. "We'll do what we need to do," she said. She took me to the emergency room at the Greater Baltimore Medical Center and I had surgery within 24 hours to repair the detached retina. Dr. Raymond N. Sjaarda, a retina specialist, performed the surgery which included inserting a gas bubble in my eye in hopes that it would provide enough pressure to keep the repaired retina in place. In my case, the pressure increased to a dangerous level within two days after surgery. It was excruciating. Laura took me back to GBMC and we met Dr. Sjaarda in his office in the evening for an emergency procedure. First he put in liquid cocaine to numb my eye, but that didn't work. When he inserted a needle into my eye to release the gas, I passed out. Laura remembers having to help the doctor revive me. "Lift his legs," he said. That brought me to. He was able to release the gas, but I was ordered to lay face down for four weeks. I was allowed to be upright for no more than ten minutes each hour.

I spent most of the time lying on my stomach on our deck at home. Since it was summer, I went shirtless. As Laura tells it, I developed such a spectacular tan that she joked I should model for Bain De Soleil tanning lotion. I spent most of the time listening to music. Laura remembers me as an excellent patient, following doctor's orders like a good soldier. I wasn't depressed. I believed if I followed the doctor's instructions and the gas bubble kept the repaired retina in place, I would be able to see again. But after a month, I could not see any written print. I could not see beyond 20 feet and I could only watch a small TV in the kitchen if I put my face within six inches of the screen. The retina repair did not hold.

I was disappointed, of course, but Laura and my sons, James and Joe, told me it was not the end of the world.

Three years later I would have the first of three corneal transplants in an effort to restore sight in my right eye. For those operations I would travel to Boston to see a cornea specialist, Dr. Kenneth Kenyon, at Massachusetts Eye and Ear Hospital and be the grateful patient of the most advanced surgical methods in the world. The first surgery was called a limbal stem cell transplant. He used a tiny instrument to remove cells from my blind left eye and implant them in my right eye in the hopes that the cells would regenerate and help me regain some sight.

Prior to every surgery I would tell doctors that I am a difficult person to anesthetize. In this instance, I woke up in the middle of surgery and noticed what looked like a tiny round saw circling above my left cornea. I immediately told the doctor. He said, "You certainly are difficult to put to sleep." I was grateful that he immediately gave me more anesthesia. I certainly did not want to remember anything about the cornea transplant.

That day in early 2001, when I was sent to a state doctor before I could use the leave bank, Laura and I walked into a large room the size of a basketball court, filled with other state employees waiting to be examined. I was ushered by a doctor I did not know to a slit lamp, a microscope with a light that would allow him to examine my eyes. Though I had stopped driving, I was ambulatory. The doctor could see that I walked to the lamp without assistance. He barely addressed me before the examination, which took just a minute. I would later learn he was an internist and occupational medicine specialist, but not an ophthalmologist. He had received a report from one of my ophthalmologists, Dr. Melanie Graham, who described in detail my "significant ocular disease in both eyes," though she concluded, "we have a gentleman who is very eager to work and who definitely has a potential for visual recovery."

After his cursory exam, the doctor ushered us to his office.

"I don't foresee you being able to go back to work," he said, with absolutely no sympathy or emotion.

He would later describe me in his written report as crudely as he addressed me in person. To him I was "an unfortunate 51-year-old right-handed male who has experienced severe ophthalmic complications from Stevens-Johnson syndrome . . . He is currently legally blind in the left eye, which is permanent. He has lost significant vision in his right eye since 1997 to the point where he is not able to drive.

"His ability to return to work," the doctor concluded, "is determined by his level of visual functionality. The appropriate administrative steps should be taken concerning Mr. Cabezas's duty status."

Apparently this specialist in occupational medicine believed a blind person could not work. Had he never heard of the Americans with Disabilities Act? The federal civil rights law was enacted for disabled persons, giving us equal opportunities in American life, including the workplace.

I was flabbergasted by his conclusion that my blindness would prevent me from doing my job.

"But I want to work," I told him.

"You can't," he said. He was very matter of fact.

As Laura drove home, I was very stoic, but I had desperate thoughts.

"So, we're down to this. What will I do? How am I going to stay busy? I'm a workaholic. There's got to be a way around this."

Laura snapped me out of my self-pity.

"Blindness," she said, "has nothing to do with your ability to think."

Since I have always believed in passing on bad news as soon as possible, I asked Laura to drive me to the office. She stayed in the reception area. I walked directly to Steve Montanarelli's office and knocked. He waved me in and I got right to the point. He was as stunned as I was to hear the doctor's conclusion.

"This is not the time to panic," he said.

He immediately called in Cindy Lewis, the office administrator, and gave her the bad news.

She was also caught by surprise.

"This is so very wrong," said Steve. "There has to be a way for you to keep working. You're my go-to guy." Steve and I had worked together for 17 years on dozens of cases, including Operation Quartermatch, the conviction of Baltimore City comptroller Jackie McLean for theft and the Baltimore liquor board corruption case. We had a father-and-son relationship. Steve had his own health problems that worried me. I knew he was suffering from cancer, but he did not speak about it. I did know, though, that he was on dialysis. For years we both worked on Saturday mornings. On one of those mornings, he walked into my office carrying a four pack of Charmin toilet paper. "You never want to be without," he said, without further explanation.

"Indeed," I replied. "Thank you sir."

I mentioned that there were other state employees who are blind. Steve asked Cindy to contact the state's human resources office to get advice.

When I left Steve's office I realized how much work had gone unfinished while I was visiting the doctor. During any given time, the OSP has about 30 open criminal investigations, not to mention open cases for more than 100 alleged election law violations. I also would need to answer voice mail messages and more than a dozen emails. I was still able to read documents and emails on the computer by setting the font to the largest size.

I went back to the reception area where Laura waited. I told her to go home without me.

"I'm going to be working for the rest of the day," I told her.

47
WHEN ONE DOOR CLOSES, ANOTHER OPENS

In 2002 Laura drove me to an office in the city on Argonne Drive, across the street from the Northeast police station, a place I knew from a lifetime ago. I was not going to see a doctor who would surgically attempt to improve my vision, or alleviate the pain in my eyes, or tell me my diminished sight disqualified me from doing my job. Instead, I was going to a place where my disability would be understood and accepted, where I would be taught how to perform my job with the help of the most modern technology. At Steve Montanarelli's direction, Cindy Lewis found a government agency called DORS (Division of Rehabilitation Services), which was part of the Maryland State Department of Education. A rehabilitation technologist would figure out how the most up-to-date computer programs could keep me working. I could hardly believe my good fortune.

As Laura signed me in at the reception desk, I thought, "Here is where I shed my fears, my disappointments and aggressions." By then, I could only see faces close up. I read with a powerful magnifying glass. I had not been able to drive a car for many years. My frustrations over my failing vision—and the threat to my career—made me want to hit something. Instead, I increased my jogging from 15 miles a week to 20. Luckily, that did the trick.

Jim Doyle, a soft spoken man, was the rehabilitation technologist who warmly welcomed us. He spent the first three hours asking me about my long history of vision problems, starting with my bout with Stevens-Johnson Syndrome all the way to my more recent detached retinas. He explained the Americans with Disabilities Act, the federal law that mandates reasonable accommodations be made for disabled persons like me. He also asked about my job at the OSP, my work habits, my typing skills (or lack of them), and my familiarity with a computer and the internet. It didn't take long for him to understand that it was absolutely necessary for me to be able to access the data in the office computer system.

I would also need some lessons in touch typing on a keyboard because I had spent my life as a hunt and peck typist with just two fingers.

Doyle and others at DORS, including an enthusiastic instructor named Melissa Day, began testing my abilities using various computer technologies that would significantly magnify type on a computer screen. Doyle also talked about new programs that allowed a computer to read text aloud to me. This was years before I could talk to the Apple computer voice, Siri, on my cell phone and ask her to call my contacts, dictate text messages without a keypad and get her answers to thousands of questions by searching the web. It was also long before the invention of Alexa, an Amazon device that I now daily rely on to answer any question, from the current temperature to historic dates. Back in 2002, that technology was a ways off, so the idea of a computer program reading documents aloud for my work was both a great revelation and a relief to me.

As Doyle later wrote in a report on my case, "Screen-reading software is a program that allows a blind or visually impaired person to operate a computer through key commands while the computer describes what is on the screen through audio feedback. Since the user cannot use a mouse, the computer is fully accessed through the keyboard with literally hundreds of key combinations."

I was given lessons on proper touch typing. DORS provided me with an extra-large keyboard with oversized key caps on each letter. I purchased small rubber bumps for some of the keys that helped me properly place my fingers. I glued on thick squares and circles, as well as very thin ones, to guide me to the proper letters. The letter "z" has a small circle, the "o" has a large, higher, circle, the "5" has a large square and the "m" has a small square, for example.

I began using a document-reading program called Kurzweil 1000, which allowed me to scan a document into my computer. With just two keystrokes I could listen to the text. I could adjust the speed of the voice. Using keystrokes, I could save a document in any selected folder or send to someone else by email. It was still a bit clumsy to use, since I could not direct the computer to scroll up and down, to help me re-listen to passages.

At a later session, Melissa Day worked with me and several other low vision students eager to learn. She helped us find the best way to read with a screen magnification program called Zoomtext that allowed us to change the font size of letters and select colors that helped us to better see the words. A ticker tape of the words ran across the screen as a continuous ribbon. Some students selected red lettering against a yellow background. For me it was black print against a white background. I could still only read very large words if I put my face close to the screen.

The magnification software turned out to be cumbersome because I had to read one giant word at a time on a 36 inch TV screen that my office bought for me. That took up too much time. The DORS staff spent many months training me on various programs and installing them in my office, along with a new computer capable to handling the software.

Eventually, the staff at DORS would introduce me to what I came to consider the Cadillac of talking computers, a program called JAWS, which stands for Job Access with Speech. It was invented in 1989 by a former motorcycle racer, Ted Henter, who lost his sight in an auto accident. Today, JAWS comes in voices in 30 different languages and works with most common computer operating systems, including Windows, Google Docs, Internet Explorer and Microsoft Office. With a keystroke, I can set the program to read to me at several speeds. I can even stop it to spell a word or read punctuation. I can scroll up and down to any place in a document. When I type, JAWS reads each letter aloud to me and then says the word.

On that first day at the DORS office, Laura and I found hope for the future. As I was leaving, I heard the sound of scraping and little wheels moving behind me. A small man, a dwarf who appeared to have no legs, came scooting by. He sat on what looked like a skateboard and he held paddles in his hands that allowed him to push the floor to move forward. As I opened the door for him, I was acutely aware of the difference between my disability and his.

I remembered a saying that put my hardship in perspective.

"Some people ask, why me?" I thought.

"I ask, why not me?"

Each additional training session gave me relief from the fear of losing my job. I knew that I would never get my old swagger back, but the realization that I was regaining control of my life brought me the comfort of confidence.

"Is there a God?" I asked myself.

"You bet your ass," I answered.

"Thank you Jesus."

48
DOUBLE TROUBLE AT CITY HALL

When I arrived at work on March 15, 2006, I was well aware that it was the Ides of March, the day Shakespeare made infamous in his play *Julius Caesar*, when a soothsayer warned Caesar "beware the Ides of March" just before the Roman dictator was assassinated.

As always, Laura drove me to the office and assisted me to the front door. I was the first to arrive at 6:45. That allowed Laura time to drive the short distance to school so she could be in her third-grade classroom by 7.

I turned on the lights for the other staffers and walked directly to the kitchen to brew a pot of strong coffee. I carefully poured water into the pot, putting my finger inside the rim until I felt it was full. Then came the hard part. I had to pour the water into the back of the Mr. Coffee machine without spilling it all over the counter. Easier said than done in the dark. I then counted three-and-a-half scoops of coffee into the basket.

I now lived in complete darkness after three failed corneal transplants at the Massachusetts Eye and Ear Hospital in Boston. With my white cane, I carefully moved around the breakroom, hallways and other common areas, sweeping the tip left to right to make sure all the chairs were pushed into the tables and that nothing else was out of place. More than once, I had tripped over evidence boxes sitting on the floor. One time I walked into a loaded hand cart. Ouch! I smacked into the top rim of the cart. My forehead didn't bleed for long.

I once even slammed into Deputy Prosecutor Mike McDonough. He was speaking so softly to an investigator that I did not hear him before I almost knocked him over. Though a big man, Mike walked so softly that I often did not hear him entering my office. I told him, "Mike, you need to put bells on your shoes so I know you're here."

Finally, satisfied that the coast was clear, I headed back to the kitchen where I poured coffee into my favorite mug. I had specially ordered it, with the words: "Another one bites the dust." Now that I could no longer see even the most magnified words, I began to rely on an invaluable service from the National Federation for the Blind, which allowed me to listen to my favorite newspapers by pushing buttons on a touchtone landline phone. A current events junkie, I began every day listening to the Baltimore *Sun*, the Associated Press, the *Washington Post* and the *New York Times*.

On this particular morning, I was still thinking about one article from the *Sun*'s most recent Sunday edition. Investigative reporter Doug Donovan chronicled a remarkable story about the Baltimore City Council president, Sheila Dixon, who had been in office for six years and was the first woman to hold the position. Donovan wrote that Dixon had given her former campaign chairman the exclusive rights to maintain the computer systems for the City Council president's office. In fact, the campaign chairman, Dale Clark, didn't even have a written contract with the city for most of the $600,000 he earned during the last six years.

I thought it was an outrageous amount of tax dollars to spend without any government oversight. The article noted that any city contract above $5,000 must be approved by the five-member Board of Estimates, which Dixon chaired. She had defied the very laws she was entrusted to uphold as head of the city's most powerful spending board.

Now, if that news doesn't pique the interest of someone investigating political corruption, I don't know what would. I immediately thought that Dixon and Clark might be involved in a kickback scheme. Perhaps she paid him the large sums of money with the agreement he would kick back some of it to her. I didn't have any evidence that Dixon might be a dishonest person. In fact, the people I knew in City Hall said they had no indication that Dixon would do anything corrupt. But I also knew that Donovan was an extremely reliable reporter and from what he'd written in *The Sun*, I thought that the City Council president's hubris might one day be her downfall.

I'd also had a front row seat to the unsavory business of government officials readily accepting kickbacks, or bribes, from contractors. I had already investigated a boiler company kicking money back to a city public works official, not to mention the owners of ten companies conspiring to bribe a city school employee for millions of tax dollars he arranged to pay them for nonexistent work.

Soon after the article appeared, I went back to the *Sun* and found previous articles about Dixon's payments to Clark. It turned out that the newspaper first reported the no-bid work with Clark's company, Ultimate Network Integration, five years before. Gady Epstein, a *Sun* reporter, wrote in 2001 that Dixon admitted her error. "I was wrong. I should have put it out for bid," she told The *Sun*.

At the time, Mayor Martin O'Malley refused to criticize her in public.

I personally believed that O'Malley would always do whatever was politically expedient to advance his ambitions. Crossing the black City Council president would not be a good political move for a white mayor, I thought. I was reminded of the saying about the precarious world of politics: "Twenty-four hours in politics can be a lifetime."

Instead, Mayor O'Malley praised her back in 2001. "I've always found Councilwoman Dixon to be very conscientious about the expenditure of public dollars," he said.

And so the payments to Clark's company continued unchecked for five more years, even after bids were later sought from other companies—and rejected. While the mayor gave no hint of concern, a *Sun* editorial in 2001 made a grim prediction: "Ms. Dixon's shaky ethical pattern is particularly troublesome because of her rising political star. The 13-year council veteran easily won the president's seat in 1999, and is being eyed as a potential mayoral candidate someday."

Soon after I finished sweeping the office for my own personal land mines, I heard my boss, Bob Rohrbaugh, pass by my office to get a cup of coffee.

I said, "Good Morning Boss," and asked if he had read the Donovan story in the Sunday *Sunpapers*.

"No," he answered. "We in Montgomery County read the *Post*," he said. I gave him my summary of the *Sun* article and said that I would forward a copy to him. Twenty minutes later, I knocked on his office door.

"What might you think of having a ten o'clock meeting?" I asked.

Long ago, I made it my business to pay special attention to all the attorneys in the office so I could learn their personalities and proclivities. Bob Rohrbaugh was the third state prosecutor I had worked for, after Gerald Glass and Steve Montanarelli.

Bob had an excellent command of the law and was judicial in his thoughts. He'd carefully analyze evidence, factoring in how difficult it might be to convict an accused person, while also being fair. He was also the type of amiable boss who would come in on a weekend to help move furniture when somebody switched to a new office. And he had a great sense of humor. Bob especially loved to make puns—and laugh at them harder than anybody in the room.

Mike McDonough, his deputy, who had worked at the OSP office almost as long as I had, was excellent at preparing subpoenas and conducting legal research. He had the patience to review thousands of documents. He was also the rudder of our operation, always keeping us on keel to make sure we never went into dangerous waters with an investigation.

On this particular morning I did not plan to ask them to open an investigation of Sheila Dixon. Even I knew I could not justify it, though I told myself, "This thing is dripping with potential."

Instead, I thought we should begin with Dale Clark. I nevertheless knew that there would be a lot of pushback with so little evidence, but I was well prepared.

After we were seated in the conference room, Bob's voice turned to me.

"It's your show. What are you recommending?"

"A self-initiated investigation of Dale Clark." As I expected, the floodgates opened with questions.

"Why should we not simply refer this to the city's Ethic's Board?" asked Mike.

"The story is not just about a conflict of interest violation," I said. "There are so many other concerns. With all due respect," I said, "is there not the potential for criminal charges? I see two: a conspiracy to defraud the city, and maybe tax evasion. "

I also thought that Dixon might have defrauded the city government by making a sole source agreement with Clark without a contract. Bob would later recall that I strongly urged him and Mike to "poke our nose under the tent."

"Do you have an investigative plan?" asked Bob.

"Yes sir. I would like to get grand jury subpoenas to secure records from the City Council and the Department of Finance as well as the Board of Estimates. We need to prove that Dixon bypassed an existing computer contract when she awarded the no-bid work to Clark.

"I also want to call a long time source who works in the Finance Department. He can get copies of the front and back of checks issued to Clark." I knew that would reveal not only how much Clark was getting paid, but where he deposited the checks. We would eventually subpoena the checks, but for now I wanted to quickly confirm what was in the newspaper article.

"I could have that information by this afternoon," I said. "Once we know where he banks and his account number, we should subpoena his bank records," I said. Of course, we would also get court approval for a "nondisclosure" order to prevent the bank from telling Clark he was under investigation.

I also suggested we perform a background check on Clark, which would tell us if he was involved in any criminal cases or lawsuits. Had he ever been arrested? Had he ever filed bankruptcy? We needed to get his phone records to see where he was calling. Someone from the office would also need to drive past his home to see if it was feasible to go back some night to make a trash rip.

When I was done, the room fell silent. Though I could not see anyone's face, I felt a thick fog set in.

"Do you have anything else?" asked Bob.

"Just my instincts, which tell me this is the right thing to do," I said.

He then told me to initiate an investigation and to call around to make sure the Maryland attorney general, the Baltimore City state's attorney, or the U.S. Attorney for Maryland were not already investigating Clark.

We always began by filling out a form that has four boxes for subjects to investigate.

"I only want to see one named subject," Bob told me. "Dale Clark."
The meeting ended. Bob told Mike to join him in his office.
"Let's talk subpoenas," he said.

By late afternoon the subpoena had been served on the city solicitor Ralph Tyler for all payments from the city to Dale Clark. We were beginning to shake that delicate spider's web, so we had to be very careful—and as quiet as possible. No matter how careful we were, though, word of the investigation would leak out to the media in less than a week.

In the meantime, I had several well-placed confidential contacts in city government. One was a legal advisor to the Department of Public Works. Another was an auditor in the Finance Department. I also still had several contacts in the police department's Intelligence Unit who might know valuable information about Dixon.

As I said, they all told me they had no indication that Dixon would do anything corrupt.

Still, her relationships with private businesses getting work from City Hall were beginning to bother me as I read more articles in *The Sun*.

When I went back for a more careful review of the news from City Hall I discovered that the deal between Dixon and her campaign chairman was not the City Council president's only questionable practice. I found a previous article by Donovan, published the month before, which noted that the Board of Estimates, headed by Dixon, voted three times to award $1 million for subcontracts to a company called Union Technologies, or Utech, that employed her sister, Janice Dixon. Sheila Dixon claimed she abstained from voting, but the record showed she had, in fact, voted in favor of her sister's company. Her action appeared to violate the city's ethics laws prohibiting her from participating in any matter involving a sibling's business activities with the city.

The *Sun* also reported that the city's Minority and Women's Business Opportunity Office revoked Utech's minority certification because the company's downtown address was only a mail drop and a phone number. I took note of the coincidence that Clark's company, Ultimate Network Integration, had the same "no show" address.

Soon after we began the Clark investigation, Bob instructed me to open a second investigation on the contracts awarded by the city to Mildred Boyer, the head of Utech.

Our investigations included subpoenas to obtain personal tax returns for Clark and Boyer. We would discover that both of them had serious tax problems. Boyer's tax returns were falsified and Clark had neglected to file his taxes for multiple years.

Within a matter of weeks we were investigating two people circling

Sheila Dixon's orbit, but not the City Council president herself.

By coincidence, a few weeks after starting our investigations, Laura and I attended a cocktail party at a beautiful home in the Baltimore County suburbs. The host, a longtime friend, was about to introduce me to another guest, a businessman.

Before the introduction, my friend whispered in my ear, "He's dating Sheila Dixon."

He then introduced me to Ronald Lipscomb, head of Doracon Contracting. Lipscomb was a very gregarious man who politely poured wine for the other guests. I thought he was a perfect gentleman.

Later I would learn that Lipscomb's construction company had purchased city property and was promised coveted tax breaks. The projects needed the approval of the City Council and the Board of Estimates.

I wondered, "Gee, how many contracts does he have with the city?"

(I was later reminded that our office had received a visit two years before from someone in the legal community, claiming Dixon and Lipscomb had a corrupt relationship. The person who gave us the tip would not disclose the name of a potential witness, so we never pursued the case.)

While we were moving full speed ahead on the Clark and Boyer probes, I really wanted our office to open a case on Dixon and Lipscomb. My curiosity was piqued after we seized Dale Clark's computers in a raid on his home with a search and seizure warrant. Strangely, his computer contained Dixon's list of contacts and appointments. It included Ron Lipscomb's business, home and cell phone numbers, as well as Dixon's appointment calendar.

One appointment mentioned a groundbreaking involving a Lipscomb company as general contractor. Another entry mentioned an awards ceremony at the Hyatt Regency Hotel. "Sheila will attend-Ron Lipscomb has ticket," a note read. Dixon was also scheduled to meet with Lipscomb and state senator Ulysses Currie from Prince George's County. (Currie was later acquitted of federal charges that a supermarket chain bribed him to help expand its business.) Still another appointment for January 24, 2003, noted that Dixon was scheduled to have dinner with Lipscomb at Fleming's Prime Steakhouse & Wine Bar. An accompanying notation read: "Sensitivity: Private and Private: Yes."

If that wasn't intriguing enough, Clark's computer files also contained proof of Lipscomb's business getting help from Dixon. One memo from her office summarized a meeting with restaurant owners seeking her help to develop an inn. To get the City Council president's support, the memo said, they could agree to "soft encouragement of Ron Lipscomb's participation as part of the development team."

I was intrigued, but I knew the time wasn't quite right to dig into the relationship between the president of the Baltimore City Council and this prominent businessman. We had to tread carefully. I knew that O'Malley had already announced his run for governor. If he won, Dixon would automatically become the next mayor. I told myself, "Patience, Patience."

49
TURNING EVERY STONE

For the next two years our office became a cyclone of activity as our investigators and prosecutors dug into the finances of Clark and Boyer. Although we found no evidence of kickbacks from them to Dixon, we charged them with tax violations (for which they pleaded guilty), and quickly turned to the clues left on Clark's computer files of Dixon's conflicts of interest involving Lipscomb.

With subpoenas we burrowed into her financial disclosure statements, bank accounts, credit card bills and travel records. Likewise, we issued subpoenas for Lipscomb and his companies. Their unethical activities underscored the lucrative development deals between construction projects of Baltimore's hit or miss renaissance and the power of City Hall to make or break them.

I thought back to my days as a young police officer when I heard Spiro Agnew was resigning as vice president of the United States after federal investigators collected a mountain of evidence that he took kickbacks for a decade from consulting engineers awarded no-bid contracts. Back then, I had no clue how to investigate political corruption and I was in awe of those agents who were so good at their jobs, they could bring down a corrupt official at the highest level of government.

Now, I thought, "I know how those agents felt in the Agnew case. I'm now one of them."

For a state investigation, I knew I was working on the ultimate case.

After 24 years, I certainly knew how to do the job. I always began with the big question: "What is the best way to get the best evidence to get to the truth?" It was paramount to turn over every stone in our path.

I was now also aware of the heavy weight on my shoulders to oversee an investigation that must be thorough and fair. Just ten months after we began, O'Malley was elected governor, automatically elevating Dixon to become the city's first woman mayor. The stakes would be high if we discovered enough evidence to indict her.

The case would be tried in the Baltimore City Circuit Court. That meant our all-white staff of investigators and prosecutors (except for me as the lone Latino) would be going into a majority black city with a largely black jury pool. Our case could not appear racist or politically motivated in any way. I began compiling a list of all the other pending investigations in our office, noting the race of each person we were investigating to make sure we weren't scrutinizing more blacks than whites.

In case Bob Rohrbaugh was accused of racism I would be ready to show him our history of racial fairness. After a quarter century in the business, I knew that while political corruption is not partial to Republicans or Democrats, it is also color blind.

Bob, of course, was well aware of the enormity of our task. As a former Assistant U.S. Attorney for Maryland, he was mindful that our office needed at least one financial investigator who could qualify as an expert witness on the stand if we went to trial. At the time, no one in our office held the right qualifications, so he hired two retired IRS agents, Woodland Morris and Martin Furman, to analyze the financial records of Dixon and Lipscomb.

Woody and Marty's personalities were as different as an ocean is from a desert, but they were equally talented and dedicated.

Woody was a congenial man who joined the rest of the staff for lunch. While I could not see it, I was told he loved to wear bright-colored shirts in banana yellow, apple red, and of course, Raven purple. Marty was a stoic man who ate lunch at his desk and did not engage in social conversations.

Once we received the financial records, the documents were scanned and date stamped. The originals were placed in the evidence room; Woody and Marty worked from the scanned copies. They would eventually review more than a 100,000 pages.

They conducted their analysis using Excel spreadsheets for each set of bank or credit card statements. Once completed, they merged the databases onto a master spreadsheet.

Another invaluable investigator was John Poliks. John was innately tenacious and always followed his instincts. If he believed there was evidence of a crime at a certain location, he simply would not stop searching until he found it. When other investigators reached exhaustion, John was just getting started. During one particular search on behalf of the Baltimore City state's attorney's office he found the smoking gun inside the pole of a shower curtain: it was a thief's list of bribes people owed him.

In one of our cases together I told him, "John, you are beating that dead horse again."

"Well it's my horse and I'll beat it when I want to," he answered.

Typically, my style of supervision was not to hover. In this case, even though our investigators were very experienced, I made sure they briefed me three times a day: the first thing every morning, at mid-day and before they left for the day. If they found any significant piece of evidence, I made sure one of us told Bob Rohrbaugh and Mike McDonough. Every evening, just before leaving, I reviewed the investigative plan and adjusted it if necessary. I was often one the last staff members to leave the office.

Naturally, we started by collecting Dixon's financial disclosure statements, which every elected official is required to file.

I was well acquainted with the Baltimore City Code: Article 8, Ethics, subtitle 6, Conflicts of Interest Part IV. Gifts:

"A public servant may not knowingly accept any gift, directly, from any person that the public servant knows or has reason to know: does or seeks to do business of any kind, regardless of amount: with the public servant's agency; or if the public servant is a member or employee of the City Council…"

When asked on the form if she received any gift (including payment of travel) of more than $50 or a series of gifts worth more than $150 from anyone doing business with the city, Dixon only listed complimentary tickets to a political fundraiser and a pass for two at the Senator Theatre.

We already knew from Clark's computer files that Lipscomb had provided tickets to events Dixon attended with him, so there was a little taste of evidence that she perjured herself.

A few months into our investigation, I was no longer the only one in the office who suspected serious ethical lapses—and possibly criminal acts—on Dixon's part. Now everybody was enthusiastically peaking under the tent.

In some investigations there is a "eureka moment" when investigators find a crucial clue to a crime that will eventually lead to an indictment. In the Dixon case, we had two of those moments.

Our first "eureka moment" came from Woody. One afternoon he came into Bob's office and told him he saw a small charge, not more than $100, on Dixon's credit card account for fur coat storage. Woody said he knew the owner of Mano Swartz Furs from a previous case and wanted to go interview him. Bob thought little of it.

"You just want to get out of the office," he jokingly told Woody

When Woody came back, he told Bob, "You're not going to believe this."

The furrier, Richard Swartz, told him that Dixon purchased two fur coats at a discount sale, a Persian lamb and a burnt umber mink coat, totaling more than $2,800. She used a $2,000 gift certificate to pay most of the cost and her credit card to pay the balance. When Woody asked about the gift certificate, Swartz told him it was the only $2,000 certificate sold during that time. He remembered the man who purchased it made the unusual request not to put the name of the recipient on the certificate. He also requested his own name be left out of the store's records, but Woody was able to track it down. It was Dennis Cullop, Lipscomb's vice president at Doracon.

Now we clearly saw intent to deceive. All of a sudden we knew the case had jury appeal.

We were on the right track

Investigators traced back several years of Lipscomb's companies closing construction deals with either City Council or Board of Estimates approval, with Dixon's full participation. Then we tracked the couple's out-of-town travel together. In just a four-month period they went to Boston; Chicago; Vail, Colorado; and New York City. Lipscomb also traveled to the Bahamas for Dixon's 50th birthday party in December 2003. When they traveled together, they went first class: they stayed at the Ritz Carlton in Vail and the Hyatt Regency in Chicago.

On one particular day in February 2004, Dixon presided over the Board of Estimates as it approved one of the city's biggest discount deals for Lipscomb and his partners. The development team, planning a multi-million dollar residential and retail project in the upscale Harbor East neighborhood, won a property tax break of almost a half million dollars a year from the Board. Dixon's official calendar noted that day that she would be out of the office for the rest of the afternoon. Shortly after 3 p.m. the couple boarded an Amtrak train to New York City. They certainly had plenty to celebrate. Doracon's vice president, Dennis Collup, bought the train tickets in advance. Dixon and Lipscomb dined that night at a Chinese restaurant near Central Park in Manhattan. He paid the $140 bill. They spent two nights at the Trump International Hotel for $1,000 a night. He paid that bill, too, as well as their train tickets back to Baltimore.

There were other Lipscomb projects that got help from the city. The City Council overrode an urban renewal plan to allow him to build a residential project in South Baltimore. And the city and state promised generous loans and a tax break so he could build a recreation center in East Baltimore.

As we looked closely at the other trips the couple enjoyed, our investigators uncovered lavish shopping sprees, including one to Chicago's famous Magnificent Mile on Michigan Avenue.

Records showed, once again, that Cullop paid for their plane tickets in March 2004. Bob came to think of Cullop as Lipscomb's "bag man," a term that was especially popular in the corruption days of Agnew and Dale Anderson when contractors arranged for "bag men" to drop off bags of cash to politicians.

Lipscomb's credit card bills showed he spent hundreds of dollars for makeup accessories and other items at Saks Fifth Avenue, the Coach store, and Niketown. Dixon's credit card bills showed she spent more than $8,000 at Saks, Coach, Giorgio Armani and St. John Boutique. One charge alone, for $570, was for a pair of Jimmy Choo sandals at Saks. It appeared that Dixon had spent more money on the shopping spree than Lipscomb. Then the paper trail took an unexpected turn. Two weeks after they returned to Baltimore, our investigators found unexplained deposits of cash into Dixon's bank account. First, $6,000 was deposited. A month later, Dixon gave her police department security officer, who also acted as her driver, $4,000 in $100 bills, instructing him to deposit the money into his own bank account, then write a check to American Express, presumably to pay her credit card bill.

"I ain't want to know," the driver told a grand jury. "Absolutely didn't want to know."

Our investigators could find no source of income that would explain the $10,000 cash. We could only presume that someone gave her cash to pay off her credit card bills.

As part of the investigation we interviewed Lipscomb, who denied giving Dixon any significant gifts. He admitted going to Chicago with her, but failed to tell us he paid for her plane ticket.

At this point in the investigation we could have charged Dixon with misconduct in office and perjury, maybe even bribery, but we wanted to be absolutely sure the case was solid as a rock. The threshold to indict the mayor of Baltimore had to be very high. On November 6 2007, after serving as the city's appointed mayor for ten months, Dixon won the mayoral election with the endorsement of every major Baltimore politician, labor organization and newspaper. We moved our investigation up a notch.

Three weeks after the election we raided Doracon's offices in East Baltimore with a search and seizure warrant, following up a few months later with another search of the company's storage units downtown. While going through personnel files seized at the office, John found cash register receipts for a large number of gift cards bought from Best Buy, Target and Old Navy.

John, of course, was curious and wondered what they were for. The receipts for Best Buy had identification numbers for each gift card, so he went to the store to see if he could identify the person who spent them.

That was the second "eureka moment" of our investigation.

Apparently the person who spent the gift cards used her Best Buy rewards number, so she could get future discounts. The buyer's name was Sheila Dixon. Now we had concrete proof of a quid pro quo for all the perks Lipscomb's company received from the city.

With the gift cards, we had tangible evidence to bring to a jury. We would not need a witness to the mayor's crimes whom a defense attorney could eviscerate. The gift cards—and what she bought with them—would speak for themselves.

I remembered the time, years before, when a grand juror asked me why a millionaire would steal a small amount of money. I said it's not the first million that exposes him, but the million plus one dollar. Here, in Dixon's case, she got caught using her Best Buy rewards number, seeking discounts, while spending someone else's money. It's all about the greed.

We moved on with our investigation, turning over more stones.

Our investigators knocked on the door of developer Patrick Turner, whose companies were involved in two multimillion dollar projects that needed City Council and Board of Estimates approval. One was called Silo Point, a luxury condo project near historic Fort McHenry. The other would have turned a vast swatch of wasteland west of the popular Inner Harbor into a new community. We knew Turner had donated at least $3,000 to Dixon's reelection committee over several years. Subpoenaed cell phone records showed phone calls from Turner's cell phone to Dixon's Blackberry and to the City Hall operator.

When we reached him in person, Turner volunteered that he bought hundreds of dollars of gift cards at Best Buy and Target because he was under the impression that the cards would be given to the poor.

As we did with the Lipscomb gift cards, we traced the purchases made with Turner's cards and found Dixon had used them herself on a digital camcorder, a PlayStation controller, and Nintendo games, among other things. Again, she used her Best Buy rewards number so we could trace her expenditures. She also left us an easy trail at Target, where she combined some of the gift cards with her credit card to make purchases.

Finally, in 2008 John and I went into Bob's office.

"We have enough to search the mayor's house," I said.

"Sit your asses down and don't move. I'm going to get a cup of coffee," said Bob.

As far as Bob was concerned we had crossed the Rubicon.

"When you go into that house," he warned John, "If you find absolutely nothing, you walk out with empty boxes if you need to because the press will be all over this. No matter what, you walk out with something." Of course, he was joking, but his comment explained the high stakes we faced.

The importance of searching the mayor's house reminded me of the expression: "If you shoot the king you better kill him." We needed every I dotted and T crossed.

The warrant signed by a judge listed ten pages of items Dixon bought with the gift cards: the mink, the Persian lamb, the Jimmy Choo sandals, a pair of Giorgio Armani shoes, a woman's Italian leather coat, and many more items of clothing. We would search for movie DVDs, music CDs, and games for a PlayStation, Nintendo and Xbox. We also were seeking receipts.

As I wrote at the beginning of this memoir, the day of the raid, June 17, 2008, was one of the most important days in my career, and in the careers of my co-workers at the Office of the Maryland State Prosecutor.

We had completed a herculean task to get to this day.

I was, of course, extremely disappointed that I could not lead the raid myself. But I put complete faith in John Poliks to lead the search and leave no stone unturned. There truly was no one I trusted more than John to be my eyes.

John and the other investigators would be accompanied by Maryland state troopers, who always assisted us on raids. We hoped to keep it quiet, so the team arrived just after 6 in the morning.

Since this was the home of the mayor, we knew that it would be guarded by an unsuspecting city police officer in a squad car, thinking he was on a typical work shift protecting the mayor's house in a quiet neighborhood. We had taken great care so no one in the city police department had advance notice; the mayor's body guards work at the police department, and they might feel a duty to tell her. At all costs we had to insure that no evidence was destroyed.

As soon as our team arrived John called Baltimore City police commissioner Fred Bealefeld at home. The commissioner sounded like he was asleep.

"Commissioner, it's John Poliks from the state prosecutor's office. I have a warrant for the mayor's house."

"Are you there now?" asked Bealefeld, his voice almost trembling. He was certainly awake now.

"Yes," said John. "I need you to tell the uniformed officer here what we are doing. Tell him not to call the sergeant, not to call the lieutenant, not to call the district commander."

"Okay," said Bealefeld.

John walked to the police car and showed the officer his badge.

"The police commissioner wants to talk to you," John said and handed the officer his cell phone.

Despite John's warnings, someone did tip off the police department. Soon, one police car drove by. Then a second car and a third. About an hour later, members of the news media began to line up across the street. At the same time, I was alone at our office when the phone rang. It was a high ranking commander of the state police. He told me that Governor Martin O'Malley was incensed that we did not give him advance warning of the raid. I frankly didn't think much of the call. We would never give anyone advance notice of a raid with a search and seizure warrant, even the governor. I didn't even bother to mention the call to John. He had more important things to worry about.

The mayor, who answered the door in her nightgown, had first refused to let the team in and slammed the door. Only after her lawyer advised her that she had to comply with the warrant did she let them in. She quickly dressed, grabbed her gym bag and left. Once inside John took out pieces of paper with large numbers printed on them. He taped one to each door and photographed and videotaped each room, so we would have a record showing where each item of evidence was found. Then the search began. John brought each item to a state trooper sitting at the mayor's dining room table to make a note of it. They found many of the items sought by the warrant, including the fur coats. Much to Bob's relief, the boxes they hauled away would not be empty.

Six months later, a grand jury indicted Dixon on 12 counts of perjury, theft and misconduct in office. She was the first Baltimore mayor to face criminal charges.

50
THE WAR ROOM

As we prepared for the trial, our staff was laser-focused on "all things Sheila." I asked John Poliks to relocate the evidence, except the fur coats, from the evidence locker into our conference room. I could hear John placing several boxes onto the large table as Bob, Mike and our newly hired assistant prosecutor, Shelly Glenn, took seats. As John removed evidence from the boxes, he kindly told me what he was doing. Now I knew that the envelopes of documents sat side by side.

Despite the compassion of my co-workers concerning my blindness, I was all too aware of the disadvantages of not being able to see the evidence. I felt like I was fishing without a pole. I was thankful, nevertheless, to be able to easily remember which records we subpoenaed. The years of going blind and being unable to read (not to mention investigating crimes on The Block without taking contemporaneous notes or wearing a recorder) left me with better recall than most people.

At one of our early meetings the room suddenly went quiet, except for a strange noise that I didn't recognize. It lasted just a few minutes and left me perplexed. I didn't dare ask what was going on. No one else said a word. Finally, I heard Bob take his seat. He asked for our suggestions on the order of evidence to be presented in court. Once the meeting was over, I asked Shelly about the noise. With a giggle she said the sound was Bob touching the evidence, running his fingers over each document, as if to magically absorb it. At first, Shelly thought her new boss was acting like a mad scientist. But later, she too began to touch the evidence.

Despite Bob's little eccentricity, I felt very confident that he was an excellent prosecutor to lead our case: he had an outstanding grasp of the law and knew how to prepare a powerful opening statement to the jury.

Bob also knew the risks we were taking and he was ready for the battle. He even dubbed the conference room "The War Room."

We didn't use the words "war" and "battle" lightly.

From the early days of the indictment our office became the enemy.

Baltimore leaders and the mayor's many public sympathizers circled their wagons around her, vilifying the OSP for charging her with what they believed were petty accusations.

Sheila Dixon was a popular mayor in a city where every elected official is a member of the Democratic Party (the entire City Council, the comptroller, the mayor, and all the state legislators) so there was no opposing party to express a disapproving view of her.

The OSP's history was demonized and demeaned: we were wrongly ridiculed for not putting away any "high profile bad guys" in the past. We were singled out for losing an important bribery case against state senator Larry Young years before. One powerful state legislator, defending Dixon, noted "there was no charge that (the mayor) was in any way bribed."

Baltimore City solicitor George Nilson, City Hall's chief lawyer hired by the mayor, sent an unrealistic affidavit to court, hoping the charges would be dismissed. He argued that Lipscomb's gifts to the mayor were not a conflict of interest, since it was his company—not the man—doing business with the city.

Even Patricia Jessamy, the Baltimore City state's attorney (a prosecutor who should know better) backed Dixon: "She is a very hard worker. . . . I hope this is resolved quickly so that she can continue conducting the business of the city."

And of course, Dixon's lead lawyer came out swinging. The legendary Arnold Weiner, who had defended Governor Marvin Mandel in his federal corruption trial, insinuated that Bob was tainted because he was appointed by a Republican governor. Then the defense attorney attacked Bob personally:

"There wasn't a bedsheet he did not look under or a lead he found too trivial to pursue," Weiner said. Since Bob lived far from Baltimore, in Montgomery County, and didn't listen to local radio stations or regularly read The *Sun*, he was somewhat insulated from the criticisms. Ever the news junkie, I listened to all the local papers from the American Federation for the Blind on my phone and tuned into the radio talk shows. None of this bothered me. Professionally, prosecutors and investigators should never be influenced by public opinion.

Shelly Glenn, an energetic lawyer who would learn how to prosecute a white collar case in the War Room and develop a good rapport with the jury, was challenged by her own mother.

"She was against me on it," Shelly remembers. "She and I had some knock-down drag-out debates." Shelly's mother cared for her children while she worked, so she faced her mother's doubts about the indictment when she came home each day. Dixon, her mother argued, was a good mayor who "has done a lot for this city."

"You don't know what you're talking about," Shelly could only respond because she could not discuss the case before the trial.

For the first time in the OSP's history, we hired a jury consultant to help us choose a jury most likely to weigh the evidence honestly.

The consultant brought a focus group of volunteers that reflected the demographics of the city's jury pool. The prosecutors asked the volunteers to sit through a mock trial and listen to arguments of the case. The volunteers then discussed the "evidence" while the prosecutors and investigators watched behind a two-way mirror. Shelly was impressed by one woman's comment about the mayor spending gift cards intended for the poor: "That ain't right," she said from the other side of the mirror. "You don't steal from poor people." That simple judgment would stick with Shelly throughout the trial. "If we can get that point across to the jury," she believed, "We can knock it out of the ball park."

In the meantime, the Baltimore City grand jury indicted Lipscomb, city councilwoman Helen Holton and John Paterakis, one of Baltimore's wealthiest businessmen who was partners with Lipscomb in developing Harbor East. Holton was charged with accepting a bribe from Lipscomb in the form of a political poll he paid for. Paterakis was charged with violating campaign finance law by helping pay for the poll.

Our case would be hampered by numerous legal obstacles, each one applauded by the public clambering in the mayor's defense, while making our prosecution team more and more concerned about the strength of our case.

Our first legal snag came when Judge Dennis Sweeney dismissed most of our original charges against Dixon. The judge ruled the mayor had legislative immunity that protected her; we should not have used her votes on the City Council and the Board of Estimates, as evidence of her wrongdoing.

The judge also dismissed charges against Councilwoman Holton for the same reason, though we still had the bribery charges against Lipscomb.

We were able to save the Dixon case by taking it to a new grand jury without mentioning the legislative votes and presenting new indictments charging the mayor with counts of perjury (for failing to report gifts on her financial disclosure reports) and theft of the gift cards.

We decided to try the gift card case first because, as our consultant's focus group confirmed, it had great jury appeal. We were not worried about getting developer Pat Turner to testify in a forthright manner. He was a straightforward man who really did believe he was buying the gift cards for the poor that he delivered to City Hall. Lipscomb was another story. He agreed to testify only as part of a plea deal, in which we dropped the bribery case and charged him with minor campaign finance violations.

Although Lipscomb went along with the plea deal, everyone on the prosecution team had an uneasy feeling about him. His willingness to testify was lukewarm, at best. His answers to our questions were minimal. I personally didn't trust him at all, but we initially believed we had no choice but to call him to the stand.

The media believed that our case hinged on Lipscomb's testimony. They touted him as the prosecution's star witness. Even though he wasn't dating the mayor anymore, we truly didn't know whose side of the fence he was on. Once on the witness stand, we all worried, Lipscomb would only halfheartedly give us what we wanted. Even worse, under cross examination he might just roll over for Arnold Weiner. That would be a disaster.

We also believed that Weiner made a tactical error at the trial's start when he showed his hand by laying out his defense in his opening statement. He said the case was all Lipscomb's fault, and that the businessman was not trustworthy. From that point on we began seriously discussing whether we were willing to take a huge risk: scratching Lipscomb from our witness list.

We spent many subsequent hours discussing the pros and cons of canceling his testimony. Finally, we all met in Bob's office on a Sunday night to hash it out. Bob played devil's advocate, endorsing Lipscomb's testimony, but the rest of us came to the conclusion that it was a bad idea. Shelly remembers John Poliks almost writhing in his chair at the thought of Lipscomb taking the stand.

Finally Bob turned to Mike McDonough and said, "The decision's been made. We're not going to put Lipscomb on the stand."

We were all very nervous but we knew it was the best decision.

"We're doing heady stuff," said Bob, more than once.

As we suspected, Judge Sweeney dismissed the charges involving Lipscomb. Of course, the public took our decision—and the judge's ruling—as a sign of weakness. That did hurt.

The trial lasted six days. I was not present because I was working on other cases and I needed to stay out of the courtroom in case I might need to testify, but I couldn't help but hear all the news reports in newspapers, TV and radio broadcasts.

In Bob's opening statement, he smacked a pile of gift cards on the edge of the jury box and showed them receipts used to buy them.

"When you are a public official," he said, "it is a breach of the public trust when you steal. When you are a public servant and you steal from the needy, it is unspeakable."

Pat Turner's testimony was strong. He came across as honest and believable. He truly did think the gift cards he bought were for charity.

We also believed the exhibits in our case drove the trial. We painstakingly connected the dots, tracing the developers to the gift cards to the purchases made by the mayor, then to the items found in her home during the raid. That part of our case was solid.

On the advice of her lawyers Dixon chose not to testify in her own defense. It was no surprise to anyone on our trial team. If Bob cross examined her, he would eviscerate her defense.

In the end, jurors had to choose one of two theories to convict her: that the mayor stole the gift cards, or that she had the right to possess them, but misused them.

The jury deliberated for seven days that left the prosecution team very tense.

During one of the very long hours of waiting, the prosecutors were sitting around their courtroom table when Mayor Dixon walked up to Bob and handed him a folded piece of paper torn from a legal pad.

"Can I speak to you?" she asked. Bob carefully looked around, wondering if he should take what appeared to be a note. It is highly unusual for a defendant to have any direct contact with a prosecutor, so he was quite surprised.

"Do I really want to do this?" he asked himself.

The other lawyers saw the exchange and, of course, they were all curious.

When Bob opened it, he was astonished. Though it was handwritten, the mayor had constructed the note as if it were a legal motion. It read:

"Motion to Give me my Coat Back

SAD (Sheila Ann Dixon), by her counsel, moves the court to order the SKUNKS (aka Rohrbaugh and company) to give back the coat that lawfully belongs to her, especially since another winter is coming."

Bob walked over to Weiner, who sat with the six other members of Dixon's legal team and showed him the note.

"Tell her she'll get her coat back after the trial—if at all," he said.

The note was so unusual that Bob kept it for years after his retirement.

The jury finally reached a verdict on the first day of December 2009.

I sat on a bench behind the prosecutors and leaned forward to listen closely as soon as I heard the jury walk into the courtroom. I only needed to hear one word: "guilty."

They convicted the mayor of Baltimore for embezzling $500 worth of gift cards meant for charity. Even though the jury acquitted her of some of the other charges, the one conviction was all we needed to prove our case.

"There's no explanation for why she used gift cards for a needy child," said one juror, expressing precisely the viewpoint Shelly Glenn had hoped for. Shelly was right. We did hit it out of the ballpark.

We were all so relieved, not to mention drained, by the verdict. I was absolutely pleased. "We are validated and vindicated," I thought. "We were right all along."

As we were preparing for Dixon's next trial over the perjury case, Bob got a call from Arnold Weiner. The mayor wanted to discuss a plea deal, rather than take her chances on another trial. Bob was surprised, but certainly willing to talk. We were not interested in having Dixon serve time in prison. Our primary goal was to get her to resign from office and let the city move on with a new mayor.

There were other complications: the jurors had become too friendly with one another, conversing on Facebook, prompting Dixon's defense to move for a mistrial. Dixon also could appeal her conviction, insist on staying in office, and leave a cloud over the city. In another scenario, the judge could sentence her to probation before judgment, essentially wiping out her conviction and allowing her to stay in office.

As Bob began negotiations, he discovered that the mayor was most interested in money, namely her $83,000 pension. Finally, after a day of negotiations, a plea deal was hashed out.

On January 6, 2010, Sheila Dixon resigned as mayor, and pleaded guilty to perjury. She was given probation before judgment, allowing her to keep her pension. The public could not pay for her attorney's fees. She was ordered to perform 500 hours of community service and to pay $45,000 to charities. She nickeled and dimed the prosecutors, dickering over the last few thousand dollars they wanted her to contribute to charity until the very last minute before they went into court.

The plea deal also extracted one more thing from the mayor: she would not get back her fur coats. They would be auctioned off, with the proceeds going to charity.

After the sentencing, Dixon appeared not to grasp that she was legally confessing to perjury.

"Your honor," she said, "those things are not true." She did not apologize for her crimes.

Baltimore is a forgiving city.

Six years later she would reemerge on the political scene and run in a hotly contested mayoral race in the 2016 Democratic primary. Despite her crimes, Dixon proved to be as popular as ever: she almost won, coming in second out of a field of 13 candidates, getting just 2,446 fewer votes than the winner.

With the case finally over, Bob put the fur coats up for auction on eBay.

A lawyer who taught ethics at the University of Maryland bought the Persian lamb to teach ethics to her students. Shelly remembers that one of Dixon's friends bought the mink. When the woman picked it up, she said, "I'm giving this back to Sis."

So it appears that Dixon may have gotten her mink back, after all.

The day of the plea deal, I was back in my office listening to the Queen song "Another One Bites the Dust" when Bob knocked on my door.

"We're going to Bahama Breeze to celebrate. You've got to join us for a drink," he told me.

At first I declined. It was not my style to toast to someone's criminal conviction, though I will always remember the champagne toast with prosecutors Jerry Glass and Gerry Ruter over our very first case when we won convictions of a judge, a gubernatorial aide and a state health official for bribery. That was 30 years back.

Now, Bob refused to take no for an answer.

"I'm ordering you now," he said. "Turn off the music."

"After all, you started this."

51
WHAT MY HEART CAN SEE

There are times when I see more with my heart than others see with their eyes.

As a blind person, I can focus my attention acutely, not only on what people say, but how they say it. I can read a mood from the tiniest giveaway in the inflection of a voice: sadness, fear, excitement, confusion. In that way, I can communicate with people better than I did when I still had my eyesight. I can provide solace if someone is sad or congratulations for an achievement. I miss very little with my heart.

Today I am at peace with my blindness. I once gave a speech to an annual DORS conference and told the audience, "The first thing you notice about me is my white cane, but don't let it worry you because it doesn't worry me."

I don't complain about my blindness, not even to Laura. But I do talk to God. After I returned to the church I found tranquility through the offering of the Kiss of Peace during Mass after the Eucharist. It is very satisfying in a spiritual way.

Once I found peace, I no longer felt a world of emptiness.

It didn't come to me easily.

It took me years to come to terms with blindness, just as it took a lifetime to come to grips with the idea of going blind. I spent decades since my affliction from Stevens-Johnson Syndrome in a cycle alternating between hope, fear and despair. Fear over every episode of blurred vision while driving on a rainy night. Fear of failing an eye exam at the police department, or a test at a firing range. Fear of having to pull a gun as a cop and not being able to aim straight.

I feared every cataract surgery, but found hope when I could see better after the cataract was removed. I felt fear—terror actually—over each detached retina, enveloping my eye in blackness; hope while I waited for the surgery to take hold; despair when it failed. On my way to Boston for each of three corneal transplants, I held out hope that always led to despair over the transplant's failure.

Once I finished fighting blindness, I had to fight the emptiness that came with the darkness: the awful feeling of being insignificant, no more than a single blade of grass among towering redwoods.

By 2007, I was completely blind. That is when I lost my swagger. I was proud of what I had accomplished in both my personal and professional life. People sought my counsel because of what I knew and who I knew, particularly in the criminal justice community. I enjoyed giving valuable advice to anyone who sought it. When my world turned dark I never heard from some of those people again. Some were in law enforcement. Some were friends. I felt devalued and humiliated. I could have judged them, but I didn't.

I was glad that others continued to seek my advice. I was grateful that my disability showed me my true friends.

After it became clear that the repairs to my detached retinas and the corneal transplants did not work, surgeons sealed shut my eye lids in my right eye to protect me from infection. But they left a tiny hole to allow just a pinprick of light to come through. When I walk to my front door, for example, I can see the white from the stair railing—not the image of the railing—just the white light. It is really all I need to get up the stairs. I love it.

Though I cannot see images through the tiny opening in my eye, I had one episode of sight that I cannot explain. It was a Christmas Eve shortly after I went blind.

Laura picked me up from work, as usual. We were in the elevator going down to the car. She was standing under the elevator light that aimed straight down on her. I held on to her elbow and turned to her.

"Oh my God," I said. "I just saw your face." It lasted barely a second, no more.

I smiled and we hugged each other.

I know I can't explain it. Maybe it was a miracle that I could see my wife's smile.

That was the last time I saw Laura's face.

I am still coming to terms with all the other beautiful sights I am missing: my granddaughters' growing faces, seeing my sons growing old. A simple blue sky and a yellow sun. Game days will no longer find me in the ballpark. I can only listen to movies and television. My life-long fraternity brothers will not call to ask me to play tennis, basketball, golf, pool, or even a game of poker.

Laura decorates the house for Christmas and trims a tree, but I will never see her handiwork.

In a restaurant I cannot cut my own steak.

As I said at the start of this memoir, I am a man who learned how to turn misfortune into opportunity. I am grateful for the help of many counselors and disability specialists at DORS for giving me the opportunity, along with the tools, to use computer software for the blind so I could keep working for another 14 years after I could no longer read. If I had been forced to retire after I went blind it is very possible that Mayor Dixon might not have been investigated. The course of Baltimore politics and elections would have been quite different.

The tools and training the DORS staff gave me also allowed me to write this memoir. I will be forever thankful to the DORS staff, Tara Hunter Payne, Jim Doyle, Melissa Day, Lou Smith and Donald Kuhn, for their patience and training.

I am also indebted to the army of ophthalmologists from Johns Hopkins Medicine, Massachusetts Eye and Ear Hospital, and the Greater Baltimore Medical Center, who kept my blindness at bay for so many years:

Roy O. Scholz
Bert Glaser
John Minkowski
Marcos T. Doxanas
Raymond N. Sjaarda
James Comber
Kimberly Rigdon
Kenneth Kenyon
Melanie Graham
Roy S. Chuck
John T. Thompson
Esen K. Akpek
James Chodosh
Teresa Chen
Lucy Young
Peter L. Gehlbach

You could sum up my life with these brief lyrics from a Jimmy Buffet song, "He Went to Paris."

Some of it's magic, some of it's tragic
But I had a good life all of the way.

EPILOGUE

I retired from the OSP in the spring of 2017 after 38 years with the office. At my retirement lunch on May 9, the staff of a dozen young prosecutors, investigators and administrative staff squeezed into our small conference room. Many of them had not been born when I started working there. They listened to very kind remarks from Mike McDonough, who took them down a memory lane of cases we investigated and prosecuted together. State prosecutor Emmet Davitt was out of town at a funeral, but he issued a very thoughtful press release:

State Prosecutor Lauds James Cabezas, Chief Investigator for the Office, at the Announcement of his Retirement

James Cabezas, Chief Investigator for the Office of the State Prosecutor, announced his decision to retire after 38 years with the office. Cabezas, who has been with the office since its inception, has indicated that May 9th will be his last day on the job.

"Jim Cabezas has had a remarkable and illustrious law enforcement career," State Prosecutor Emmet C. Davitt stated. "Prior to joining this office, Jim was a highly respected and well-liked Baltimore City police officer who spent several years deep undercover investigating organized crime ties to Baltimore's "Block." Having served under all four State Prosecutors, from the first, Gerald Glass, to the administration of Mr. Davitt, to the law enforcement community and the public, Jim was the face of this office."

As Chief Investigator, Cabezas has been a participant in every major investigation and prosecution that the OSP has undertaken. In recent years, he played an active role in the criminal investigations and successful prosecutions of Baltimore City Mayor Sheila Dixon, Anne Arundel County Executive John Leopold, Prince George's County Delegate Tiffany Alston, and the 2010 voter suppression robocall case involving political operative Julius Henson and former Ehrlich campaign manager Paul Schurick.

"Not only has Jim been an outstanding Chief Investigator and an excellent mentor to countless younger investigators over the years, he's just a wonderful person," Davitt further commented. "He never forgets that he is here to serve the public. His patience and empathy in dealing with the often difficult or upset callers, complainants and witnesses contacting the Office always impresses me.

"I speak for all who have served in the Office of the State Prosecutor over the last 38 years when I say 'Jim, you will be missed. Congratulations and enjoy your well-earned retirement.'"

Davitt was the fourth Maryland state prosecutor I worked for. I began with Jerry Glass and his deputy Gerry Ruter, both of whom went on to practice private law.

Steve Montanarelli followed Glass. He died in 2004 of multiple myeloma cancer.

The third Maryland state prosecutor, Robert Rohrbaugh, retired and lives in Florida.

Mike McDonough retired in 2018.

Two months after I retired I opened a consulting business called The Chilo Group LLC. I advise bar owners to make sure they are in compliance with the city liquor laws. I also counseled a young man who was addicted to opioids.

At the end of the 2017 school year, Laura also retired after 30 years teaching in Baltimore County's elementary schools. We celebrated our 25th wedding anniversary on June 19, 2018.

Ours has been a blissful marriage. It is perhaps the greatest gift God has ever given to me.

James and Joe have been devoted sons, not just to me, but to their mother, Dee, who retired after working for 25 years for the Giant Pharmacy. Unfortunately, she passed away in October, 2018 after a long illness. James has two daughters, Autumn, 13, and Alexis, 15. Both are good students and are very active in theater. Indeed, they are the apple of my eye.

Sadly, my daughter Diana died at the young age of 34 due to complications of influenza in 2001. Dee and I think she began abusing alcohol after her daughter died of Sudden Infant Death (SIDS). Baby April was only four months old. The image of her little white coffin will forever be in my mind.

Joe and Diana's biological father, Elmer Skaggs, convicted in 1974 of first-degree murder, robbery and housebreaking, was serving a life sentence when he was released in 2013 after an appeals court ruled that his jury was given improper instructions. Joe heard that Skaggs moved to Kentucky, but chose not to contact him.

My sister, Esther, is now retired after working as a seamstress for 20 years for Kent Fisher Furs. We are still very close and share the wonderful memories of our parents before their untimely deaths.

On every Mother's Day I listen to Connie Francis singing "Mama."

When the evening shadows fall
and the lovely day is through
Then with longing I recall
the years I spent with you

Mama, I miss the days
when you were near to guide me
Mama, those happy days
when you were here beside me

Every November. 11, Pop's birthday, I listen to Eddie Fisher's hit, "Oh My Papa." The words are very fitting:

Oh, my pa-pa, to me he was so wonderful
Oh, my pa-pa, to me he was so good
No one could be so gentle and so lovable
Oh, my pa-pa, he always understood
Gone are the days when he could take me on his knee
And with a smile he'd change my tears to laughter
Oh, my pa-pa, so funny, so adorable
Always the clown, so funny in his way
Oh, my pa-pa, to me he was so wonderful
Deep in my heart I miss him so today

Pop's murder went unsolved for 44 years. In 2016 I mustered the courage to investigate it myself. The decision took a huge amount of emotional energy. On one hand, I told myself, "Just leave it alone." But another part of me knew that I could potentially solve it. I also remembered my raw thoughts of Pop at his funeral.

"Here is a fair man who was cheerful in all weather, who never shirked a task," I thought. I had pledged to live my life by Pop's example. Now, nearly a half century later, I was ready for the task.

I had initiated my investigation by speaking with a woman I knew as Misty, a bartender who worked at the Tic Toc Club in 1970. She knew my father as a customer. She also knew another customer, a strong-arm extortionist, burglar and safecracker named Theodore "Teddy" Kittelt, who occasionally partnered in his crimes with the notorious Dominic "Crow Bar" Corozza, well known in Baltimore's underworld. Misty confirmed that Pop and Kittelt knew each other as bar patrons. Misty also knew Kittelt's wife, a dancer named BJ, who told her that Kittelt murdered Pop to steal his money. I also spoke with a former bookmaker and bartender from The Block, who did not know Pop, but knew Kittelt. The bartender also believed that Kittelt killed Pop to steal his money. I theorized that Pop and Kittelt arrived at Pop's home by taxi cab the night of the murder.

I also learned that Kittelt was murdered two years later. His body was found with four gunshot wounds in the trunk of a car in Baltimore County, so I knew there would be no arrest in the case.

I subsequently met with Baltimore police commissioner Kevin Davis, to tell him who I believed had murdered my father. I requested that Kittelt's fingerprints and/or his DNA be compared with evidence collected at the crime scene.

In May 2018 I was finally contacted by a homicide supervisor of the BPD. After explaining that the unit was somewhat overwhelmed with work (with homicide rates at historic highs), he told me the original case folder was located, but a sergeant and detective searched the police department's storage lockers, without finding the original evidence. My own police department lost the evidence in my father's murder. I was extremely disappointed to learn that the police department that had been so crucial in my life had failed me in the end.

The department has since closed the case unsolved. Since my theory that Kittelt murdered Pop was not disproven, I stand by my conclusion. The BPD might have bungled its task to solve Pop's murder, but I did not.

Although I'd lost contact with my fraternity brothers from high school during the years I worked as a deep covert on The Block, I renewed my friendship years later when I contacted one of them, Mike Beatty, also known as the radio DJ Batman of Ocean City, Maryland.

Mike helped me plan a long-overdue reunion with more than 25 of our frat buddies. It gave me a chance to explain why I'd dropped off the radar so many decades before. It gave me great relief. We now meet every five years in Ocean City. Sadly, eight of them have died.

I am indebted to my longtime friend Charlie Walas, who taught me so much about conducting criminal investigations. After becoming disillusioned with the erosion of professionalism in the police department, he resigned in 1988 and came to work with me at the OSP. He later moved on to breed German shepherds and to work in several security jobs.

Several others who helped shape my life have also passed:

My dear friend John O'Neill, who became chief of the counterterrorism section of the FBI, died in the September 11, 2001, terrorist attack on the World Trade Center in New York City, where he worked as security director. He died while attempting to save lives.

Howard Glashoff, best man at my wedding to Laura, died of a heart attack in 2009.

Wayne Carneal, whom I met during my first year on the police force, remained a close friend until he died in 2018 of a heart attack. I am godfather to his daughter.

Dr. Roy O. Scholz, my ophthalmologist from the age of eight until I was nearly 30, was the first in a long line of dedicated eye doctors who kept me from going blind for many decades. He died of cancer in 1985.

I sadly report that the racism and corruption in the Baltimore Police Department I witnessed in the early 1970s has not only continued, but has escalated.

In April 2015, riots broke out after a young African American man named Freddie Gray died from injuries suffered in a police paddy wagon. Pharmacies were looted and thousands of opioids flooded the streets, provoking more violence.

Matters only got worse with the federal convictions of eight police detectives on the city's elite Gun Trace Task Force. They were convicted of arresting innocent people, robbing them of tens of thousands of dollars, planting drugs, and charging the police department with hundreds of hours in overtime they never worked. One officer was even accused of selling the very prescription drugs stolen by rioters after Freddie Gray's death.

In just a decade the BPD went through nine police commissioners, including one who only served four months in 2018 after he was charged with failing to file his income taxes for several years. In 2017, the city entered into a consent decree with the U.S. Justice Department, promising to reform the police department after a federal investigation found pervasive discriminatory and unconstitutional police practices. A little more than a year later, a federal judge said he doubted the BPD had the leadership to carry out the changes.

I still go down to The Block now and then because there are so many drug-related crimes going unsolved by the BPD. Though it's been more than 30 years since I worked as a deep covert, I still have informants there, their numbers tucked away in my talking cell phone. Of course, when I go to The Block, someone needs to drive me there. Often, it's Charlie Walas, who watches my back just as he did in the old days.

I always take precautions, as a blind man should when visiting what is essentially an open air drug market. I wear a coat or vest (even in the summer) to make it appear as if I might be concealing a gun. I leave my white cane at home. It would only draw the attention of a predator. But I nevertheless am safely watched over once I arrive. A doorman at one of the strip clubs takes my arm and walks me to whomever I am meeting. I always remember to tip him.

Once I introduced an informant to a young city narcotics detective. Another time a stripper told me her ex-boyfriend was staging a hijacking of a tractor trailer he was driving full of food to be delivered. I have spent years sending tips to the BPD about gang-related drug activities and other crimes on The Block. I give police comprehensive information, including names and cell phone numbers of Block employees selling narcotics for the Bloods gang. None of my tips have resulted in any investigation or arrests. What's more shocking is that the city's red-light district is right under the BPD's nose, just one block from police headquarters and the Central District police station. There is even a surveillance camera mounted on the police building facing directly onto The Block.

Still, I have not given up on my old police department. I may have retired, but I have not stopped working. My situation is no different from a retired teacher, a nurse, or a social worker, who commits his or her life's work for a cause. I have never liked the thought that retirement results in the loss of an institutional mind. I understand that I am not what I once was. So what? That I am a 69-year-old blind man will not deter me.

ACKNOWLEDGMENTS

This memoir could not have been written without the assistance of family, friends and colleagues. We thank those who confirmed and augmented Jim's memories, provided photographs and gave their time to read the manuscript and offer constructive criticism.

Jim is especially grateful to his wife and best friend, Laura, who never complained about his typing at 3 a.m. She spent many hours wisely improving the manuscript by reviewing chapters, making helpful suggestions and choosing photographs.

Deborah Weiner, our meticulous copy editor, caught many errors and improved the manuscript in innumerable ways.

Chris Broussard and Brian Megargee, our talented graphic designers, produced the book's handsome cover, designed the interior, and created the photo section.

Bill Barry, our patient photographer, took the back-cover photo, as well as the Cabezas family portraits.

The Daily Record gave us permission to use the photo by Maximilian Franz of the prosecution team walking to the Baltimore Circuit Courthouse for the trial of Mayor Dixon in 2009.

Jim's sister Esther Kueberth provided pictures from Jim's early life and shared her childhood memories of life growing up with Jim in East Baltimore and on the estate of the Evergreen House. Jim's sons Joe and James also helped recall family events and reviewed the manuscript.

The crucial chapters about the investigation and prosecution of Mayor Dixon could not have been written without the reminiscences, insight and patience of former State Prosecutor Robert Rohrbaugh, former Deputy State Prosecutor Thomas "Mike" McDonough, former Senior Assistant State Prosecutor Shelly Glenn and former Special Agent John Poliks.

We are grateful to the many readers of individual chapters or the entire manuscript whose thoughtful observations greatly improved the book: Michael Olesker, John Minkowski, Emily Clay, Kelley Harrison, John

"Mickey" McEntee, Charlie Wilhelm, Doug Dunlap, Marina Sarris, Linell Smith, Laura Lippman, David Simon, Kevin Abell, and Erwin Burtnick.

Thanks to two librarians for locating old newspaper articles for us: Paul McCardell, the *Baltimore Sun's* librarian, sent us news clips from the *The Evening Sun*. Nancy Harrison Gage, a student assistant at the University of Maryland College Park Special Collections, sent articles from the *The News American*.

Gerard Shields, spokesman for the Maryland Department of Public Safety and Correctional services, gave us vital information about criminals we mentioned.

Others who answered questions or provided documents include Rick Barger, Charlie Walas, Genie Gunthrop, Mike "DJ Batman" Beatty and Lou Otremba.

--James Cabezas and Joan Jacobson

Eyes of Justice

Made in the USA
Middletown, DE
26 April 2019